To

Mike

Love from

Rose.

Xmas 1997

IRELAND

IRELAND

NICK CONSTABLE &
KAREN FARRINGTON

PRC

ACKNOWLEDGMENTS

The photographs for this book were kindly supplied by Bord Failte, the Irish Tourist Board except for the following: the National Museum of Ireland provided those on pp51, 52/3 (Top), 66, 67 and 176; John Cleare those on pp26, 27, 60, 178, 179. David Lyons supplied those on pp25, 147, 151, 153, 155, 161, 163, 165, 167, 169, 196–225 (All); Sunburst Library provided 232/3, 236, 237, 239. 241, 243, 244, 245.

Photograph Page 2: *The coast at Youghal, Co Cork.*
Photograph Page 3: *The Rock of Cashel, Co Tipperary.*

First published in 1997 by
Promotional Reprint Company,
Kiln House,
210 New Kings Road,
London SW6 4NZ.

ISBN 1 85648 431 9

Printed and bound in China

Contents

INTRODUCTION

Ireland has always been a land of troubles. From the constant squabbling of the early Gaelic chieftains, through to the barbarism of the Vikings, the ruthless military efficiency of the Normans, and the twisted logic of Oliver Cromwell's religious bigotry, the island has known hardly a decade's peace in 2,000 years. Today, in spite of courageous attempts by democratic politicians to find a lasting solution to the nationalist/unionist divide, the shadow of conflict hangs as dark as ever over the country.

But this is not a book just about Ireland's problems, however closely the problems of partition can be linked to the actions of previous centuries. Instead, it aims to find defining moments in Irish history and look at how these have shaped the country's distinctive culture and environment. Inevitably, the legacies of past wars feature heavily. To many of the old Celtic kings, war was their whole reason for being; an affirmation of their power and a constant source of inspiration to their historians, poets and storytellers.

It must also be said that Ireland is a place worth fighting for: anyone who has seen an Atlantic storm hit the rugged west coast, strolled along the hauntingly beautiful yellow beaches, watched sunlight spearing the clouds onto purple-clad mountains, smelled the peat fires of the villages and the sweet, rain-washed air, tramped the wild boglands and watched the mist roll in across peaceful loughs; anyone who has experienced one or more of these things knows something of the magic of the place.

It is worth looking briefly at the geography of Ireland, if only to do some scene-setting for the historical events considered later — a more detailed survey is given in Part One. Ireland has four main provinces — Munster in the south, Connacht in the west, Leinster in the east and Ulster in the north — comprising 32 counties. In very general terms, the country looks like a saucer with jagged edges — its central limestone plains surrounded on almost every side by dramatic mountain scenery. Aside from the lowland midlands, with its bogs and gentle pastureland, a journey through the Irish countryside produces a constantly changing panorama. Travelling across the Silvermine mountains, near Nenagh, for instance, you can find yourself moving from craggy heights into Tipperary's rolling dairy country within the space of a few miles. Similarly, a car ride across the Mayo plains, beneath the rounded mass of Ben Nephin, will take you quickly into one of the country's most desolate districts — the peatlands of the north-west.

Irish mountains, particularly, are inspiring. Because the ranges are small and set in isolated groups around the plains, they seem to tower much higher than their 610-915m (2-3,000ft) would suggest. Each range has its own character, the result of very different geological processes, and so the sandstone ridge and valley scenery of the south-east is a striking contrast to the volcanic basalt of Antrim or the glistening quartzite of mountains such as Mayo's Croagh Patrick or Donegal's Errigal.

The Ice Age also left its mark on the landscape, particularly in the lowlands. Here features such as eskers and drumlins — geological terms derived from Gaelic words — can be easily spotted. Eskers are low, curving ridges of gravelly soil deposited by rivers of melting ice over thousands of years. They were among the first early trackways, providing a firm footing across marshy wetlands, and some Irish roads still follow them. One of the most interesting eskers, called the Pilgrim's Road, runs for several miles along the Shannon's east bank from the old monastery at Clonmacnoise to the Shannonbridge crossing.

Although the land itself has changed little since the days of Ireland's first inhabitants, the scenery is drastically different. This is largely because the native deciduous woodland which covered most of the country was ruthlessly hacked down during the early days of British colonialism. The British navy earmarked the best oaks for its frigates (ancient woodland around Lough Derg, on the River Shannon, proved particularly popular for this) and vast tracts of forest were cut for iron-smelting charcoal. When, in later years, English landlords began fencing off their estates and reclaiming forests for agriculture, the Irish peasants had little choice but to strip unenclosed woods for their building materials and their fuel. The effect has been to turn today's Ireland into one of the least wooded of all European countries. Where forests once flourished, the land now bears a man-made creation of patchwork fields divided by neat stone walls and hedgerows.

The country's main industry is, and always has been, farming. Agricultural land is best in the east and south-east where good quality soils allow some large arable farms. The further west you go, the more the soil deteriorates. Here the focus is on livestock farming — dairy and beef cattle on the pasture and sheep on the open moors and mountains. It is this concentration on farming which has helped keep the Irish countryside economically buoyant and, as a result, the population is evenly spread. Even in the wildernesses of the north and west, farms and cottages can usually be

Opposite: *The Caha Mountains in Co Cork. The range is among the most evocative sights in all Ireland, rising from the shores of Bantry Bay to reach heights of 610m (2,000ft) and above.*

seen and small towns and villages are scattered almost everywhere. Indeed, apart from Dublin and Belfast, Ireland has no major cities and only towns such as Cork, Limerick, Waterford and Derry can be considered large by European standards.

So much for the shape of the land. Geography and geology are mostly exact sciences and there is little room for argument and speculation over interpretation. History, (especially Irish history) however, is a different matter again. Here the problem is too much biased interpretation, coupled with a tendency among the early 'praise poets' to habitually over-egg the pudding. Contemporary accounts of just about any early historical event in Ireland have to be read with an eye to the writer's own interests — specifically the patronage offered him by his lord and master.

Our coverage of Irish history — Part Two of the book — begins with the very first Stone Age inhabitants, the men and women who are the only citizens of 'pure' Irish stock that the land has ever known. There are some romantic tales which more than suggest that Ireland was 'taken' by a wave of intrepid Celt invaders, a people who became the nation's founding fathers. In fact all the historical evidence suggests this scenario is distinctly questionable. The Celts, as we shall see, were just another bunch of warriors with colonial ambitions. They do not appear to have seized the land by force, but then they didn't need to. At the time the Celts began arriving from Britain and France the native population of Ireland must have been so small as to be almost insignificant. Even if they'd wanted a fight they would have had to look hard to find an enemy. Most likely Celtic colonisation was a gradual process which happened peacefully over hundreds if not thousands of years.

The sad truth is that our knowledge of early Irish history remains terribly sketchy. Up until recently, most archaeologists were still insisting that the Romans never invaded the country. They explained away Roman hoards and artifacts and a Romano-British grave as the result of sporadic trading and exploration. Then in 1996 came confirmation of a massive fortified settlement at Drumanagh, which seems to have been a beach-head for the Roman army on campaign in Ireland. At a stroke, a whole swathe of domestic historical theory was exposed as fundamentally flawed. While this is no fault of the archaeologists, who can work only with the information available, it is a useful reminder that few things about this period are certain.

The decline of the late Roman Empire may have given Irish Celts the confidence to conquer new lands of their own. They took control of Scotland through the Dál Riata, a tribe from Co Antrim, and there is good evidence that Irish tribes from Munster, such as the Dési and the Úi Liatháin, settled in western Britain from north Wales down as far as Devon and Cornwall. Perhaps this Celtish invasion was to assist the Britons in driving the Romans out — although around this time Irish warriors were also attacking the west of Britain simply to plunder and loot any settlements they could find. It was on one such raid that they captured a young boy from a wealthy family and took him home to work as a slave. In later years, Irish nationalists imbued with a romantic view of their heritage, must have shuddered at this cruel twist of history. To think that the most famous of all Irish saints, St Patrick, was a Brit! Once the Romans had been forced out of Ireland, the country was temporarily free of any further outside hostility. But there was certainly no peace. Gaelic tribes lived in a state of constant war with

Above: *The ancient art of turf cutting is still common in much of rural Ireland. Here a family from Achill, Co Mayo, load up for the trip home.*

each other and the internal politics of the following 500 years is a maelstrom of confusion. There would be occasions when some leader with enough military clout would declare himself 'High King' of Ireland, a title which usually meant little outside his immediate sphere of influence. However the Úi Néills dynasty, the country's most powerful tribe, were able to make their claim for kingship stick over very large areas indeed, especially during the 9th century. As we shall see Ireland came very close to uniting under a single king, although it never actually happened.

The Viking wars, which began at the end of the 8th century, had a devastating effect on the Christian communities of Ireland. Monastery after monastery was sacked, whole villages were razed and the country's greatest treasures exported back to Scandinavia. At first Gaelic coastal settlements were helpless against such fast, sea-borne raids but later the tribes began to hit back with some success.

Fears that the country would be over-run by Vikings during the middle of the 9th century proved groundless and although the longboats returned early in the 10th century this second period of raiding lasted little more than two decades. One of the greatest battles in Irish history took place at this time — the Battle of Dublin (919). This engagement has sometimes been portrayed as a showdown between the greatest of the Úi Néill warriors and the cream of the Dublin-based Vikings. In fact, petty rivalries and jealousies meant the makeup of the two sides was actually far more complicated, with Viking fighting Viking and Irishman fighting Irishman. For all their undoubted military and economic strength, the Vikings imprinted surprisingly little of their culture on the Irish way. True,

Above: *Once the haunt of outlaws and tribal bands, the Ring of Kerry is now tramped by thousands of visitors every year. This view shows a stretch of the rocky coast near Cahirdaniel.*

their language is credited with naming three of the four provinces (Munster, Ulster and Leinster) and some towns such as Dublin, Waterford, Wexford, Wicklow, Howth and Carlingford were named from Old Norse words. But aside from this, and a few words borrowed for the Gaelic language, there is surprisingly little to remember them by. Perhaps their greatest positive achievement was the maritime trade they brought to Ireland. Dublin at this time was one of the most important ports of the Viking world and was the centre of many trade routes. This might seem odd to us today because the city is seen as something of a European outpost. But in Viking times Dublin held a key position as a halfway stop-over between Gibraltar and Norway. Despite the huge distances involved, navigators of the day seem to have been well used to the sea lanes.

The next group of colonial hopefuls to land were the Normans. At first sight it might be thought their seizure of Ireland was the result of some carefully worked-out political strategy. Nothing could be further from the truth. It was a random, haphazard, chaotic affair in which successive English kings turned out to have very little say. Even when Henry II landed near Waterford in October 1171 at the head of a large army it was as much to keep his own barons under control as seize new territory for the Crown. Over the preceding two years the ousted Irish king of Leinster, Dermot MacMurrough, had recruited some mercenary Norman lords to help him reclaim his kingdom (including Dublin). Such was their degree of success that Henry saw the dangers of a powerful new kingdom arising on his vulnerable western borders. His very presence was enough to bring both Irish and Norman leaders into line beneath his rule.

Yet the problem for the English king and his successors, was keeping them there. As more and more Norman barons began flooding in to Ireland to claim estates, it became apparent that they cared little for any edicts issued by some far-distant monarch. This was a time of rising population in Europe — and therefore rising food prices — and the barons wasted no time cashing in. They guarded their investments by building motte and bailey castles (for which they received feudal grants from the Crown) and, almost by accident, completed a highly effective colonisation of the country. This was fine in times of plenty — but when populations began to fall, and Europe became devastated by plague, many of the barons abandoned their Irish estates and headed home to more comfortable country seats in England. From the middle of the 14th century there arose a revival in Gaelic culture — and outbreaks of civil war among Irish chieftains jockeying for positions of power.

Throughout this book the theme of religious freedom and the survival instincts of the Catholic Church, crop up time and again. The Viking raids were a dark time for the priests, but these were as nothing in comparison to the systematic persecution which lay ahead. When Henry VIII set the Reformation in train he tried to impose his model of the English Church onto Ireland and set about replacing his Catholic government officials — even though their loyalty to the Crown was absolute. For many of these Catholics this was a time of traumatic personal conflict. Their king demanded they should recognise his spiritual authority; their church demanded that they should not. Attempts by some Dublin lawyers to find a compromise were doomed from the start and the seeds of 400 years of religious strife were duly sown in fertile soil.

The mutual mistrust between England and Ireland deepened under Elizabeth I with the establishment of the first Protestant settlements or 'plantations'. For decades there was no let-up in the siege mentality prevailing among Irish Catholics, who were soon confronted with a deluge of aggressive new Protestant colonisers taking advantage of iniquitous laws to grab land and property when and wherever they could. In the first few decades of the 17th century at least 100,000 Britons crossed the Irish Sea to make new lives for themselves. By 1641 the Catholic lords could take no more, and they retaliated by becoming the persecutors. At least 2,000 Protestants were slaughtered and thousands more were stripped of their clothes and turned out into the streets. Such appalling acts were further exaggerated by church leaders in England and Scotland to the point where it was believed the Irish had massacred virtually every Protestant in Ireland.

It was against this background of suspicion and hatred that the most formidable army in Europe, headed by Oliver Cromwell, arrived in Ireland intent on revenge. It was an army fuelled and fired by a combination of religious zeal and an eagerness for plundering and it reminded Catholics everywhere of their perilous position under a Protestant monarch. Not until the crowning of James II, a Catholic king, in 1685 would there be a general sense of relief.

James II was removed from the English throne in 1688 and his attempt to regain it took place in Ireland. James's defeat by William of Orange in the two key battles of the 'Glorious Revolution' — at the Boyne in 1690 and Aughrim the following year — ushered in the era of Ascendancy, a culture in which wealth, land, education and the best jobs became Protestant luxuries and in which the poor would be thrown to the mercy of poverty, disease and famine. This period culminated in the Act of Union in 1800 when Ireland legally became part of Britain.

The 19th century is dominated by disease, hunger and the Great Famine of 1845–8, which would see over a million die and a diaspora of emigration, much of it to the New World. Together these factors would halve the pre-famine population to under four million by 1900. It is unsurprising that this tragedy sparked off campaigns for tenants' rights, home rule and — ultimately — rebellion.

Daniel O'Connell, the 'Liberator', pursued Catholic equality which was delivered in limited form in the 1828 Catholic Emancipation Act. Charles Stewart Parnell, leader of the Home Rule Party, would see support for his movement from British Prime Minister Gladstone. However, plans for Home Rule were shelved because of the European conflagration in 1914 that would lead to world war. Because of this, it would be the revolutionaries that would strike the blow that freed Ireland from 900 years of oppression. After the abortive Easter Rebellion of 1916 had been put down, its leaders callously executed in Kilmainham Gaol, it would take another five years of struggle before the Anglo-Irish Treaty of 1921 granted independence to the south.

Civil War followed as those in favour of the treaty battled others who wanted to see all Ireland given independence. It would be some years before coexistence was possible in the south; in the north, of course, the final vestiges of the civil war continue to this day. In 1932, Eamon de Valera, who had escaped execution in 1916, became *Taioseach* (Prime Minister) of the country leading his *Fianna Fáil* (Soldiers of Destiny) party; he would remain in power until 1948 and be reappointed for further terms in office in the 1950s.

Neutral during World War 2, Éire (as the country had become in 1937 when it declared its complete independence from Britain) would stay a member of the Commonwealth until 1949 when it became the Republic of Ireland. In 1955 the Republic joined the United Nations; in 1973 it became a member of the European Economic Community and the country began to thrive. Today the Republic, under the benign control of its first female president, Mary Robinson, has modernised and found its place in the world. Irish culture has blossomed in the form of literature, dance and music, and has won a worldwide audience.

The chapters ahead are not intended to give an exhaustive account of Irish history. Neither do they try to draw lofty conclusions about the reasons for today's Republican-versus-Unionist conflict. The aim is rather to offer a glimpse of Ireland's colourful and fascinating history, of some of her sufferings and her triumphs but, most of all, of the people who made her.

Above: *The ruins of King John's castle, Carlingford Co Louth.*

Opposite above: *The still of the evening captured at Lough Talt, Co Sligo.*

Opposite below: *A reminder of Ireland's war torn past at Rosslare, Co Wexford. The south-east coast saw many invasions — from the first Celts to the 'shock troops' of Oliver Cromwell.*

PART 1:
THE LAND

1 Geology and Geography

Ireland, like its people, is blessed with unique character. Within the space of a few hundred miles the countryside embraces a geological pot pourri of gentle rolling hills, rugged 3,000ft mountains, wild moors and bogs, sweeping inland plains, compact massifs and, in its striking eskers and drumlins, intriguing legacies of the Ice Age. Despite this pedigree, the uninitiated sometimes consider it to be Europe's afterthought; a small, lonely island whipped by the Atlantic, ravaged by rainstorms and wrapped in perpetual mist. Only when they glimpse the magic of Ireland – perhaps cloud shadows racing across the Cork and Kerry Mountains or the huge skies of Connemara above a wild ocean – only then can the casual visitor recognise the truth. This is God's own country.

The huge variety in the landscape is obvious, even to the untrained eye. The red sandstone heights of the South for instance are very different in shape to the quartzite peaks of Donegal or Mayo. Equally, the contrast between the central limestone plains and the coastal mountain ranges – the geographical features that give Ireland its saucer shape appearance in cross-section – are apparent in any lengthy cross-country journey.

The one recurring theme in the Irish countryside is water. Apart from the twisting 2,000-mile coastline, boasting some of the finest unspoilt beaches in Europe, there are dozens of spectacular hill loughs created by the gouging action of glaciers during at least two Ice Ages. Add in the Shannon network of interlocking rivers and lakes, which covers around one-fifth of the land mass, and it is easy to see why the place is considered an angling Mecca.

The country has four provinces – Leinster (12 counties) in the east, Munster (6 counties) in the south-west, Connaught (5 counties) in the west and Ulster (9 counties) in the north. The political division of Ireland is dealt with elsewhere in this book but it should be noted that 'Northern Ireland', which is under British rule, and Ulster are not one and the same administrative region. Three of Ulster's counties – Monaghan, Cavan and Donegal – form part of the Republic. The other six, Londonderry, Antrim, Tyrone, Fermanagh, Down and Armagh are collectively known as Northern Ireland.

Ireland's geological regions are so clearly defined that it is easier to look at each separately, crossing provincial boundaries where necessary. The midlands is perhaps the best place to start, not least because within its apparently unremarkable scenery lie some real gems for any walker who has ever pondered over an unusual feature of the land.

The Midlands

Glacial drift (rock and soil deposits left by the ice) can be found across much of the midland plain, although it only becomes noticeable where it has been fashioned into distinctive eskers and drumlins. Ireland has excellent examples of both, indeed the geological terms are derived from Gaelic words.

Eskers are low, snaking ridges of sand and gravel that were laid down by rivers of melting ice running beneath the main glaciers. Centuries later they were used as primitive highways across the surrounding marshes and today you can still find yourself driving along one. Perhaps the best known is the Pilgrim's Road, which runs for seven miles along the Shannon's east bank towards the ancient abbey of Clonmacnoise.

Drumlins appear as whale-shaped hills and are best seen on the northern and western extremities of the central plan. They are found in groups – so-called 'basket of eggs topography' – and are aligned in the direction of the ice flow. Although the outer shells are made up of glacial deposits, there is sometimes a central rock core acting as an anchor for the rubble around it. There are submerged examples in Clew Bay, forming a fascinating group of islands, while both Co. Down and north east Roscommon boast classic drumlin country of 200ft high hills divided by hollows around half a mile across.

Today the Midlands, or Central Plain, has become Ireland's most important beef-producing area, as becomes obvious when you encounter the numbers of butchers, slaughterhouses and stockyards in market towns like Ballyhaunis and Tullamore. The scenery may be uninspiring in comparison with the rest of the country yet from the quiet lanes off the main routes west there are superb views across the country's pastoral heartland.

Cork and Kerry

If fairies really do live in Ireland then their capital city must surely lie somewhere in the Cork and Kerry Mountains. This south-west region exudes a mystical atmosphere that somehow survives even at the height of the tourist season, when cars and coaches battle it out on trips around the Ring of Kerry and the Dingle Peninsula. The rocky coves and bays of the west coast lie within a few miles of the Killarney Lakes, while a little further inland rises Ireland's highest mountain, the 3,414 ft Carrauntoohil, part of the gloriously-named MacGillicuddy's Reeks. Grasslands extending high into the hills bear testament to the amount of rain blown in from the Atlantic, and this is certainly no place to be caught in a storm. But for a taste of true Irish wilderness there is no better region to travel. It is easy to escape the tourist honey-pots and explore the quiet headlands of the Mizen, Sheep's Head and the Beara or, further inland, the untouched expanse of the Boggeragh and Derrynasaggart Mountains.

Previous page: *A typical Connemara landscape of windswept mountains and peat bogs.*

Opposite: *Valentia Island, Co. Kerry, linked to Portmagee on the mainland by a seven-mile (11km) causeway.*

Thatched cottages are an essential and timeless part of the Irish landscape as building techniques have changed little over the centuries. A properly thatched roof is totally waterproof, provides vital insulation and can last half a century.

Above: *A cottage near Lough Corrib, Co Galway. This wild part of Ireland is said to be the spiritual home of the writer James Joyce.*

Left: *An Irish paradise; a farmstead on the coast of Co Donegal.*

Opposite: *A cottage nestles alongside the River Erriff, beneath the uplands of Co Mayo.*

The Burren

Like the countryside of Sligo, this curious carboniferous limestone plateau stretching across northern Co Clare was a lasting inspiration for Yeats. After the breathtaking scenery further south it can be difficult to immediately appreciate its beauty, yet the treeless landscape with its thin, stony soil and scatterings of white rock has a peculiar charm of its own. Alpine plants flourish in the unlikeliest crevasses while entrances to underground rivers, caves and holes are common in the grey, porous rock. It was not, however, appreciated by Cromwell's army. According to local folklore, soldiers complained that there were 'too few trees to hang anyone, too little water to drown anyone and too little earth to bury anyone.'

Mayo and Connemara

Connemara, in the west of Galway, lies between the dark waters of Lough Corrib and the cliffs of north of Galway Bay. It is perhaps the heart of old Ireland, an area where Gaelic Irish is still widely spoken, where the donkey is crucial to many people's livelihoods (especially as a transporter of newly-cut peat) and where the old Celtic traditions of singing and storytelling have survived intact. Most of the farms lie scattered along a narrow coastal belt between high mountains and a sea that seems forever to be on the boil. The sight of a full-blown Atlantic storm moving towards the simple, whitewashed homesteads is enough to make any visitor wonder whether scratching a living in Connemara is worth the candle. Little wonder that the weather is an ever-present topic of conversation among the locals.

Mayo, a county on Ireland's north-west extremity, is separated from Connemara by Lough Mask, one of a dozen large lakes in the area. North of the county town Westport lies the country's largest offshore island, Achill, which forms the westernmost edge of the Nephin Beg mountain range. An undulating L-shaped island, Achill is almost entirely covered in bog and heathland. Its north and west coasts contain some of the most stunning cliff scenery anywhere in Europe, with 2,200ft peaks rising sharply from the ocean. Mayo's eastern plains have a quieter, secluded air to them with dry-stone walled pastures interspersed by the occasional dense patch of woodland.

Donegal and North Sligo

Co Donegal, in the far north-west, is a remote and often inhospitable terrain. Its mountains run north-east to south-west across most of the county and on a typical day the peaks will be concealed beneath a cold, grey mist. The north has some fine sea loughs; the west is dominated by sandy beaches but the one thing they have in common is a feeling of emptiness. Away from the scattering of villages pegged out along the coastal strip there are precious few signs of civilisation. A few roads fan out north-east along the valleys, the busiest being the most southerly – the route between Donegal town and the communities at Ballybofey and Stranorar.

The country north of here is dominated by the Blue Stack Mountains, towering above the picturesque Lough Eske with its sinister island fortress once used to hold enemies of the O'Donnell clan. Further west is the mountainous South Donegal peninsula, ending in the awe-inspiring 2,000ft high Slieve League cliffs. The landscape here is as lonely as anywhere in Ireland and yet the towns and villages of the south coast, particularly the fishing port of Killybegs, are lively places with a strong sense of community.

Sligo town is sited on the edge of another limestone outcrop, a flat-topped ridge culminating in the magnificent Ben Bulben mountain at the Atlantic end of the Dartry range. In his poem 'Under Ben Bulben', Yeats conjures up something of the stern, work-a-day feel of the place, its people hardened to the practicalities of life by the daily struggle to survive:

Under bare Ben Bulben's head
In Drumcliff churchyard Yeats is laid
An ancestor was rector there
Long years ago, a church stands near
By the road an ancient cross
No marble, no conventional phrase
On limestone quarried near the spot
By his command these words are cut
'Cast a cold eye
'On life, on death.
'Horseman, pass by.'

North of the Shannon

This region is bounded to the north and west by the long finger of the Ox Mountains, separating Sligo and Mayo, and the south-east Sligo ranges of the Bricklieves and Curlews. Further east limestone again stamps its mark on the countryside with undulating hills occasionally split by a bog, forest or pastureland. Along the fringes of Co Roscommon lies the thickly wooded Lough Key, from where the Boyle River flows east on its way to link with the Shannon near Carrick. To the north lies some fine drumlin country and the narrow river valleys, bald peaks and countless small lakes of Co Leitrim.

The Shannon, Ireland's longest river, runs from a source above Lough Allen, near Carrick, to join the Atlantic a few miles west of Limerick. The banks are thinly populated and so the lack of heavy industry and sewage effluent makes the Shannon one of Europe's cleanest major waterways. In recent years it has sustained a vital segment of Irish tourism – namely the joys of inland cruising. The river is perfect for novices; apart from a short non-navigable stretch in its upper course, the gradient down to Limerick requires only six locks.

The Eastern Counties

Much of the farmland around and above Co Dublin – in Meath, Louth, Monaghan and Cavan is drained by the slow, wide River Boyne and its tributary, the Blackwater. Here the invading Normans and the Anglo-Irish built their grand estates and planted fine deciduous woods, many of which thrive today. The Boyne meanders through unspectacular grassy plains, entering the sea at Drogheda. But the region also has its wilder side in the heathery uplands of the Cooley and Carlingford peninsulas and along the rocky cliffs of Clogerhead. County Dublin, increasingly the commuter belt for Ireland's capital city, still retains old traditions of

Opposite: *The Doonbriste stack, at Downpatrick, Co Mayo, an area of stunning cliff scenery.*

Agriculture is the lifeblood of Ireland but, despite generous help from the European Community, it remains as tough a life as ever. Broadly speaking, the south-east and east midlands have most of the arable land — elsewhere pasture and hay are the order of the day.

Above: *Cattle wander freely across the desolate limestone plateau that forms The Burren, Co Clare.*

Right: *Connemara ponies soak up the sun.*

Overleaf: *Grazing sheep complete a tranquil rural scene on Achill Island, Co Mayo.*

vegetable-growing and dairy farming although the expansion of Dublin City has maintained huge pressure on the countryside from property developers. Thankfully, many beauty spots have escaped the urban sprawl; Killiney Bay, to the south, is a jewel for city workers anxious for fresh air while northwards lie the neat, flat fields of the Skerries and Rush and the unspoiled peninsula of Howth Head.

The Wicklow Hills

The Wicklows, in Ireland's south-east corner, are a true granite massif with comparatively few river valleys and a 200 square mile area of moorland which rises comfortably above 1,000ft. The brown and purple hills can be a bleak place on a stormy day, with hardly any tree cover and few settlements. Until the 18th century many of the higher moors were barely explored and (rightly) acquired a reputation as the haunts of highwaymen and outlaws. There are only two east-to-west passes – the Sally Gap and the Wicklow Gap – while most north-south traffic now uses the tight coastal plain between Dublin and Wexford. South of the hills, defining the Wexford-Carlow border, lies the narrow Blackstairs Mountains chain with its highest peak, Mount Leinster.

The Southern Country

This is ridge-and-valley scenery, with the picturesque Blackwater and Suir rivers sandwiched between the heights of the Knockmealdowns, the Monnavullagh and Comeragh hills south of Clonmel and the Galtees south of Tipperary town. The contrasts between the rich grazing land, which produces some of Ireland's finest cheese, butter and cream, and the sheer mountains surrounding it give the region a clear identity. The Galtees are a particularly strong landmark, easily identifiable for miles around, while to the north-west rise the enchanting Silvermine Hills and the lower reaches of the largest of the Shannon waterways, Lough Derg.

Northern Ireland

In the Giant's Causeway, Co Antrim surely has the Ireland's most visually striking geological feature. According to folklore it was built by giants who wanted a bridge to cross between Ireland and the West of Scotland (where Celtic tradition is equally strong). The scientific explanation is that the promontory was formed by volcanic lava pouring into the sea. This cooled quickly, creating thousands of tightly-packed hexagonal basalt columns.

Sadly, thousands of visitors who gaze in wonder at the Causeway never get to explore the rest of the stunning Antrim countryside. The headlands of Fair and Torrs Head rank among Europe's wildest and most beautiful coastlines, while inland the Nine Glens of Antrim have inspired poets and writers for centuries. Glenariff is particularly interesting, with its Mare's Tail waterfall and classic U-shaped glaciated valley. Antrim, together with counties Armagh and Tyrone, also forms one of the shores of Lough Neagh. This is the largest lake in the British Isles, measuring 18 by 11 miles with a maximum depth of some 40ft. It is filled by ten tributary streams and drains from its north end down the River Bann.

Co Down is dominated by the great purple mass of the Mourne Mountains, an area of rounded uplands, shaped by the ice and rising to 2,798ft at Slieve Donard. from where it is possible to see the English coast on a fine day. The south of the county has the splendid Carlingford Lough, a type of fjord which once saw the brunt of Viking invasions. The Lough is part of a geological fault line, the Gap of the North, which has been an important link road for centuries. Armagh, Ulster's smallest county, also has its share of moor and mountains although the further north and west you go the more farmland you find. Farming in Armagh wears its Gaelic heritage proudly; the myriad interlocking dry-stone wall fields bear witness to the practice of splitting lands between the family.

To the east, Londonderry, Tyrone and Fermanagh together offer a huge variety in the landscape. Fermanagh is the North's lake district, with around one third of the county underwater. Good grazing land is at a premium and in the limestone uplands to the west the soil is so poor that few farmers have attempted to scratch a living from it. The result has been that many indigenous species have flourished undisturbed by chemical fertilisers. Tyrone, the 'heart' of Ulster, is mostly covered on its northern flanks by the Sperrin Mountains, the highest of which (Sawel) stands on the Londonderry border. These lonely hills are known to contain gold deposits and for centuries panners have worked the streams in the hope of eking out a living. Londonderry is a county of rugged coves, wide sandy beaches, sheltered woods and valleys and belts of open moorland. The traditional linen industry still survives, although the continuing 'Troubles' have left the local economy heavily reliant on UK Government subsidies.

Major Cities

Dublin (pop. 1 million) is the Republic's capital and traces its history back to the first Christian Celts. It's reputation as a major European sea-port was established under the Vikings and it became the country's administrative centre following the influx of the Anglo-English. Its characteristic wide streets and beautiful squares show many Georgian influences and it has become an important university and cultural city. Today the main industries are distilling, brewing (it has the world's largest brewery), clothing, glass and food processing.

Belfast (pop. 304,000) is the capital of the north. It is viewed around the world as a city in fear, although without be-littling the deaths of hundreds of innocent people, this is simply not the case. First-time visitors are often surprised at the normality they find in the bars and shops and the infectious sense of fun possessed by the inhabitants. Belfast rose to prominence as a 19th century industrial town and its economy is now based on shipbuilding, electronics and engineering.

Opposite above: *Near Lisdoonvarna, Co Clare.*

Opposite below: *The deserted village Slievemore on Achill Island, Co Mayo. The country's largest offshore island, Achill forms the western-most edge of the Nephin Beg mountain range. An undulating L-shaped island, it is almost entirely covered in bog and heathland. Its north and west coasts contain some of the most stunning cliff scenery anywhere in Europe, with 2,200ft peaks rising sharply from the ocean.*

Cork (pop 128,000) grew up around St Finbarr's 6th century monastery and is today a cosmopolitan city with a culture and energy to rival Dublin. It has some striking buildings, particularly churches and cathedrals, and its industry exports bacon, dairy produce, livestock and beer.

Limerick (pop 52,000) is another city founded on a monastery. Historically it was a key strategic port on the mouth of the Shannon and its prosperity today is largely down to light industries attracted by the nearby Shannon international airport.

Sligo (pop 56,000) was a bustling port in the 19th century with distilling, brewing, linen, milling, rope and leather-making forming its manufacturing base. The surrounding countryside has always been devoted mainly to agriculture, although there are some coal, lead and copper deposits. The area was hit very hard by the famines, devastating the local economy for decades.

The beauty of Ireland is timeless and unspoilt. While their mountains may not be as large as others in Europe, they are rugged and beautiful to walk. These pictures show scenes from the Wicklow Mountains less than an hour's drive from Dublin – the haunt of warlords and rebels 'beyond the Pale' – and from the Sperrin Mountains of Co Tyrone just south of Londonderry in Ulster.

Above: *Glendalough Upper Lake seen from the Wicklow Way, which runs 132km (82 miles) from Marlay Park in Dublin to Clonegal in Co Carlow, traversing the Wicklow hills.*

Opposite above: *The Sperrin Mountains in Co Tyrone. View to the south from below Dart Pass to Glenelly valley.*

Opposite below: *The upper valley of the River Liffey, looking south towards Mount Mullaghcleevaun (849m -2,784ft).*

PART 2: THE HISTORY

2 The First People

Throughout the Ice Age, which lasted from about 1.7 million years ago to around 11,000BC Ireland was geographically linked to the European continent. For much of this time the country was covered by an ice cap, which advanced and retreated according to the various warm and cold phases in global weather patterns. It is possible that a population established itself during one or other of the warm spells, although there is no evidence for this yet. Present thinking is that the first humans in Ireland arrived somewhere between 8000BC and 6500BC and that they crossed from Britain along one of several land bridges that existed at the time. Many wild animals also made the crossing but some, such as beavers, roe deer, wild cattle, otters and snakes never made it over in time (to this day there are no snakes in Ireland). As the climate warmed, so the ice melted and sea levels rose — causing the land bridges to disappear forever beneath the waves.

These first human settlers were hunter-gatherers. From analysis of settlements such as Mount Sandel, in Co Derry, they seem to have dined on the likes of duck, pigeon and grouse, along with nuts and berries. Fish was also a major part of their diet — the remains of eels, flounder, salmon and sea bass have all been identified at Mount Sandel — and pig and hare may have been hunted with the help of dogs. Weapons were mainly flint arrows and spears, although stone axes were also made — most notably from factories at Tievebulliagh and on the isle of Rathlin in Co Antrim. These porcellanite axes were probably Ireland's first large-scale exports and have turned up in far-flung archaeological sites right across the British Isles.

The early Stone Age Irish would have spent much of their time on the move, seeking out new hunting grounds in winter and then perhaps returning to established sources of food in summer. Ulster and Leinster probably saw the first colonies, but exploration inland must have been severely limited by the dense forests and scrub. Lakes and rivers were the only way to travel at speed.

Initial colonisation of Ireland was followed by the second key event in the country's pre-history — the development of agriculture and a more stable, ordered existence. Farming techniques were adopted in Ireland somewhere around the 4th millennium BC, spreading from the Middle East where they had emerged some 3,000 years earlier. The first Irish farmers began enthusiastically clearing forest for cultivation and by 3400BC the first farm animals had been introduced. Cattle, sheep and goats seem to have been brought over in an already domesticated state by settlers arriving from Britain. The prevailing theory is that these Neolithic colonists came from south-west Scotland to the counties of Antrim and Down, which they could see on a good day with the naked eye over the North Channel. Longer voyages may have been made further south across the Irish Sea, but the chances of cattle surviving in small open boats, their legs tethered, must have been much slimmer.

Above: *Staigue Fort, Co Kerry, is one of a number of early stone fortresses which may have been influenced by Scottish designs.*

Opposite: *The so-called 'Bog Roads', such as this one in Co Longford, were a communications lifeline for the early Irish. Much of the land was either impenetrable forest or impassable marsh.*

Previous page: *View of Kilkenny Castle from the banks of the River Nore. This Norman fortress was the meeting place of the Irish Parliament in the 13th century.*

One of the oldest known Neolithic houses in either Britain or Ireland has been excavated at Ballynagilly, near Cookstown, Co Tyrone. It dates from about 3200BC and was square-shaped, covering around 40sq m (430ft). The walls were formed of planks of oak driven into a shallow trench and the roof was probably thatch. Later houses used stone foundations with wattle-and-daub packed between wooden posts.

While these domestic houses are now little more than chemical remains in the soil, there are plenty of surviving monuments on which we can judge the skills of the megalithic builders. Their great tombs, stone circles and standing stones are among the most evocative features of the Irish landscape. The sheer scale of these early engineering projects still inspires wonder today.

The geological wonderland that is Craig Cave at Castleisland, Co Kerry.

3 Tombs, Circles and Stones

Above: *Proleek Dolmen, a typical portal tomb at Ballymascanlon, and* **(Opposite)** *another fine example at Haroldstown, Co Carlow. The word Dolmen comes from an old Breton phrase meaning 'stone table'.*

Beneath its fertile soil Ireland has one of the richest archaeological treasure troves anywhere in Europe. This is partly because less intensive farming methods over the years have helped preserve the past. But it is also down to the sheer productivity of the ancient megalithic builders. There are at least 1,200 known megalithic monuments in Ireland and probably many more which have disappeared over the years.

This area of pre-history is sometimes forgotten by those who seek to establish the 'real identity' of the Irish. It is probable that the first megalithic builders arrived from France in two or three distinct waves, absorbing into the resident population slowly and smoothly. They were a people whose customs and beliefs, rituals and laws are unclear to us today. But bearing in mind the scale of the building projects they undertook (megalith means 'large stone' in Greek), they must have been not only committed and resourceful but also driven by some powerful faith.

Most megalithic monuments in Ireland were built somewhere between 2000 and 3000BC, although modern radio-carbon dating methods are not always accurate. There appear to be four main types:

• Court Cairns: Well over 300 of these have now been identified, mostly north of a line between Galway and Dundalk. Only about a tenth of them have been properly excavated but the items recovered are much the same. They include cremated human bones, typical round-bottomed 'Western Neolithic' pots, flint and chert arrowheads and the odd axe or knife.

The purpose of court cairns is debatable. Very little pottery is ever found intact, suggesting either that many tombs were disturbed by later peoples or that their contents were moved in from earlier burial sites (perhaps to appease the spirits and nature gods). The cairns consist of a narrow mound of earth with a small courtyard at one end leading into a narrow passageway. The passage is often sectioned off into a series of chambers.

It is likely that these tombs were the pagan equivalent of a parish church, acting as a cult centre for communities of around 50-100 people all living within a couple of miles radius. Perhaps the cairns were a way of establishing ancestral rights over a particular ground. Certainly, studies of megaliths in Co Leitrim suggest that they were positioned on light, well-drained, upland soils ideally suited to early farming practice. This implies that they stood close to domestic settlements as important focal points for the communities they served. Among the most interesting are at Creevykeel and Treanmacmurtagh in Co Sligo, Ballyalton and Audleystown in Co Down, and Browndod in Co Antrim.

• Portal Tombs (also known as dolmens): These are the most dramatic of the Irish megaliths and something no visitor to the country should miss. They are above-ground tombs and one theory is that they evolved out of the court cairn design (the sites of the two types closely tally). When seen against the skyline, portal tombs can eerily evoke the magic of Ireland's mysterious past and it is little wonder they became an integral part of the nation's folklore. Who could blame later peoples for believing them to be the dining tables of giants? — The term dolmen originates from old Breton words meaning stone and table — and no doubt their massive capstones were designed to impress Neolithic tribesmen. Some of these stones weighed 102kg (100 tons) or more and appear to have been hauled into place on wooden rollers. The number of willing hands needed to pull them the final few metres up a temporary earthen ramp is a matter of guesswork, but it was possibly several hundred.

Portal tombs were often built close to the sea and along river valleys. Good examples include Legananny, Co Down, Kilclooney, Co Donegal and Ballykeel, Co Armagh.

• Passage Tombs: These were perhaps the first great architectural designs of prehistoric European culture. They rank alongside the temples of Malta in importance and are Western Europe's modest equivalent of the Egyptian pyramids or the Mycenaean burial chambers (the idea of an above-ground passage and tomb covered with an artificial mound is the same). Passage tombs are usually found in countries bordering the eastern Atlantic, such as Portugal, Spain, France, Scandinavia, Wales, Scotland and, of course, Ireland.

The Irish examples are arguably the most fascinating. They tend to be sited together in large cemeteries such as Newgrange, Knowth and Dowth and Loughcrew in Co Meath, and Carrowmore and Carrowkeel in Co Sligo. Often there is one very large tomb easily distinguishable from the others — almost as a cathedral among a scattering of churches. These larger versions are not always found in the centre of a cemetery. At Knocknarea near Sligo town the grave of Queen Maeve looks down on smaller passage tombs making up the main Carrowmore cluster.

Studies of the tombs have shown that they were used both for cremation and burial rituals. The Irish Tourist Board archaeologist Patrick Hartnett established that the one at Fourknocks, Co Meath, contained the remains of some 60 people, yet these bodies would not have been interred in one mass service. Rather, passage tombs were the equivalent of the graveyard vaults used by wealthy families of recent times. Passage tombs were mostly a final resting place for several different generations, although some may have been constructed specifically for a great tribal chief.

The items placed with the dead are more difficult to fathom. In addition to the usual pottery, there are often carved bone pins which may have fastened leather bags containing the cremated remains of the dead. As these pins are usually burnt, however, it's perhaps more likely that they clasped a cloak around a dead body as it lay on a funeral pyre. Other grave goods include stone pendants or talismans, usually made out of soapstone or limestone and often fashioned in the shape of a hammer or axe. Most enigmatic of all are the large balls of chalk or stone which have turned up. Their significance remains a mystery.

Sadly, some of the secrets of the passage tombs may already have been lost for ever. So called 'excavations' (which in reality were little more than grave robberies) of the 19th and early 20th centuries destroyed much vital archaeological material. One of the worst cases occurred at the remarkable Loughcrew passage tombs — known locally as The Hill Of The Witch — near Oldcastle, Meath, where more than 30 mounds are grouped together. No decent records were kept of the items taken, which presumably are now in private collections somewhere. But at least those responsible didn't remove a crude stone basin, probably used for rituals, neither could they take the large stones decorated with Neolithic art — U-shapes, sun symbols, snakes, spirals, 'fishbone' lines and zig-zags.

Fortunately for today's archaeologists the three great passage tomb clusters of Meath's Boyne Valley, namely Newgrange, Knowth and Dowth were not subject to similar raids and have produced numerous important finds. One of these was the Knowth mace head, a superb ceremonial implement carved from flint and mounted on a wooden handle.

Before leaving passage tombs it is worth mentioning Newgrange's hallowed place in Irish folklore. According to the early analysts it was both the final resting place of the kings of Tara (more of which later) and entrance to an underworld populated by the supernatural Tuatha de Danainn (people of the goddess Danu). Newgrange was also said to have been the home of the god Dagda and his son Oengus.

• Wedge Tombs: These are Ireland's most common megalithic monument, with almost 400 located — mostly west of a line between Cork and Derry. The rectangular shaped burial chamber was often higher towards the front and roofed with large stones which were encased in a wedge-shaped earthwork mound. Wedge tombs are thought to be the later megaliths and may have been the work of Bronze Age man after 2000AD. Some have suggested they were designed by a 'new wave' of colonists from France, who landed in southern Ireland and spread their influence north and west. Among the most interesting are those of Baurnadomeeny, Co Tipperary, Labbacallee, Co Cork, Ballyedmonduff, Co Dublin, and Moytirra, Co Sligo. Moytirra excavations have produced some of the best examples of 'beaker' pottery in all Ireland.

The precise social and religious significance of the four different types of tombs is still largely guesswork. There was almost certainly a belief in the spirit world and it is possible that keeping an ancestor's bones in the village where he lived was a way of laying down land rights. Whatever the truth, the tombs were not the only sacred sites. Stone circles, of which there are around 200 in Ireland (mostly in the south-west and Ulster), must surely have hosted religious gatherings — perhaps for the worship of the sun and stars or to pay homage to pagan nature gods. The purpose of standing stones, prevalent almost everywhere in Ireland, is less clear. Some appear to form alignments with the more important circles, while others might have been markers for ancient trackways or gravestones.

One of the most elaborate circles is at Grange, in Co. Limerick, where the prehistoric builders erected stones up to 2.7m (9ft) tall. Grange is surrounded by a large earthen bank with a clear entranceway on the eastern side. The land within the stones was originally floored with clay, raising it about 61cm (2ft) above that outside, and it clearly held great significance for those who used it. But the assertion that Grange, and similar circles in Cork and Kerry, were sophisticated lunar observatories is debatable. There is some small evidence that stones were set to correspond to a point on the skyline marking the rise or fall of the sun, moon and stars. Why though, if this were all that was needed, did the Neolithic builders not rely simply on two key stones to make an alignment? At the moment all we can say with certainty is that the movement of celestial bodies influenced the siting of circles and standing stones. Dromberg circle in Co Cork, for instance, is set up along the line of the winter solstice sunset.

Whenever prehistoric stone circles are discussed, there is inevitably speculation about the use of some form of sacrifice by the religious leaders of the day. A combination of ancient mythology, folklore and over-imaginative film scripts have today conjured up images of men in white cloaks and hoods cutting the throat of some terrified virgin tied to a sacrificial stone. Such scenarios seem unlikely, but it would be wrong to pretend human sacrifice did not happen. One henge-type circle on the moor at Curragh in Co Kildare has a central grave in which was found the remains of a young woman. The position of the skeleton is highly unusual and does suggest that she was buried alive. The head was probably upright, one hand and one leg were pressed against the side of the grave and the legs were apart. A few miles from this site, though probably unconnected, we find the Punchestown standing stone which, at 6.4m (21ft), is the tallest in Ireland.

Outside Cork and Kerry, the Ulster stone circles are the most dramatic. Particularly noteworthy is the Beaghmore cluster near Cookstown, Co Tyrone where three pairs of circles and a single one studded with 884 small boulders have been built within a few hundred metres of each other. The site also contains numerous cairns and standing stones but the reasons behind its layout are unknown. One academic has speculated that a line of four stones nearby could have been used to pinpoint the rising moon on the horizon in about 1640BC.

Finally, we come to the other intriguing aspect of prehistoric architecture — a trend which probably followed the wedge tombs and stone circles — the stone rows. In Ireland the vast majority of these were short, comprising only three to six stones, but there were many more of them than in England, Scotland and Brittany. There are around 30 four-to-six stone rows, nearly 60 three-stone rows and well over a 100 stone pairs. The short rows seem to be independent of circles or tombs and are much more common in the south and west. Ulster has a dense concentration of both long and short rows.

Extensive research by the archaeologist Ann Lynch in south-west Ireland has proved conclusive links to astronomical alignments. Of the 37 short rows she plotted, 23 showed significant alignments to the solstices and/or the major extremes of the moon. But this does not necessarily imply that Neolithic or Bronze Age astronomers had an advanced scientific understanding. These were people who spent much of their lives staring at the night sky and the movements of the sun, moon, stars and planets would have evoked far more general interest, and undoubtedly far more significance, among the population than they do today. The stone rows may simply have been an aid to observation, and therefore to the timing of rituals and festivals.

The emergence of the Irish rows seems to have coincided with exploitation of the first copper mines. Irish copper and Cornish tin combined made bronze, and the start of the Bronze Age in Ireland (from roughly 2000BC) must have seen an eruption in trading links between these two lands and Brittany — another major outlet for bronze items. One offshoot of this trade would have been an exchange of ideas and the Bretons, who built Europe's most impressive stone row complex at Carnac, may well have exported their beliefs to the Irish and Cornish. It was the dawn of a new era, a time in which metalworking was the growth industry. For Ireland, it was the beginning of a golden age.

Opposite above: *The massive capstone of the Browneshill portal tomb, Co Carlow, is thought to weigh more than 100 tons.*

Opposite below: *The Carrowkeel passage tombs in Co Sligo form one of Ireland's most important early cemeteries.*

Above: *Another view of the partially-collapsed Browneshill dolmen.*

Left: *A decorated stone from the great tomb complex at Knowth, in the Boyne valley, Co Meath. This form of prehistoric art is more common in the east of the country.*

Opposite: *The Burren, Co Clare, has numerous examples of Ireland's commonest megalith — the wedge tomb.*

Above: *Beneath a threatening Irish sky, the graves at Carrowkeel have a truly atmospheric quality.*

Left: *The Neolithic settlement at Lough Gur, Co Limerick, (now reconstructed) has yielded important clues to the spread of 'Beaker' pottery in the north of Ireland.*

Opposite: *Ireland's tallest standing stone at Punchestown, Co. Kildare, stands more than 6.5m (21ft) high.*

Above: *A general view of the Knowth passage grave complex. It ranks alongside the temples of Malta as prehistoric Europe's greatest monumental architecture.*

Left: *The Catstone megaliths of West Meath.*

Opposite above: *A view through the remains of Creevykeel Court Cairn, Co Sligo. It is more than 61m (200ft) long and has an entrance 'court' measuring 15 by 9m (50 by 30ft).*

Opposite below: *Stone circles such as this one at Carrowmore may have combined religious, social and scientific purposes.*

Above: *The impressive stonework forming the roof of Newgrange, Co Meath is easily Ireland's best known megalithic monument. Conservative estimates suggest that Newgrange, which is orientated to the mid-winter sunrise, may have taken 30 years to build.*

Left: *The squat Aghnacliff dolmen in Co Longford.*

Opposite: *Another stone circle from the Carrowmore cemetery in Co Sligo. The site's religious significance may date from as early as the 4th millennium BC.*

Above: *The purpose of these standing stones at Oran, Co Roscommon remains a mystery.*

Right: *Hundreds of visitors every year come to view the Creevykeel court cairn.*

Opposite above: *One of Ireland's largest stone circles is the Grange, in the Lough Gur area of Co Limerick. The area within the circle was raised by an 45cm (18in) deep clay floor.*

Opposite below: *Another view of the Grange stones.*

Derrintaggart stone circle stands on the Beara Peninsula, Co. Cork.

4 Buried Treasure from a Golden Age

The discovery of copper sometime after 2000BC heralded the start of an Irish metalworking industry which became renowned in western Europe. In archaeological terms this was more accurately the beginning of the Bronze Age, a time of new technology for the prehistoric Irish and the arrival of many economic changes. The country's copper mining centre was Cork and Kerry and it is thought they together produced a remarkable 375,920kg (370 tons) of finished copper. Given that the total number of pre-1400BC copper and bronze objects discovered in Ireland amounts to little over 748kg (1,650lb), the Irish must have built up a healthy export trade. It is difficult to imagine all that metal being lost in the soil or melted down for a fast buck by succeeding generations.

Digging out copper was a hard life. The miners would cut a passage downwards into the copper vein and then enlarge it into a small, rocky room. They would heat water on an underground fire (this depended heavily on the oxygen available) and throw it onto the surrounding walls to shatter the ore-bearing rock. They would then scrape off the ore using rough pebbles fastened to their hands by rope. This Cork and Kerry copper industry left behind the only known examples of prehistoric mines in Europe, outside Austria. There are at least 25 mine shafts clustered together on Mount Gabriel, near Schull, Co Cork, although flooding has prevented all but two from being properly explored. They seem to date from between 1500BC and 1180BC.

Copper quickly become a status symbol. Ownership of a mine would give a family both kudos and wealth and there must have been many prospecting parties dispatched to find the tell-tale traces of green malachite and blue azurite in rocky areas of the countryside. Bronze (a mixture of copper and tin) and gold also emerged at this time and quickly became sought after. A bronze dagger or axe head was far superior in its strength and cutting edge to stone. Furthermore, the metal was easily worked — it would be poured molten into a stone mould, cooled and hammered into shape — and could be 'customised' with magical symbols to impress both its owner and his enemy!

Irish bronze metalworking reached a high point early in the Bronze Age. Metal axe production then fell quite dramatically (the reasons are unclear) and there seemed to be a tendency for the original Irish styles to be dropped in favour of longer weapons with curving blades. These were probably modelled on English designs, which in turn copied continental fashions. Gradually new weapons became widely available — the spearhead, the rapier and, by around 800BC, the sword. While the southern Mediterranean's Bronze Age chiefs were being engulfed by waves of central European barbarians, the west was left alone to develop its own distinctive bronze and gold industry. For Ireland it was the apex of a Golden Age.

Intriguingly, as well as producing vast quantities of metalware the Irish were very keen on burying it. Numerous treasure troves have been dated to this era and there must have been a number of reasons why concealment was so important. The obvious one is that wealthy families and metalsmiths took precautions to protect their assets during times of war or unrest. But there might also have been a religious aspect. Many of the hoards have been discovered in rivers, marshes and other sites close to water. Perhaps the Bronze Age was a time of climatic change in western Europe and rain was either in short supply or too prevalent. Were the treasure hoards ritual offerings aimed at calming the wrath of some nature god? If so, the owners were happy to donate in large quantities. Hoards such as the Dowris, found between two lakes in Co Offaly during the early 19th century, amounted to more than 200 items.

Among these were five swords, leaf-shaped spearheads, numerous axe heads, gouges, chisels, knives and instruments which may have been razors. There were also 'crotals', thought by some to be weights used in trading but by others to be modelled on bulls' scrotums and made to the specifications of a European fertility cult. In support of this second theory there were also 26 bronze horns, each skilfully cast in two separate pieces; these were undoubtedly modelled on bulls horns.

Most interesting of all was the Dowris 'bucket' made of decorated bronze sheets, which was imported from central Europe sometime after the 8th century BC. This may well have been an important vessel for religious ritual, along with a cauldron found nearby. In early Irish mythology cauldrons played a critical role in appeasing the gods — particularly Dagda, the god of health and plenty. It is not difficult to imagine the meat-filled Dowris cauldron

Opposite above: *A golden collar, part of the hoard found at Broighter, Co Derry, and now held by the National Museum of Ireland in Dublin. Ornaments such as this, and the torc* **(Opposite below)**, *were highly-prized among the jewellery-loving Celts. As metalworking techniques improved, La Tene artwork flourished across the land.*

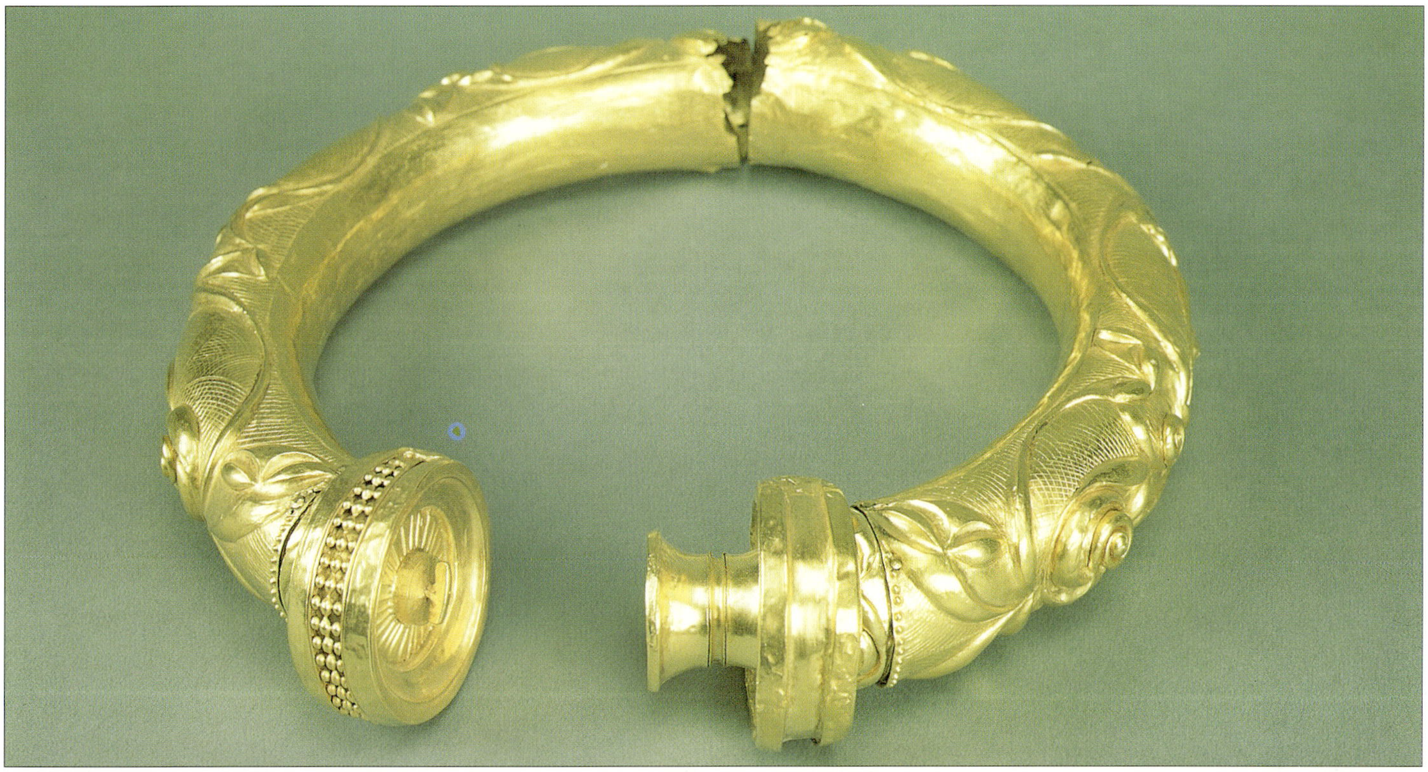

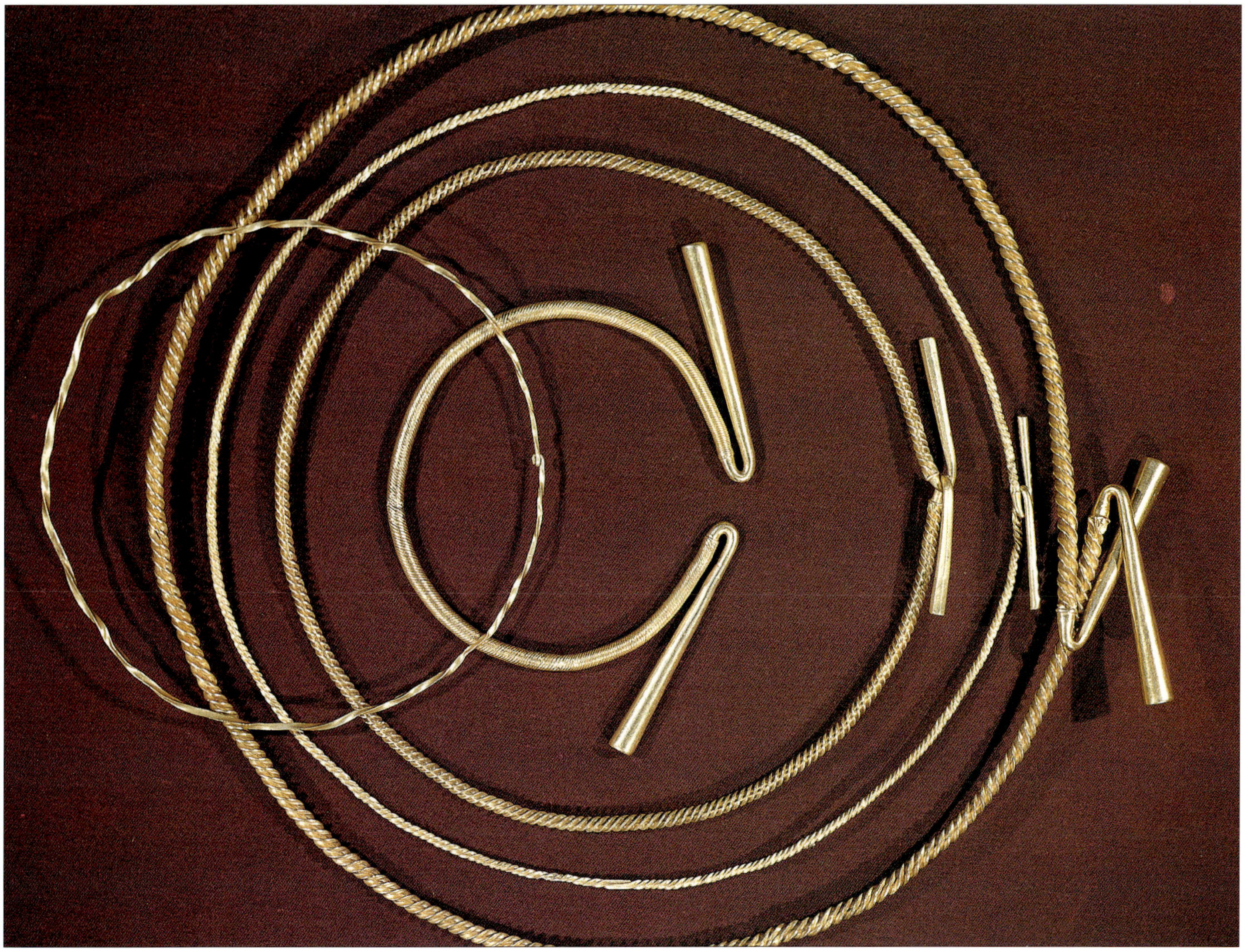

being carried in to an open-air ritual feast, its arrival heralded by the horn-players.

Gold hoards are also relatively common in Ireland and in them lies confirmation of the country's lofty status as a major European goldwork producer. The quality of the materials, and degree of craftsmanship, matches or exceeds any other Late Bronze Age society. Irish ornaments were surely highly prized throughout the ancient world.

The most dazzling hoard so far discovered is the 'Great Clare Find' of 1854, when 146 objects were dug up close to the Mooghaun North hill fort, Co Clare. The treasure was discovered by a construction gang working on tracks for the West Clare narrow-gauge railway. It is believed to be the largest single discovery of gold Bronze Age pieces outside the Aegean. Unfortunately much of it was melted down for hard cash, though not before casts were made (these are now in the care of the National Museum at Dublin). The priceless hoard included golden collars, neck-rings, bracelets and cloak-fasteners.

At least two other noteworthy Clare hoards have been found — at Gorteenreagh and at Gleninsheen. Gorteenreagh threw up an ornamental 'lock ring' which, it is thought, was used as a hair decoration. At first glance the ring appears to have been decorated with very fine concentric scratches. But under a microscope these 'scratches' appear as tiny strands of wire, less than a third of a millimetre thick. Few jewellers today could make the wire, let alone fit it onto the ring.

The location of these Irish gold mines is tantalising; the Wicklow Hills were certainly a rich source, although by no means the only one. It is likely that the Sperrin Mountains, in Co Tyrone, contained some veins and many of the rivers probably washed down more gold than they do today. It seems unlikely that the smiths ever needed to import their raw materials, which in any case would have been an expensive and hazardous task.

All counties bordering the River Shannon estuary and its lower reaches seem to have had a tradition of gold-making (judging by the number of ornaments that turn up). One explanation is that it was a convenient place from which to export; another is that foreign goldsmiths arrived by ship there and decided to stick around. Either way, influences from abroad clearly impressed the Irish and elements of German and Scandinavian designs began to creep into their work. There also seems to have been a trading link from the southern Mediterranean, across southern France and up the western seaboard of Europe. Irish gold ornaments would be exchanged for spearheads, swords and new axe designs, as well as more mundane products.

In terms of its standing in Western Europe, Ireland was relatively richer in the Late Bronze Age that it has ever been — either before or since. A strong indication of this is the way economic prosperity set off a huge expansion in farming. Pollen samples from around 800BC show the land was largely heath, bog, bracken and peat. Yet by 400BC large tracts had been re-claimed as grassland or for the planting of grain. The great irony for the Irish today is that so little else is known about this period in their history. We have hazy theories on religious beliefs, absolutely no clue as to the political and military situation and a dearth of reliable evidence about family life. The hopes and fears of Ireland's late Bronze Age remain an enigma and we can only hope that some still-to-be-discovered settlement will bring further enlightenment.

Above: *The fabulous Tara brooch, a potent symbol of Ireland's Celtic heritage. The 8th century brooch, discovered at Bettystown, Co Meath, is fashioned from gold, silver, copper, glass, enamel and amber.*

Opposite: *The economic importance of the River Shannon estuary was rooted in its Celtic metalworking industry. Later, fortifications such as this sprang up along its banks.*

5 Romans in Ireland

For years historians remained convinced that Ireland had escaped the Roman conquest of Europe. There was so little evidence of any permanent settlement; no sign of a fort or even of a temporary camp. The bits and bobs of Roman relics which turned up were explained away merely as imports brought in by travellers and traders. Ireland was seen as some kind of heroic twilight of the Celtic peoples, defying the march of the legions in a way Britain had failed to match. Then, in the mid 1980s, this 'official' version of history began to fall apart.

Gradually word spread among the country's leading archaeologists of a newly discovered site at Drumanagh, 24km (15 miles) north of Dublin. At first it was considered to be only a small encampment, the temporary home of a Roman expeditionary force sent to discover what lay beyond the western seas of Britain. But as time went on, and more fieldwork was carried out, the extraordinary truth began to emerge. A small group of archaeologists was granted access under conditions of strict secrecy. The National Museum of Ireland took possession of several valuable Roman items but decided not to put them on display. The concern was that treasure-hunters armed with metal detectors would descend on the site in their droves and plunder the evidence.

It was not until January 1996 that the true scale of the Roman settlement was revealed. Drumanagh appears to have been a massive Roman coastal fort which must have housed hundreds if not thousands of people. The 1,618sq m (40 acre) site was probably a beachhead constructed to support Roman armies on campaign in Ireland during the 1st and 2nd centuries AD. The first coins discovered bear the names of the emperors Titus, Trajan and Hadrian, which indicates a Roman presence at least between 79 and 138AD. Later the fort seems to have developed into an important trading post.

The Drumanagh excavation is likely to prove the most important in the history of Ireland. Archaeologists believe it fits in perfectly with Roman activities along every frontier in the empire and it will certainly help explain the widespread scatter of Roman artifacts already dug up across Ireland. Although nothing is yet certain, it seems Drumanagh helped establish a considerable Roman influence across much of the country's east coast. One discovery which supports this is the grave of a Romano-British warrior chief on Lambay Island, 4.8km (3 miles) off shore. Another is the theory that for many years the Romans tried to interfere in Ireland's internal politics by re-establishing kingdoms for Irish noblemen exiled in Britain.

Among these exiles was the late 1st century chieftain Tuathal Techtmar, who is thought to have tried to reclaim his lands with the aid of a Roman-trained and equipped mercenary army. Another, separate, Roman-backed campaign may have led to the founding of Cashel, an important ancient town in Tipperary whose name is derived from the Latin word Castellum. During the ninteenth century fragments of surgical equipment belonging to a Roman eye surgeon were discovered in Tipperary but it was so out of keeping with the area's known history that it was dismissed as a freak find. Now it seems the surgeon's tools, along with just about every other Roman find in Ireland, will have to be carefully reassessed.

Above: *Ogham Stones such as this one at Kilmalkedar, Co Kerry, carried the first Irish writing — believed to have been inspired by contact with Roman numerals.*

Opposite: *One of Ireland's most distinctive castles is the Rock of Cashel, Co Tipperary. There is thought to have been a fortress here since Roman times.*

6 The Coming of the Celts

Of all the foreigners who settled in Ireland, none left a cultural legacy to rival the Celts. They were proud and resourceful, brave and intelligent and they established a way of life and language that persists even today. It was the Celts who first defended Irish soil from invaders during the Viking Wars, and they mounted the first Irish attacks on foreign soil (their raids on western Britain during the 3rd and 4th centuries AD).

Yet there is absolutely no evidence that the Celts colonised Ireland through some massive invasion force. Their arrival was gradual — over hundreds if not thousands of years — and their customs and skills became ingrained rather than imposed. For all the fearsome raiding of the Norsemen and the brutally efficient Norman armies, it was the Celts who really shaped the Irish society we know today.

But who were the Celts and where did they come from? To answer this we have to look to the heart of Europe around 500BC. Writers at this time began making references to a barbaric, illiterate, warlike race who occupied much of the Alpine region along with parts of central France and Spain. They were named the Keltoi by the Greeks and the Celtae by the Romans, although there was no suggestion that they had their own empire. True, the Celts shared a religious heritage and a broadly common language but there were also major differences between the tribes. The political order would range from large regional Celtic governments to kings commanding little more than a few settlements. In addition and contrary to popular opinion, they were by no means all followers of the Druids.

The Celts had obviously been around for many hundreds of years before they were 'recognised' by the annalists. Celtic speakers probably occupied pockets of land throughout Europe (including Ireland) early in the Bronze Age and continued migration would have established them further and further north and west. But it was the rise of the so-called La Téne Celts in the 5th century that really grabbed the attention of Greek and Roman political and military leaders.

La Téne Celts get their name from a distinctive style of highly decorative art — on metalwork, pottery, graves and in settlements. The name comes from a site in Switzerland where, in the mid-19th century, archaeologists discovered some extraordinary Celtic treasures. The La Téne designs which flourished in centres like these would dominate British and Irish artwork for well over 1,000 years.

But in 400BC it was not La Téne culture that concerned the Romans and the Greeks. A number of large, powerful tribes had begun storming across the Alps and into northern Italy. Some settled in the Po Valley, attacking and plundering Rome around 390BC. Others moved east into Greece and it is thought they may have sacked Delphi in 279BC. That was the end of the Celts colonial history. From the 2nd century on, the all-powerful Roman Empire flexed its muscles, conquering their lands and imposing an entirely new law and language. As the Romans moved inexorably across western Europe, the La Téne Celts found themselves forced to adapt. Only the fringes of the Roman Empire — Scotland, Wales, western England, Brittany, the Isle of Man and parts of Ireland — were left in relative peace to develop in their own distinctive ways. It is no accident that today these sanctuaries remain the only places where the Celtic language is still spoken; that it has survived at all is largely thanks to pressures from nationalist groups in the areas concerned.

Unravelling Ireland's Celtic past is, in many ways, just as difficult as tackling its Bronze or Stone Age periods. For one thing, the Celts left no records of their own. For another, it is almost impossible to be sure how widespread they were at any one time. Very often all we are left with are the tainted or fictionalised writings of later historians.

The celebrated Greek geographer Strabo, who lived around the time of the birth of Christ, was only too well aware of this. In his Geography of the Ancient World he writes of Ireland: 'Concerning this island I have nothing certain to tell, except that its inhabitants are more savage than the Britons, since they are man-eaters as well as heavy eaters, and since, further, they count it an honourable thing, when their fathers die, to devour them, and openly to have intercourse, not only with the other women, but also with their mothers and sisters.' Strabo knew that the travellers' tales he'd heard were likely to have been embellished and he went on to warn his readers: 'I am saying this only with the understanding that I have no trustworthy witnesses for it...'

According to the much later Book of Invasions which medieval scholars argued that pre-Christian Ireland had been conquered by waves of intrepid invaders, the country's founding fathers were apparently Celts and a people called the Fír Bolg. While these shadowy groups bear similarities to Gaelic tribes living in France and Belgium, there is no clear evidence of any 'invasion'.

Despite the absence of hard facts, it has been possible to draw some conclusions on the lives of the Celts in Ireland. These ideas are based partly on Greek and Roman historians, partly on surviving language and place names and partly on archaeological analysis of settlements, land use, excavations of forts, farms and tombs, weapons and tools and the skeletons of the people them-

Opposite above: *Part of the stone fortifications at the Grianan Aileach hill-fort in Co Donegal. Here Celtic architects created a large, stone wall as a central defensive point within a number of earth ramparts.*

Opposite below: *Prehistoric stonework displayed in the National Heritage Park at Ferrycarrig, Co Wexford.*

selves. Archaeology is very far from being an exact science but at least it has given us a few clues.

Celtic society in Ireland was a haphazard collection of family tribes, each ruled by a king. These tribes would occasionally come together (perhaps for a counsel of war) to strike deals and form political alliances. But Celtic politics was a precarious business and there was no sense of any national identity.

Within the tribe, the pecking order was clearer. Beneath the king would come the warrior nobility, followed by those considered to have special skills — Druid priests, storytellers, artists, craftsman and seers. Among the early Celts the king would have had strictly limited powers and any important decisions would have been taken by vote of all free men in the tribe. This semi-democracy seems to have broken down in later years with tribal leaders becoming more autocratic.

One easy way of judging the importance of a king was to cast an eye over his jewellery. The Celts could not get enough trinkets and they held a significance way beyond fashion or petty vanities. Jewellery conveyed a person's wealth and standing in society, it could be imbued with magical symbols and it served as an heirloom to assist with the tangible handing down of power. Brooches, bracelets and anklets of enamelled bronze, necklets (particularly copper, iron or gold torcs), elaborately crafted bronze chains and ornate belts were all much in vogue. Jewellery was worn as much by men as by women and certain styles may have been emblems of rank, age or authority.

Political life was male-dominated, although occasionally noblewomen such as Connacht's Queen Maeve took very prominent positions. The best known example of a powerful female leader however emerged across the water in Celtic Britain where Boudicca, Queen of the Iceni, massacred around 70,000 Romans before her revolt was ruthlessly crushed. The historian Cassius Dio said of her: 'In stature she was very tall, in appearance most terrifying, in the glance of her eye most fierce, and her voice was harsh; a great mass of the tawniest hair fell to her hips; around her neck was a large golden necklace; and she wore a tunic of diverse colours over which a thick mantle was fastened with a brooch. This was her invariable attire. She now grasped a spear to aid her in terrifying all beholders and spoke . . .'

Celtic women shared their menfolk's sense of pride along with a determination to avenge personal insult. When Chiomara, wife of the Galatian leader Ortiagon, was captured, enslaved and raped she persuaded the Roman centurion who had violated her that she could be ransomed. A deal was struck, the ransom was brought to a secret meeting place and the gleeful centurion walked away with his ill-gotten gains. Hardly had he turned his back when she ordered her kinsmen to slaughter him. She then cut off his head and presented it to her husband. 'Woman, a fine thing is good faith', scolded Ortiagon. 'A better thing only one man should be alive who had sex with me,' she replied.

Chiomara's sense of chastity aside, the Celts were a people of moral contradictions. On the one hand there are signs that women participated in sex with a number of different partners, and that noblemen had several wives. On the other, many Celtic marriages seem to have been solemn affairs in which both sides pooled equal amounts of wealth and pledged fidelity and respect to the other. The idea that men had power to legally murder their wives now seems to be more fable than fact.

Feasting and drinking were fundamental rituals of life and as trade routes developed with the Mediterranean demand for wine grew inexorably. Wine would be served up in large quantities, as much a status symbol as proof of generosity, and allowed a king to emphasise his wealth and authority over the subordinate nobles sitting in order of importance down the table.

One curious aspect of Celtic feasting was the presence of a 'praise poet', a bard who would recite sycophantic songs and poems extolling the great deeds of the leading warriors and, of course, the king. Interestingly, there would often be a satirist (a kind of court jester) as well. He would direct jibes at some of the inflated egos around him and was a much feared face at the table. In a society where pride and image was everything, the voice was indeed sometimes mightier than the sword.

If feasts were ritualistic, war was even more so. Celtic armies were very often alliances of different tribes and on the battlefield these tribes would march and fight together. Each would have its own standard — usually an animal figure — which served as a rallying point for re-grouping. The standard often had its own religious significance and fighters would bow down to it, convinced of its magical powers.

Where two armies met, the actual fighting could be delayed by several hours while a bizarre display of rituals was performed. Sometimes champions from either side would face each other in single combat, boasting loudly of their past victories, their bravery, their skills and their great ancestry. Once this charade was over a psychological war would begin with flamboyant false charges and spectacular rapid movements by charioteers and infantrymen. Above it all a war chant would strike up, backed by the sound of sword on shield and swelled by the haunting sound of the battle horn. In this way the Celts hoped to un-nerve their opponents and in this they were no doubt very often successful. Only in continental Europe, where the Celts found themselves up against highly disciplined, well-trained Roman legionnaires, did the tactic tend to founder.

By around 200BC the Iron Age in Ireland was becoming well established. The use of iron meant lighter, stronger weapons, tools and chariots — factors which must have had far-reaching military and social effects. It is hard to say exactly when the Celts began to work iron, but it was certainly not an overnight revolution. The likeliest scenario is that iron began to emerge way back in the Bronze Age, perhaps as early as the 6th or 7th century BC, and gradually gained acceptance among the smiths. Even when its use was widespread it did not totally replace bronze, which remained popular in jewellery and for the decoration of horses and chariots. The Celts religious beliefs remain a mystery to us today, mainly because nothing was ever written down. Their priests were often Druids (there were a few other holy sects such as the Vates) and there can be few faiths throughout history which operated with

Opposite: *Excavations at the Drombeg stone circle, Co Cork, revealed a flat-bottomed pot containing cremated human remains. It had been intentionally broken before it was buried.*

such obsessive secrecy. This of course helped the Druids defend their power base in Celtic society. Because they were so secretive they were feared, and because they were feared their views carried great influence. The fact that so many novices were picked from the ranks of the nobility was a further prop to their authority.

It seems the roots of Druidism were in Britain. Caesar tells how the novice priests of western Europe were sent there because the country had a reputation for offering the most thorough induction training. However, the legendary meeting place of the Druids was in Gaul. The priests, for whom the oak was a sacred symbol of 'earth power', were said to congregate in an oak forest somewhere in the Carnutes tribal area each year, when they would elect a Chief Druid. This chief would hold sway over all priests and tribal loyalties had to be cast aside in deference to him.

Despite their shadowy reputation, priests were familiar faces in any settlement and would mix and talk with their kinsmen quite freely. They were dowsers and healers, as well as the teachers, judges and guardians of tribal history. They had the power to mete out punishments, such as excommunicating tribesmen from sacrificial gatherings. They were both prophets and personal advisers — suggesting 'lucky days' on which to do important business. They acted as mediators between ordinary mortals and the gods.

Druids supervised the training of priests (this could take up to 20 years because all Druid philosophy was committed to memory and novices had to learn long tracts of law, verse, history and magic formulae). They organised the calendar (one reason for the astronomical connections with prehistoric stone circles) and, although they were themselves excused military duties, they helped draft treaties and negotiate peace. When the time came for a Druid meeting, or the enactment of magic, they would cut themselves off from outsiders. For many ordinary mortals the only sight of a Druid in his religious cloak and hood would come with the performance of a sacrifice.

The frequency and method of human sacrifice in Ireland is an area easily distorted by events on the continent. There is little doubt that the Druids in Gaul and central Europe inflicted the most hideous ritual murders on both their kinsfolk and their enemies. There are stories of giant wooden cages, filled with straw, people and animals, being set alight. Of sacrificial victims being hurled into deep pits to die a lonely, lingering death. Of men being stabbed in the back to allow dispassionate Druid seers to foretell the future from their death throes. Of prisoners-of-war being forced over ritual cauldrons to have their throats cut; and even of volunteers for sacrifice, whose duty was to bear important messages to the gods. Whatever the exaggerations of early historians, both animal and human sacrifice was an indisputable part of the Druid way. One 'sanctuary' of the Gauls at Ribemont-sur-Ancre has revealed the bodies of at least 1,000 people, aged between 15 and 40, many of whom had been ritually decapitated and dismembered. The fact that these activities happened on the continent does not automatically mean that they occurred in Ireland. But, given the free exchange of ideas between Celts and Druids of different countries, the chances are that some form of human sacrifice was practiced.

Opposite: *Settled in pre-Christian times, Lower Lough Erne contains many islands. In the Romanesque church on White Island stand enigmatic statues of Celtic saints, they are probably from the remains of an earlier monastery dating from around the 9th-10th century.*

The main purpose of these gruesome rituals was to appease the wrath of the gods. They were closely linked to the four main Celtic religious festivals — Imbole (1 February), linked with Brigid the Irish goddess of childbirth, Beltain (1 May), linked to sun worship and fertility, Lughnasa (1 August), the harvest festival, and Samhain (1 November), the start of the Celtic year and the day barriers to the underworld were lifted. Samhain is still celebrated in many parts of the world today as Hallowe'en, a contraction of 'All Hallows Eve'.

No book about ancient Ireland can be complete without some mention of the country's treasure chest of Celtic myth and legend. Many of these began as folk stories, surviving in verbal form from generation to generation, but later they were carefully written down by the monks. The most famous is the Ulster Cycle featuring an epic story called the Tàin Bo Cúailnge (Cattle Raid of Cooley). This is the Irish equivalent of England's King Arthur or Scandinavia's Beowulf and recounts the heroic deeds of Ulster's King Conchobar mac Nessa and his circle of warrior chiefs and noblewomen. The greatest of these fighters was Cú Chulainn (Hound of Culann) and the amazing magical powers he possesses. The Tàin is made up of many different tales with extravagant titles such as The Tooth Fight of Fintain, The Bloodless Fight of Rochad and The Missile Throwing of the Charioteers. It is impossible to do it justice with brief extracts but the story of how the Hound of Culann got his name at least gives a flavour of the epic. The story below is an abridged paraphrase.

One day the smith Culann made ready a feast for Conchobar, king of Ulster, and sent word asking the king to travel with only a few companions, since his smithy did not provide a good enough living to feed a large host. Conchobar therefore decided to bring along just 50 of his bravest knights. As the journey began, the King noticed a young boy fostered at his palace playing against 150 others. The boy defeated each of them with ease in ball games and at wrestling and soon the king called him over to invite him to the feast. The boy replied: 'Master Conchobar, I have not yet finished playing but I shall follow you later on.'

When Conchobar arrived at the feast Culann asked if anyone else was following. The king had already forgotten the young boy and said 'no'. Culann then unleashed his giant, ferocious hound to guard the approaches to his fortified home. But at that very moment the boy came into sight and the hound sprang to savage him. Untroubled, the boy cast down his ball and hurley, grabbed the hound with his bare hands and dashed it to death upon a stone. The Ulstermen ran to the boy and took him back to Conchobar. The king was greatly relieved, for he now discovered that the child was Sédanta mac Sualtamh, son of his sister. Remembering his duties as host, Culann welcomed the boy but mourned the death of his dog for it had given loyal service in defence of his property. The boy replied: 'I shall raise a puppy of the same breed for you and until he is ready to serve you I shall protect you and your cattle myself.' Cathbad the Druid then stepped forward and told the youth: 'Then you shall be called the Hound of Culann (Cú Chulainn)'.

7 Gaelic Family Life

If the Church evolved without rigid structures, the same could not be said of Gaelic society generally. The law was obsessed with a man's status. If you were a peasant seeking compensation for some wrong, your chance of a big payout was infinitely less than if you happened to be the regional king. Because of this, the divisions between the three main classes of kings, lords and commoners were well defined. A king inherited his position, along with lands, power and wealth. A lord was judged not only by his wealth but also by the number of commoners who relied on him for a living. It was sometimes possible for a commoner to claw his way up the social ladder but it was far more usual for hard-up lords — their family assets divided between both legitimate and illegitimate sons down several generations — to end up on the breadline.

Among the commoners there were still more divisions. First among these was the freeman, usually a land-owning farmer who was ensured full legal rights. A typical freeman was described in the 8th century legal document Críth Gablach as follows:

'There are always two vessels in his house, a vessel of milk and a vessel of ale. He is a man of three snouts: the snout of a rooting hog which banishes shame at all times, the snout of a bacon pig on the hook, and the snout of plough under the sod, so that he is able to receive king or bishop or scholar or judge from the road, against the arrival of every party of guests. He is a man who has three sacks in his house always for each season: a sack of malt, a sack of sea salt for the salting up of one of his beasts, and a sack of charcoal for iron working, He has seven houses: a corn-kiln, a barn (his share in a mill so that it grinds for him), a dwelling house of 27ft [8.2m], a lean-to of 17ft [5.2m], a pigsty, a calf-fold and a sheep fold. He has 20 cows, two bulls, six oxen, 20 pigs, 20 sheep, four farmyard hogs, two sows, a riding horse with enamelled bridle and 16 sacks of seed corn in the ground. He has a bronze cauldron into which a hog fits. He has parkland in which there are always sheep, without need to change ground. He and his wife have four outfits. His wife is the daughter of his equal, wedded in lawful matrimony.'

Freemen who couldn't quite muster such impressive assets were placed lower in the social scheme of things. Even lower were men with no land or property and below them were the senchleithe, serfs bound to their local lord and master. Most lowly of all were the slaves, freely traded by Gaelic and Viking warlords.

Slaves became especially common between the 9th and 11th centuries and often ended up as subsistence workers in one of the major monasteries. Some slaves were prisoners of war taken by Vikings in foreign lands, others were children snatched with the specific intention of selling them into slavery. In times of famine, poor families would hive off their offspring as slaves as a last resort to prevent starvation.

Above: *The Cashel Folk Park in Co Tipperary provides a fascinating insight into early Gaelic life.*

Opposite: *Round towers such as this at Kells, Co Meath, are often difficult to date. Building methods, designs and techniques were sometimes repeated for hundreds of years.*

The relationship between freemen and lords was called Clientship and was supposed to strike a fair bargain between both. It was in effect a leasing agreement in which the lord would agree to grant his client a 'fief' (usually some livestock or land) and in return the client would make regular payments. There were two categories within the system — free clientship and base clientship.

Free clientship required the freeman to swear himself to the service of his lord, including a promise to fight for him if required. This arrangement allowed noblemen to amass their own private armies which could then be enlisted in the service of a regional king. Free clients were entitled to a share of their master's plunder in any raid or battle but the payment demands on them were high. It was a form of service which lords used to exact heavy rates of interest on the fiefs they advanced.

Base clientship was a rather more work-a-day contract which ensured lords a comfortable standard of living. A lord would first pay the client a handsome advance consistent with his legal standing. Then he would offer him a fief, perhaps of dairy cows, livestock or farm equipment, which would again be tailored to the man's ability and personal wealth. The lord would also promise to

protect him and to fight for him whenever he needed legal compensation for a theft or injury. In return the master could expect a regular supply of food and labour.

The typical annual return on a fief of two dozen dairy cows would be one dairy cow, three calves (of varying quality) half the dripping of a year-old bull, a cauldron of milk, a vessel of cream, 20 loaves, a 10x20cm (4x 8in) pat of butter, two fistfuls of onions, two leeks, and a 0.3m (3ft) long flitch of bacon.

In addition, a lord could invoke a handy clause in the contract entitling him and a group of friends to one night's feasting in the home of the client between each New Year and Shrove Tuesday. For the freeman, this must too often have been a dread occasion. A gluttonous and drunken bunch of nobles would not only eat enough food for two weeks but would quite likely turn a house upside down as well.

Family life was chaotic enough without the input of unwelcome guests such as these. At the lower class levels, two or three families often lived inside a single dwelling. Divorce and re-marriage was widespread, despite the entreaties of the church, and among the nobility it was usual to have a number of wives to ensure a good supply of heirs. This was both a curse and a blessing on the lords. On the one hand they had plenty of reliable manpower available to help manage their estates; but on the other their dynasties were condemned to less and less influence as assets were scattered among generations of heirs.

Ireland in the 7th century had a population of between 500,000 and 1,000,000 people, a level that fluctuated according to the effects of plague or famine. Farming was the driving force of the economy, although huge forests covered much of the countryside and the lowland midlands and western hills were agriculturally poor boglands. With mountains and moorland fringing every kingdom, Ireland was a wilderness punctuated by a scattering of cultural havens (the monasteries) and tens of thousands of small fortified farmsteads.

These farms were built like mini hill-forts with a central round-house 6x8m (20-27ft) in diameter surrounded by either an earth rampart (a rath) a dry stone wall (a cashel) or a more-heavily fortified combination of the two (a dun). All farm outbuildings and labourers' quarters were sited inside the enclosure apart from corn kilns (where corn was dried around an oven to circumvent the wet climate) which were thought too much of a fire hazard.

There was also a fourth structure, called a crannog, which was almost certainly imported from Scotland. This was an artificial island in the form of a house-platform at the centre of a shallow lake. It arrived in Ireland quite late — around the 6th century — and was popular because of its obvious defensive qualities. Another British architectural import was probably the souterrain, found only in Ulster. This was a stone-built, oddly-shaped underground chamber; history has shed no light on its purpose.

There was no straw on Irish farms, land was instead kept in reserve for winter grazing, and only the rich had a mill (or even a share in one). Cultivated land was divided into strips near the farmyard while livestock would be sent out in summer to graze common ground on the moors. Responsibility for tending these animals would fall on to the women, as would the salting of butter and cheese making — both vital for building up winter food supplies. Milk formed a major part of the diet, cow's milk for the rich, sheep's milk for the poor.

Above: *More round towers at Ardmore, Co Waterford, Clonmacnoise Monastery* **Opposite left** *and Timahoe, Co Laois,* **Opposite right.** *The towers had obvious defensive qualities in a land where Gaelic chiefs were perpetually at war with each other.*

Ploughing would begin in March. A sure sign of a farmer's wealth was ownership of a full plough and oxen team; lowlier families had to make do with spades. The most important crops were oats (used for porridge and crude bread), barley (for beer and bread), wheat (used to make bread for sale to the very wealthy) and corn. Vegetable production was small scale and apples were just about the only cultivated fruit, although families used wild berries and nuts to supplement their diet.

This was not an economy in which food was widely traded. Families worked to keep themselves alive and a failure of the crops, or widespread disease in livestock, had catastrophic results. Famine increased the likelihood of death from diseases such as smallpox, dysentery, pneumonia and rabies. Disease resulted in whole communities shifting around (which spread more disease) and in the worst years civil unrest erupted.

The most convenient authority to blame for disaster was the church, which responded in the only way it could by sending high-profile emissaries out to the worst affected areas with relics of the saints and prayers for deliverance. At these times the doctrines of Christianity would be openly challenged by many who still held a candle for the old magic and the pagan gods. The bishops relied heavily on the passing of new laws demanding respect for God and curbing violence among the masses. Without the practical support of the regional kings and their armies the Church's task would have been nigh on impossible.

8 The Viking Wars

The wind is fierce tonight
It tosses the sea's white hair
I fear no wild Vikings
sailing the quiet main

Thus wrote a 9th century Irish monk along the margin of his manuscript as he sat shivering in a cheerless cell. His simple prose perfectly sums up the mood of the time; an era when no coastal settlement was safe and every church and monastery lived in fear of the plundering longboat crews.

Ireland, like the rest of Europe, was living the nightmare of defending against these strong, fearless warriors capable of mounting lightening-fast attacks with ruthless efficiency. The Vikings came for plunder, for political expediency, for colonial ambition and for new commercial opportunities. To the Irish kings, for whom centuries of continuous strife had always involved the same standard military scenario, the effect must have been shattering.

The Vikings earliest known assault on Ireland came in 795AD when they burned Rathlin. Over the following four decades there was sporadic raiding of the coast, these appear to be mainly treasure-hunting escapades. In 798 the St Patrick's Island monastery near Skerries, Co Dublin was burned and the shrine of the monastery's patron, Dochonna, broken up. The Norsemen also demanded a heavy tax or tribute on the surrounding farming community. This was payable in heads of cattle — a heavy blow to the fragile rural economy.

Mostly the invading crews were Norwegian, called Finn-gaill (White Foreigners) but there were also a few Danes Dubb-gaill (Black Foreigners). Quite how and why the Irish writers of the day used these colours to distinguish between their foes is a mystery. To most people the invaders were simply Norsemen — men who would publicly hang three-score of their prisoners at once; who would gleefully sack and burn whole towns, and who would snatch loved-ones at will for sale into slavery.

The Vikings though didn't have it all their own way. Historians of the day recorded how in 811 Ulaid warriors wiped out a band of raiders, how the following year another group was slaughtered by the Co Mayo-based Umall and how the king of the Eoganacht, Locha Léin, inflicted devastation on a coastal war party. Yet these were small victories — in the eye of the gathering Viking storm, they were of no significance.

In the 830s the Norwegian attacks became much larger military operations. The first push inland came in 836 when Vikings poured into the territories of the southern Úi Néill, seized hundreds of captives and killed many more. Within 12 months Norse fleets of up to 60 ships were sailing into the rivers Boyne and Liffey in what was surely a terrifying spectacle for the locals. With their garish red, gold and green sails, bows ornately carved with evil-looking monsters and the sun flashing off shields lashed to their sides, such fleets must have seemed like the Devil's own navy coming to visit.

It is worth mentioning here the design of the longboats because it was this design, as much as the ferocity of the soldiers on board, that gave the Vikings such an edge. A boat of the Gokstad type, typical of the 9th century, would be around 22m (75ft) long, 5.5m (18ft) in the beam and with a keel of almost 17.5m (58ft) hewn from a single piece of oak. The hull would be supported by some 19 frames and cross beams and was overlaid with a pine deck (some planks often left loose to permit storage below the waterline). Each carried around 32 crewmen — these were not ships made to move large armies — and relied mostly on sail power.

With a favourable wind and sea, the Gokstad vessel was easily capable of voyaging 120 miles a day, allowing on-board supplies to be kept to a minimum. But the ship's greatest attribute was its ability to manoeuvre superbly close to shore. A draft of around 1m (3ft) allowed it to discharge warriors directly onto a beach, and often the Irish would know nothing of an attack until the moment it happened. On the very few occasions they tried to pursue the invaders, their task was hopeless. The Vikings would simply turn into the wind and make off by oar, leaving their victims' cumbersome ships floundering behind.

The first Viking to leave a permanent mark on Ireland was Turgeis, from Norway, who arrived in 840 with a powerful fleet on the north coast. He quickly established himself as the head of all Norsemen in Erin and soon had most of Ulster under his control. His capture of Armagh brought him fabulous wealth and immense power and he and his kin are credited with establishing the great Viking settlements of Dublin, Wexford, Waterford, Cork and Limerick. He is said to have robbed the monasteries of Clonmacnoise and Clonfert and encouraged scores of renegade Christians to troop into churches to transform them into heathen temples. In Armagh he was said to have settled himself down at the altar declaring that he was the heathen High-priest. At the altar of Clonmacnoise his wife Ota reportedly chanted spells to Thor. How much of this was true, and how much the fevered imaginings of outraged monks, is difficult to tell. But it is possible that Turgeis tried to package himself as a leader by promoting sacrifice as a way of ensuring favourable seasons.

Throughout the 840s Viking aggression reached a new peak of intensity and for the first time a fleet appeared on Lough Neagh. The crews first systematically robbed the monasteries and villages

Opposite: *Carlingford — home of the Danish Viking fleet in 850BC. Two years later Carlingford Lough was the scene of a major naval engagement between Danes and Norwegians.*

around its shores and then pushed out in search of greater booty — first to Louth (where they captured leading churchmen and scholars), then to Armagh, and finally to Dublin, from where they harried Leinster in 842. Their Dublin settlement included a warriors' cemetery at Kilmainham, to the west of the city, from which archaeologists have since recovered a number of important finds.

For a time it seemed as though Ireland would be swamped by the invaders. The Shannon river system was in Viking control, great cultural centres such as Clonmacnoise, Seir, Birr and Clonfert were sacked and a steady flow of riches from the nation's monasteries were transported to the Norsemen's formidable garrisons at Dublin, Waterford, Youghal, Wexford, St Mullins, Cork and on the Shannon estuary. Yet already the new settlers were doing deals with the natives — one alliance between Viking and Irish in 842 resulted in the death of the abbot of Linn Duachail.

But Turgeis and his like were not unbeatable. Away from the coast — where Viking naval power was unmatched — they were just local kings as vulnerable as any other. So it transpired in 845 when Turgeis was captured by Mael Seachlainn, king of Meath, and drowned in Lough Owel. That same year the abbot of Terryglass and Clonenagh and the deputy abbot of Kildare took up arms against the invaders — among several leading churchmen to do so. Both were killed in action at Dunamase.

Turgeis's death heralded a bad run for the Norwegian Vikings and they suffered a series of reverses. Ironically, the worst of these was inflicted not by the Irish but by a strong force of Danes which in 850 put into Carlingford Lough in Co Down and set up a garrison. The following year they pushed into Dublin where they routed the Norwegians and rewarded their Irish allies with much silver and gold. But Danish control of Dublin was short-lived. In 853 a large contingent of Norwegian royal ships under Prince Olaf Amlaibh arrived in Ireland and most Danes and Norwegians quickly accepted him as undisputed Norse leader. Some Danes fled to England, unable to live as inferiors, while a few Irish kings were forced to pay heavy wergeld (compensation) for the death of Turgeis.

Olaf ruled much of southern Ireland for the next 18 years, his sovereignty occasionally disrupted by voyages back to his homeland (for reasons unclear). His brother Ivar, Lord of Limerick, minded the shop while he was away but the nation was still far from being dominated. The more powerful Irish kings were in no mood to cower and in 866 Finnliath, king of the northern Úi Néill, went on the rampage along the north coast destroying many Viking garrisons. By now, apart from a few irregular attacks, the first wave of the Norse invasion was over. Olaf died in Norway in 871 and Ivar and his heirs proved unable to rule with the same authority. Over the next few decades the Irish kings once more began to extend their influence.

But the Norsemen had not forgotten Ireland and in the early 10th century they returned in force. A large fleet sailed into Waterford harbour in 914 and this was reinforced by further ships the following year. The plundering began all over again — especially in Munster and Leinster — and when the high king of the Úi Néills , Niall Glúndub, tried to drive them out he failed to achieve an overall victory. First his Leinster army was routed and then he and his greatest warriors were killed in the Battle of Dublin (919). Over the next 30 or so years the Vikings reigned unchallenged, although they became more and more preoccupied with strengthening their hold across the water in York. From 950 onwards there were few new raids and the Norsemen's influence was now as settlers and traders, rather than invaders.

Arguments still rage about the ways the Vikings changed early Ireland. They certainly brought a revolution in the importance of navies as military forces and their trading brought untold riches into the country — itself a boost to the economy. On the negative side they butchered and executed many of their opponents (often unnecessarily), destroyed scores of sacred sites and stole many Celtic treasures. Yet the level of violence they employed was hardly new. The Irish kings were every bit as bloodthirsty and equally capable of robbing a monastery or two when they had the mind. From an abbot's point of view it made little difference whether an attacker was a murderous Viking or a murderous Irishman — the toll in lives and treasure was pretty much the same.

In fact, despite all the depredations, most of the Irish monasteries survived intact. This is partly because the Irish Vikings tended to concentrate their forces in specific, defendable areas rather than trying to hold down entire kingdoms as they did in England. There was certainly no Irish equivalent of the Danelaw, the huge tract of Viking-controlled country north of a line between Chester and the Thames. So it was business as usual for the Irish monks; at Cork, for instance, they lived side by side with the Norsemen, only occasionally enduring a raid. Such was their tenacity that there was never once a break in the succession of abbots.

Some have tried to suggest that the Vikings 'heathenised' Ireland by encouraging married clergy, lay abbots and nepotism in church and government offices. However all these vices existed before anyone had heard of the Norsemen and remained long after they had been absorbed into the genetic stock. Keeping a sought-after church position within the family was accepted behaviour in the 7th century, and common in the 8th. Later, it may have been convenient for the Church to blame the invaders. In fact, after a few generations, there was increasingly little to tell the Vikings and the native Gaelic kings apart.

Above: *When they weren't fighting, Vikings enjoyed a mental challenge. This game board dates from around the ninth century.*

Opposite above: *A hand carved model long boat.*

Opposite below: *A well-preserved Viking coin.*

9 Kings at War

Whatever their habitual excesses, Gaelic kings were regarded as useful allies by the Church. They were able to impose order, by force if necessary. They could carry out capital punishments (something the early Irish bishops were all in favour of) and they were a powerful ally in ensuring God's law was followed. It was for this reason that the bishops courted royal patronage by consecrating kings, a practice later adopted elsewhere in Europe.

Kings were to be revered and respected and they were entitled to their taxes (though of course not from the church). But the bishops also encouraged fair and civilised behaviour among rulers. They were not to mount raids against their own people or impose punitive taxes; neither could they pass unjust laws.

Surprising as it may seem, the Church held great influence over the kingships and its authority was rarely challenged. When in 809 the Ulaid tribe attacked a church belonging to Armagh, and killed its priest-in-charge, the powerful King Áed Oirnide exacted terrible revenge by invading their lands and putting Ulaid leaders to the sword.

But who were these kings and how did they carve up the country? This remains one of the most confusing features of early Christian Ireland, not least because historians of the day tended to over-egg the pudding in recording the great adventures and victories of their rulers. Occasionally, claims would be made of the emergence of a tríath a single High King said to rule 'through the kingdoms of Ireland from sea to sea.' This implies that his subjects were aware of — and accepted — an all-conquering lord and master. In fact there is little evidence to back this and if a tríath did surface his tenure must have been brief. Ireland, with its ever-expanding genetic melting pot of native Irish, Briton, Celt, Roman, Gaul and Scandinavian, was anything but a united kingdom.

Nonetheless, many leading scholars of the time were keen to promote the myth of togetherness. By the 7th century much frenzied research was going on into ancestry and the Book of the Taking of Ireland later argued that all the great families and dynasties were actually united by descent from a single group of ancestors. This idea became a shibboleth which proved hard to dismantle, even though it was fiction. It was a convenient way for some warring kings to wrap their petty feuding in the cloak of unity.

The class system applied to kings as much as it did to commoners. There were the rí túaithe ('petty kings' with limited lands), the ruiri (supposedly overlords of several rí túaithe) and the rí ruirech, or provincial kings. For many years it was the petty kings who held sway and their kingdoms expanded or contracted according to the bargains they struck and the alliances they made. But by the 8th century they were really no more than landed noblemen. Real power lay in the hands of the family dynasties who ruled and contested the provinces. Of these dynasties the greatest was the Úi Néill, although even they were sub-divided into branches and feuding factions. No one should blame students of the period for feeling bewildered by it all.

The Úi Néills claimed to be Kings of Tara, a phrase traditionally taken to mean high kings of all-Ireland. Their ancestor was a warrior called Niall Noígiallach, one of the barbarian Irish who raided the western shores of Britain during the Roman occupation and who even ventured as far as the Isle of Wight. His ancient seat was Ràth na Ríogh (Fort of the Kings) at Tara, Co Meath, which some believe was the centre of a fifth Irish province, called Mide. The 'Stone of Destiny', a stone structure within the fort, was said to have been the place where kings were crowned, although the stone was originally a phallic symbol used in the fertility rights of a much earlier culture. Whatever secrets it holds, Tara was certainly a settlement of major historical significance. Roman objects dating to the 3rd century AD have been found on the site, suggesting that travellers or Roman soldiers on campaign were received there. The Úi Néill ruled much of Ulster, the north-west and the midlands. There is some doubt about when the family split into its two main branches — the northern and southern Úi Néill — nor is it clear precisely why the split occurred. The politics is further complicated by the separation of the southern group into two factions (the Síl nAeda Sláine and the Clann Cholmáin) and the northern group into two more (Cenél Conaill and Cenél nEógain). From time to time rulers would claim over-kingship of the entire Úi Néill clan. The first of these rose from the Clann Cholmáin in 743 and, with one exception, this faction kept its stranglehold on the overkingship for more than a century. But power in Ireland has never been a certainty. For hundreds of years the Úi Neills squabbled amongst themselves and with the powerful tribes from the south. It was only when the Vikings arrived in force that the Irish began to appear more unified. Even then, it was a unity born of necessity rather than desire.

Elsewhere in Ireland the feuding was much the same. In the 8th century the Úi Dúnlainge ruled much of Leinster, allying themselves closely with the bishops of Kildare and fighting regularly with their rivals, the Úi Chennselaig, in the south. Leinster gradually fell under Úi Néill influence and by the mid-9th century its kings had installed puppet rulers to govern on their behalf.

Opposite: *A Viking raiding-ship in the Ferrycarrig National Heritage Park, Co. Wexford, an open-air museum renowned for its reconstructions of Ireland's ancient history.*

Connacht's two mighty dynasties were the Úi Fiachrach and the Úi Briúin (both claimed ancestral links with the Úi Néill). For much of the 7th century the province was controlled by Úi Fiachrach but once the Úi Briúin emerged it gained ground fast. By 725 it had established an aggressive nobility and regional government which provided a base from which to seek power over the entire country.

In Munster the Eóganacht dominated between the 7th and mid-10th centuries. It had a proud history on the battlefield and its King Cathal (721-42) was hailed King of Ireland (mainly by his Munster subjects). The Eóganacht's claim to produce the country's most Christian kings was, however, dealt a severe knock by the actions of King Feidlimid, who died in 847. He was ordained Bishop of Munster but devoted much of his time to sacking monasteries such as Kildare, Durrow, Fore and Gallen. He was an accomplished general and his raids on the Úi Néill forced them to meet him for peace talks. Yet by the mid-900s the peace had crumbled and the Eoganacht quickly became a spent force. Its place was taken by the Dál Cais of north Munster.

The story of the Dál Cais, and its titanic struggle against the Úi Néill, is a key period in Irish history. It is the story of how Ireland almost achieved its Holy Grail, the crowning of an undisputed high king. Almost... but not quite.

In 976 Brian Boru became king of Dál Cais and within three years both Limerick and Munster were totally under his control. He struck a deal with the Ostmen (the name the Vikings now called themselves) of Waterford to use their fleet and then marched on into Connacht and Leinster. He was engaged by Mael Sechnaill II, the overking of the Úi Néill, but there was no decisive battle and in 997 the two rulers sat down at Clonfert to carve up Ireland between them. Brian got Dublin and Leinster to add to his kingdom but it was not enough to satisfy him. After crushing an uprising in Dublin he set out on a mission to conquer the entire country and by 1011 he seemed on the verge of success. The Úi Néill was in tatters and no other provincial king could muster a realistic force against him. Then came news of another revolt in Dublin and Leinster.

The revolt was orchestrated by Dublin Ostmen and backed by their Viking friends from the Isle of Man and the Western Isles. They marched against Brian and fought one of the bloodiest battles in Irish history at Clontarf during Easter 1014. Brian's army won, although he died in battle on Good Friday, along with many capable leaders on both sides. Trying to work out what actually happened at Clontarf is a tricky business. If any records of the battle were made then they were eagerly passed on to the saga writers — the authors of the heroic tales which blend fact with folklore in Norse and Celtic tradition. As a result, the battle was depicted as a great struggle between the Irish and the Vikings for control of the nation — this was not so. The Vikings were by now well settled and scattered and certainly not an occupying army. The battle of Clontarf was far more about the ambitions and petty rivalries of Irish leaders. Its sad legacy was that it ended the life of the one man who really could have united the provinces of Ireland under one throne — Brian Boru.

According to the sagas, the two sides faced each other between Tolka and Liffey, a few kilometers inland from Dublin Bay. Those fighting for Brian and 'Ireland' included Brian's son Murchad, his grandson Tordelbach, Mael Seachlainn and his warriors from the southern Úi Néill and Ospak, of the Isle of Man. Against them, their flanks partly guarded by the sea, were the 'Vikings' — Sigurd the Stout of Orkney, Brodir of Man, Maelmordha with his Leinster army and the Dublin ostmen under Dubhgall. This was a battle in which Viking fought against Viking and Irishman against Irishman. Even brothers ended up on different sides.

The saga writers didn't let them down. There were stories of how Brian Boru's ex-wife Gormflaith was promised as a prize of victory (along with Dublin as a dowry) to both Sigurd and Brodir. How the Icelander Hall of Sida coolly knelt to tie his bootlace as his men fled from the advancing Irish. Asked why he had not run he replied: 'I cannot get home tonight, for my home is out in Iceland.' His life was spared. Then there was the death of Brian himself, slaughtered as he knelt praying for God's help in Tomar's Wood. Brian's son Murchad was killed within an ace of victory and the grandson Tordelbach drowned as he hunted enemy soldiers near the weir of Clontarf. In all 4,000 of Brian's men, and 7,000 of their opponents (including the leaders Sigurd and Brodir) fell in battle — many of them fell as they fled back to their Dublin stronghold and their ships.

The Úi Néill high king Mael Sechnaill II hoped to fill Brian's shoes but in reality he was just another provincial ruler with big ambitions. For a century and a half Ireland returned to a familiar political minefield with only Turlough O'Connor, king of Connacht, emerging as a contender for true national power. When he died, the leading force was once again an Úi Néill — this time Muirchertach Mac Lochlainn.

Mac Lochlainn allied himself with the king of Leinster, Dermot MacMurrough, and together they decided to wrest control of Dublin. The city — still dominated by Viking noblemen despite the result at Clontarf — was by now undisputed capital of the nation. Far from being kicked out, the Vikings had continued trading, maintained their kings and princes and replenished their treasure chests. Dublin was among the greatest cities of the Viking world, an economic goldmine and a place where ambitious rulers could hire high quality, Norse-trained mercenaries. He who ruled it, could rule Ireland.

But the Dubliners had some powerful allies in the form of Rory O'Connor, king of Connacht, and the one-eyed king of Bréifne, Tighearnán O'Rourke. Together this alliance fought successfully against Mac Lochlainn, who died in battle in 1166. An isolated Dermot MacMurrough was driven out and found himself devoid of any powerbase. O'Rourke, whose wife Dervorgilla had been abducted by Dermot 14 years earlier, exacted revenge by insisting that his sworn enemy was removed from the Leinster throne.

Dermot decided he must regain his rightful seat by force and he fled to England to enlist a mercenary force. In doing so he changed the course of Irish history. By inviting the English to help him he sparked the Norman invasion of Ireland and destroyed forever the dream of a native Irish High King.

Opposite: *Early art decorates a grave at Newgrange, the legendary seat and burial place of Ireland's greatest Gaelic kings. For centuries the mound at Newgrange was believed to conceal an entrance to the land of the pagan gods*

10 The Norman Invasion

The victory of Rory O'Connor over Dermot MacMurrough and Muirchertach Mac Lochlainn resulted in Rory crowning himself high king of Ireland in 1166 (a purely theoretical claim). Dermot swore to take revenge and the same year he travelled to England to ask the young King Henry II for help in raising an army. But Henry was cautious. His power in England was still shaky and he saw little profit in getting dragged in to a conflict far out to the west. Instead he granted his Norman barons permission to aid Dermot, if they so wished.

Dermot began his recruitment drive in Bristol, a port which had long had close contacts with Dublin. He signed up three of the most powerful Welsh lords — Richard Fitz Gilbert de Clare and the half-brothers Maurice FitzGerald and Robert FitzStephen, sons of the Welsh princess Nesta. Dermot promised de Clare (nicknamed Strongbow) the hand of his daughter Aoife and the whole of Leinster. FitzGerald and FitzStephen were offered Wexford and surrounding lands.

It proved an effective alliance. Between 1169 and 1171 the Normans retook Leinster, including Dublin, and began expanding outwards into Meath and Bréifne. Henry realised their ambitions were far greater than he had imagined and belatedly tried to stall them by ordering a ban on exports to Ireland, with the intention of cutting off their supply line. He also instructed Strongbow not to enter Ireland — an unreasonable and unrealistic demand seeing as the baron was already there!

By the late summer of 1171, Henry realised he could dally no longer. Dermot MacMurrough had died in May and Strongbow had enforced the deal making himself new Lord of Leinster. Attempts by the Leinstermen to revolt had been ruthlessly crushed and Henry now faced the prospect of a new, independent Norman kingdom on his vulnerable western seaboard. On 17 October 1171 the king landed near Waterford in command of a large, well-trained army and prepared to stamp his authority on the situation.

It was perhaps the first time in 400 years that an invading force arrived without any kind of fight. Strongbow had intercepted the king before Henry had even left England, begged forgiveness and promised that Leinster would be held only as a fief. Perhaps in awe of Henry's power, the Irish kings quickly followed suit. On the leisurely march to Dublin they lined up to pay homage — the chiefs of Leinster, Cork's King Dermot MacCarthy, Limerick's Donal Mór O'Brien, Bréifne's Tighearnán O'Rourke, Airgialla's Murchadh O'Carroll and the king of the Ulaid, Donn Slébhe MacDunleavy.

Nationalists with a romantic view of Ireland later agonised over such dismal resistance to the invading 'English'. But, as historians have pointed out, Irish kings had little to lose and, perhaps, the chance of protecting their own lands and interests from accession. In any case, none of them had much notion of unity and mistrusted each other every bit as much as they mistrusted Henry.

Henry presented himself as a reformer of the Irish Church, but he had to tread carefully. The English Archbishop St Thomas Becket — murdered by Henry's hit men for trying to assert church independence — was not long dead and it was too soon for the king to proclaim his papal authority over Ireland. He began by convening a great synod, or national gathering, of Irish church leaders in the winter of 1171/2. The aim was to organise the Irish clergy on similar lines to the English system and, allegedly, to improve discipline and moral fibre.

Far from opposing Henry, the Irish bishops, like the kings, welcomed him. After Henry's penance and reconciliation with the Church in May 1172, they sent a steady stream of letters to Pope Alexander III extolling the great improvements he had made. Predictably, the Pope confirmed Henry's right to rule Ireland, urged him to defend the Church, warned the Irish kings to stick by their oaths of allegiance and instructed the bishops to excommunicate any who disobeyed.

Below: *The Norman barbican at St Lawrence's Gate, Drogheda, Co Louth, dominated the castle's walled defences. The first fortifications in the town were probably constructed by Hugh de Lacy in the 1180s.*

Opposite: *A sundial stands in the grounds of Kilmalkedar Church on Co Kerry's Dingle Peninsula.*

Henry left Wexford on 17 April, 1172, his attention drawn elsewhere in his kingdom. Behind him he left garrisons in Dublin and other major seaports (such as Cork and Limerick) and granted his own Norman favourites land and income rights in Dublin. One of his loyalist supporters, Hugh de Lacy, was given Meath and later became constable of Dublin. He effectively acted as governor of Ireland and wasted no time killing Tighearnán O'Rourke (in the middle of a so-called parley). By 1175 he and Strongbow had quelled the last few pockets of Irish resistance and set about dividing the country up into baronies to be distributed among their own friends and supporters.

That same year, 1175, Rory O'Connor signed the Treaty of Windsor with Henry, which named Rory as high-king of all Ireland outside Leinster, Meath and Waterford. Rory had most to lose from Henry's arrival because he still saw himself as Ireland's overall ruler. The Treaty of Windsor was billed as a great coup for him but, like so many other Crown deals, it withered on the vine. Rory was soon told he could have Connacht alone — and then only if he paid the tributes demanded.

Neither Henry nor Rory were able to control their followers properly. The invading Norman barons grabbed land where they could, taking little notice of Crown instructions, while the Limerick king Donal Mór O'Brien burnt the town to prevent it becoming a Norman garrison. But though he had not planned colonisation, Henry began to have more of a stake in making it work. In 1177 he made his son, Prince John, Lord of Ireland and went back on promises to keep the kingdoms of Meath, Limerick and Cork for their respective Irish leaders. Soon the country was being governed by Dublin-based bureaucrats who according to King Henry's own advisor, Gerald of Wales, were 'neither loyal to their subjects nor formidable to their enemies.'

The Norman rush to colonise Ireland was fuelled by a sharp rise in the population of Europe. Food prices were high; labour costs were low and there was a steady migration of people in search of better living conditions. The sparsely populated Irish countryside with its rich farming potential was therefore an economic magnet to the power-hungry barons. They received feudal grants to defend their new territories and this resulted in boom time for builders of motte and bailey castles. The motte was a high, circular earthen mound within which rose the bailey, a strong wooden (or occasionally stone) tower. Once these baronies were well established the Normans looked to create towns nearby, places where they could trade the food surplus produced by their labourers. Kilkenny, Trim and New Ross all evolved in this way, attracting much foreign immigration.

Opposite: *A typical Norman gate set into the walls at Wexford. Efficient defences constructed by the invaders forced native Gaelic chiefs to reassess their battlefield tactics. No longer could they dictate the rules of engagement.*

According to a poll of Dublin's merchants at the end of the 13th century the new citizens were arriving from throughout England and Wales, as well as from France and Flanders. These people were not only knights and noblemen, many hundreds of colonists were peasants and cottiers who, despite a lowly birth, were made freemen in the new land. To make way for them, the native Irish were pushed out from the best farmland to the barren forests, mountains and marshlands.

Only one Irish family made it into the ranks of the Norman nobility — the FitzDermots of Rathdown, whose ancestors were sometime supporters of Strongbow. The rest lived almost as exiles in their own land, often in small, isolated communities, although they still had to pay their taxes and they could be requisitioned to fight on behalf of their lords. For many of these serfs or betaghs life was not much changed. For others, such as the poorer landowners, the Normans' arrival meant demotion. No longer were they classed as free. As betaghs they were bound to the soil and the service of their lord.

In the eastern plains the Normans imposed their language and culture quickly. Norman-French became the language of the aristocracy and, in Dublin, the wattle architecture of the Vikings was replaced by large, timber-framed houses and an ever-expanding use of stonework. Among the great churches, which until now had been constructed in Irish-Romanesque style, there appeared a new trend imported from Britain — the Early English Gothic style. The raw materials for these buildings came from England, as did the decorative stone carvings and gargoyles.

Even greater changes began to appear in the Irish economic structure. Viking trade aside, Ireland had been largely a subsistence economy. Now that the Norman lords were running more efficient farms, the country was transformed into a wealth-generating market economy. Seaports along the eastern coast flourished on the trade in surplus fruit, crops and vegetables to England and the continent. This income enabled the barons to build their great stone fortresses of the 13th century, symbols of their power, their wealth and their system of justice.

As the lord of Ireland (later king of England as well) Prince John was suspicious of everyone, even his father's Dublin governor Hugh de Lacy. At first he treated the Irish chiefs with disdain and contempt, although after becoming king he realised the need for more diplomatic language to retain their loyalty. Under John the system of government became a monstrous bureaucracy in which his King's Council seemed to breed civil servants. As the 13th century progressed, these men met regularly with the principal Norman barons. The Great Councils, as they were called, became the basis for an Irish Parliament.

Yet even now, the seeds of Irish nationalism were being sown. The bards composed prophecies detailing some of the terrible things which would one day happen to the Normans (these were really adaptations of similar sentiments voiced against the Vikings) and there was talk of a messenger from God. In 1214 there was much excitement when a holy man calling himself Aodh the Deliverer emerged claiming he was the fulfilment of a prophecy. He was later found to be a fraud.

In their songs and poems, the folksingers began to foster a hatred for their new colonial masters. One poem of the period, written in the kingdom of Bréifne, swears revenge for the Norman murder of King Tighearnán O'Rourke:

Numerous will be their powerful wiles
Their fetters and their manacles
Numerous their lies and executions
And their secure stone houses...

Though great you deem the success of the Foreigners
You noble men of Ireland
The glorious Angel tells me
That the Bréifnians will avenge Tighearnàn

Poems such as these became the forerunners of the first Irish protest songs. Many hundreds of years later, similar sentiments would emerge from the Irish nationalists fighting for self-rule.

Below: *One of several round towers which controlled the city walls of Waterford. The fortifications probably date from the mid-13th century.*

Opposite: *A Romanesque doorway at Kilmore, Co Cavan.*

Overleaf: *The small, though well-designed, castle at Claregalway, Co Galway is based on Norman ideas and dates from around the 16th century. Its defensive features include a 'murder hole' — an opening from which the castle's occupants could direct fire onto unsuspecting assailants.*

11 Hillforts and Castles

There are somewhere around 50 hillforts across Ireland, mostly scattered in the south of the country. They are thought to have been built during the Iron Age, or possibly Late Bronze Age, but their exact purpose remains a matter of debate. Some were sited at such a high altitude — Caherconree, Co Kerry, for example lies at 610m (1,800ft) — as to make full-time occupation unlikely. Is it possible the forts offered temporary refuge to which tribes retreated in times of unrest? Were they centres of government? Or were they primitive stadia for annual festivals and gatherings? All we can say with certainty is that they seem to fall into three main categories.

The first type are forts with just a single rampart, often surrounding a defensible hilltop or burial mound. Some historians have argued that Iron Age builders deliberately picked cairns and sacred sites to give their construction an aura of respectability — a bridging of old and new cultures. This is a neat theory, but it doesn't always fit the evidence. At Freestone Hill Fort, Co Kilkenny, the builders don't appear to have given a fig for the sanctity of the graves of their ancestors; to save hauling too much stone from outside the immediate area they simply demolished the Bronze Age cairns around them.

The second category of hillfort, more common in the southwest, has two or more well-spaced earth ramparts and occasionally features stone walls as additional defences. There are a number of excellent examples — Ballylin, Co Limerick (which covers 202sq m [50 acres] and is among the biggest), Mooghaun North, Co Clare, the Grianán of Aileach, Co Donegal, and the spectacular Dún Aenghus, on the Aran Isles. Dún Aenghus also makes use of a defensive measure known as chevaux-de-frise, in which massive blocks of stone are placed in an irregular jumble to slow down advancing warriors. Some historians have suggested this technique was brought to Ireland by Spanish or Portuguese settlers fleeing the Roman conquest of Europe. The idea is certainly possible, though unproven.

The third category covers three promontory forts — Luriegethan and Knockdhu, in Co Antrim, and Caherconree (mentioned above). The Antrim sites may have been constructed by invaders voyaging up the Irish Sea from Britain or France.

It is impossible to know how long hillforts remained in active use. However the centuries between the arrival of Christianity in Ireland, and the Viking Wars, may have seen them occupied temporarily as strategically important ground during tribal wars. By the time the Normans arrived in Ireland only seven fortresses of significance were mentioned — and these were more likely to have been timber constructions.

Castle building got into full swing following the Norman invasion and continued right up until the Cromwellian campaign of the mid-i17th century. As building work could be carried out only during periods of relative peace and stability, the first Norman castles were rather thrown together. They comprised a motte — a mound of earth dug out from a circular ditch — on which a wooden tower would be constructed as the baron's personal residence. To one side of the motte would be the bailey, a flat enclosed area encompassing a hall, chapel, kitchen, stables, barns and smithy.

In Ireland these castles are of vastly differing size and shape. Some were considered useful enough to be habitable as late as the 15th century, while others were little more than observation posts and were quickly abandoned once Norman control became well established. Almost all the motte and bailey castles date from before 1216, though other than that little is known of their history. So many records were destroyed in Ireland's traumatic past that almost every medieval building has to be dated by comparing it to similar structures in Britain.

The country's oldest mortared stone castles are probably at Carrickfergus, Dundrum and Carlingford — all these date from between 1185-1200. Other early examples are Dublin, Kilkenny and Limerick, each constructed between 1205 and 1230 and each featuring a quadrangular court with high corner towers and a double-tower gatehouse. Later, rectangular courts with D-shaped towers came into vogue as at Roscommon Castle; built by Edward I on similar lines to his massive fortress at Harlech in North Wales.

Conditions inside these early castles were rudimentary and far from private. Glass windows were virtually unknown (wooden shutters were used instead) and to make the most of the available light, the walls were painted with whitewash. Some of the more important rooms had rugs or wicker mats and occasionally biblical paintings and tapestries. Latrines were built into the castle walls — the resulting smell from below can only be imagined — but there was little privacy for anyone. Even the lord and his wife would share their bedroom with several senior servants, relying only on a curtain around their bed to keep out prying eyes. Lowlier household members would have to make rough beds out of rushes and lie around the fire in the main hall, or perhaps in the kitchen. If a bed was available, four or five people at a time would have to huddle together inside it to keep warm.

Furniture was a rare luxury and usually of simple design. A lord and lady would usually have their own personal chairs in a hall

Opposite: *Reflections of the past — the ruins of Dromineer Castle, Co Tipperary.*

or bedchamber; the rest of the servants would have to make do with benches. Apart from this, the only other furniture would be a few large tables and wooden chests for storing clothes, plate, cooking utensils and family heirlooms.

By the days of the Cromwellian campaign, living conditions were better and furnishings rather more elaborate. A report prepared by Hardress Waller, owner of Castletown Tower, Co Limerick, on valubles captured from him by Irish rebels gives some idea of what the landed classes of the time regarded as valuable. Waller lists:

'Eleven downe and feather beds, six flocke beds with boulsters, pillowes, blancketts, rugs and caddoes (rough overblankets) to the said beds. Candlesticks, chamberpotts, stills (distilleries) and such like things of pewter and brasse. Hangings for a large dyning room and two chambers of tapestrie and divers other hangings and curtaynes for windows. Two very rich Turkey carpetts. A clocke. A chest of books.'

Above: *The remains of Carrigogunnell Castle, Co Limerick, which stand on a volcanic crag overlooking the River Shannon. It has a fascinating history and saw action in both the Cromwellian Wars and during the Glorious Revolution.*

Opposite: *Odeas Castle, near Corofin, Co Clare.*

The period between 1310 and 1430 saw little new castle building in Ireland. The invasion of Edward Bruce, the general economic decline in Europe and the ravages of the Black Death meant few barons had either the time or the money to devote to extra defences. The Gaelic chieftains, who were therefore enjoying something of a comeback, built a few plain towers (probably Buncrana, Co Donegal and Roslee, Co Sligo were among these) but they were far too busy destroying abandoned Norman fortresses to bother about building their own. One notable exception is the Archbishop of Dublin's castle at Swords, Co Dublin, which appears to be 14th century.

In 1429 the Irish Parliament approved a £10 subsidy to landowners in the English Pale counties of Dublin, Meath, Kildare and Louth to improve defences. This sparked off a spate of tower building, mostly to the modest specifications required by the statute — towers had to be a minimum of 15m (40ft) high, 6m (20ft) long and 5m (16ft) wide. They incorporated a number of designs peculiar to Ireland, such as parapet machicolations (slots for shooting arrows or dropping stones) above the entrances, double-stepped battlements and murder holes (openings set in the roof of an entranceway down which stones could be dropped). There are plenty of surviving examples, such as Roodstown and Milltown in Co Louth and Dunsoghly, Athgoe and Dalkey in Co Dublin. By 1449 Parliament decided enough fortresses had been built and a limit was placed on new constructions.

Among the largest of the Irish tower houses are at Blarney, Co Cork, Ballycarbury, Co Kilkenny, and Donegal and Greencastle, both Co Donegal. All of these are late 15th century and Donegal became a model for many later towers in Connacht and Munster. Its design placed the great hall on the top storey, allowing it to have narrower walls and bigger windows — features which would have compromised the tower's defensive integrity further down. This arrangement allowed the hall to have a central hearth with a smoke hole in the roof. Munster also has some very fine round tower castles, such as Ballynahow and Newtown.

From the 1580s onwards some new towers were built by settlers on the plantations of Munster and Ulster. However Elizabethan and Jacobean manor houses with no fortifications — a common sight in England and Wales — were unpopular. English families wanting more room and comfort than a tower, but still concerned about defence, would compromise by building stronghouses. These were strengthened by additional wings to permit all-round fire, open wall walkways, turrets, machicolations and pistol-firing positions beneath main windows. Good examples include Rathfarnham, Co Dublin, Portumna, Co Galway, Raphoe, Co Donegal, Kanturk, Co Cork, Burncourt, Co Tipperary, and Manorhamilton, Co Leitrim.

Although castles are traditionally seen as family seats, their ownership changed hands many times through force of arms. Ballymote, Co Sligo, is a case in point. It was built around 1300 for Richard de Burgo, fell to the O'Connors soon afterwards and then to the MacDiarmadas. It was later re-claimed by O'Connor and surrendered to the English in 1571. In between times it was held by the MacDonaghs, who lost it to Richard Bigham in 1584. In 1588 it was burnt by the O'Connors, then recaptured by the MacDonaghs in 1598, sold to the O'Donnells and, in 1602, handed over to the English. The Taaffe family then held it from 1630-1652, it was re-taken for a time by Captain Terence MacDonagh and re-captured at the end of the 17th century by Lord Granard. After all that, one can only admire as foolhardy any attempt to establish the identity of the 'real' owners.

Above: *Cahir Castle, Co Tipperary. The castle dates from the 13th century but its most impressive fortifications were added during the 15th and 16th centuries. In its heyday it was regarded as one of the strongest castles in Ireland and rebellious owners caused grave problems for Queen Elizabeth I's government.*

Left: *Leamaneh Castle, Co Clare. Legend has it that the widowed lady of the house kicked a Cromwellian soldier out of an upper window.*

Opposite: *Fitzmaurice Castle, Ballybunion, stands in lonely vigil above the Co Kerry coastline.*

Bunratty Castle, Co Clare, was founded in 1277 by the Norman lord Sir Thomas de Clare. It withstood four Irish attacks but by 1306 had been burnt twice.

Above: *The remains of Ballintubber Castle, Co Roscommon, which became a key centre for Catholic resistance during the war against Cromwell. In 1642 it held out against the government forces of both Lord Raneleagh and Sir Charles Coote.*

Left: *The magnificent interior of Bunratty Castle.*

Opposite: *Until 1922, 13th-century Dublin Castle was the centre for English government in Ireland*

Above: *A view across the old walled garden at Leamaneh Castle.*

Left: *The huge tower of Blarney Castle, Co Cork, which is said to conceal a secret underground passage.*

Opposite: *The elegant castle and gardens at Ayesha, Dalkey, Co Dublin.*

Above: *Ormond Castle at Carrick on Suir, Co Tipperary*

Left: *Perhaps Ireland's best known piece of folklore involves the kissing of the Blarney stone. The stone forms one of the massive lintels supporting the castle's parapet and the kisser has to dangle upside down through a gap in the walls. For those who accomplish the feat, the reward is said to be 'the gift of the gab'.*

Opposite: *A general view of Blarney Castle.*

Another view of Ballintubber Castle, Co Roscommon.

Opposite: *Whytes Castle at Athy, Co Kildare.*

Above: *The ruins of Carrigogunnell. It was surrendered to Lord Deputy Grey in 1536 by Mahon O'Brien and eventually passed to Michael Boyle, later Archbishop of Dublin. The castle was blown up by General Ginckell in 1691.*

Right: *One of Ireland's most beautiful hillforts — the Grianan of Aileach, Co Donegal.*

Overleaf: *Another view of Ballintubber Castle, Co Roscommon.*

12 The Gaelic Revival

By the early 14th century the haphazard powerbase of the Norman (now known as English) barons was already breaking down. No longer were they first call when the king's Irish administrators needed military muscle. As often as not, this work would be contracted out to whoever's personal army was (a) capable, and (b) not in a state of revolt. This amounted to the privatisation of the military and it became increasingly difficult to tell the sides apart.

Among the competing forces were, of course, the native Gaelic chieftains. But there were also the 'kerns', small mercenary bands who fostered their barbarian image by going barefoot into battle, and the galloglass — Scottish mercenaries from the Western Isles. The only certain thing was that the English no longer held overall battlefield superiority.

For the ordinary Irishman, this chaotic organisation served only to make the wearying process of earning a living still harder. The Crown began to franchise out tax collection to any two-bit landowner with a small private army. Such a system of 'coign and livery' effectively gave the agents free rein to collect their own income and, unsurprisingly, it became a glorified protection racket. From 1297 onwards the Crown recognised this by limiting the spread of armies to the wild frontier lands where Norman rule was most questionable. There soon followed a tacit acknowledgement of Ireland's divided state from the Anglo-Irish Parliament in Dublin. Between 1310 and 1366 it struck deals with a number of Gaelic chieftains giving them the right to arrest lawbreakers. These villains could be tried by the king's courts in the 'land of peace' (principally the east), but by the chiefs themselves in the 'land of war' (the rest of the country).

By the end of Edward II's reign in 1327 the breakdown in Irish government had translated into a full blown crisis. Europe's population expansion (and the hike in food prices to which it was linked) had ended and many of the fortune-seeking barons who had so eagerly colonised Ireland were now back home in their more comfortable English estates. As a result, half of all colonized Irish territory was owned by absentee landlords. This in turn led to bitterness among those English lords who stayed. They accused their compatriots of failing to maintain armies and defences; thus allowing the native Irish to regain the initiative.

The rise of Scottish nationalism added a further complication. In 1314 Robert the Bruce, king of the Scots, won his great victory at the Battle of Bannockburn, routing the English forces. Robert was keen to consolidate and extend his power and had long been sounding out both the native Irish and the English colonists for support. But when in May 1315 he despatched an army headed by his brother Edward to invade Ulster, he made a basic political blunder.

The Scots claimed to be supporting the revolt of the Irish king Donal O'Neill. This immediately alienated the English colonists, despite the fact that Robert the Bruce was related through marriage to one of their most senior figures — the Red Earl of Ulster. Instead of uniting both the native Irish and discontented English colonists against London, the Scottish army turned them against each other. Edward Bruce was defeated by the English baron John de Bermingham at the Battle of Faughart, Co Louth, in 1318. By then much of the country had been devastated, a situation made worse by a succession of bad winters and a famine in northern Europe.

For Robert the Bruce, defeat in Ireland was little more than a setback. In 1328 the English throne formally recognised Scotland as an independent state and a more peaceful period lay ahead. But in Ireland the chaos continued. Throughout the rest of the century a constant stream of complaints were sent winging across the Irish Sea to London. The Anglo-Irish Parliament warned of crumbling defences and of don't-care absentee landlords; of incompetent crown administrators and of the complete disintegration of the colony's economy. The result, warned Parliament, would be an unstoppable rise of the Gaelic chieftains and the increasing defection of the so-called 'degenerates' — English noblemen rallying to the Irish cause.

These forecasts proved disturbingly close to the mark. The spread of the Black Death in 1348-9, coming so soon after failed harvests and a general collapse in agricultural fortunes, resulted in colonists of all backgrounds heading back to England in the hope of reviving their fortunes. Irish taxes could no longer be relied upon by the English exchequor as easy income.

There were a number of attempts to stop the rot. Edward III and later Richard II, mounted a series of military expeditions aimed at whipping the Irish kings and the English rebels into line. But it was a hopeless task as well as a huge drain on resources. One of the worst ideas was to surround rebel territory with strategically-placed garrisons able to react instantly to any sign of trouble. These castles succeeded in quieting rebel voices. But they proved fantastically expensive to maintain and failed to re-conquer so much as a metre of land for the forces of 'civilisation' and the king. Already at court, talk of the 'Irish Problem' was commonplace.

The Irish, naturally, were jubilant. Here at last was the long-promised renaissance of the Celts, a chance to re-assert national identity and unite with the rebel English to drive the crown out. A poem written for the inauguration of King Niall Mór O'Neill in 1364 began:

Opposite: *A weathered portrait stares from the walls of Drumlane Church, Co Cavan.*

> Ireland is a woman risen again
> from the horrors of reproach...
> she was owned for a while by foreigners
> she belongs to Irishmen after that

Well, sort of. As with many aspects of Irish nationalism, the 14th century Gaelic resurgence was not anywhere near so clear-cut. Far from concentrating their efforts against the Crown, the Irish chiefs spent a great deal of time squabbling among themselves. This was understandable, given the way they had been governed by the English barons. The barons had adopted a divide and rule policy, giving every Irish leader equal status — irrespective of claims that certain kings were more important that others. With the old system in disarray, the Irish were once again free to contest rights to overlordship of the regions. Feuds enshrined in centuries of folklore were duly dusted down by a new generation of rulers.

This twist in Ireland's internal politics brought about a revival of Gaelic culture, particularly poetry and history. The 'praise-poets', responsible for fawning odes on the greatness of various leaders, were highly valued as medieval public relations men. Historians, meanwhile, strove to show how certain lands were the legitimate property of a particular patron king. But the downside of Gaelic ascendancy was evident in the devastating internecine warfare which plagued the lives of ordinary folk. Parts of Ulster and Munster, previously fertile agricultural pastureland, became virtually deserted in the turmoil.

The result of all this was that native the Irish as well as the English rebels wasted men and vast resources in pursuit of often impossible goals, while the Crown virtually abandoned hope of squeezing additional wealth out of the colony. The only real winners were the Anglo-Irish nobility, namely the loyal Crown subjects and government administrators who ran things in the east. Although they had lost territory, they retained a secure stronghold in the counties of Louth, Meath, Dublin and Kildare. To emphasise the point they built the Pale, a defensive earthen rampart designed to keep out the barbarians lurking in the rest of the country. This monument later provided the English language with one of its most useful clichés; the phrase 'beyond the Pale' signifies anything that goes outside the bounds of civilised behaviour.

Gradually, as the warring factions of the native Irish settled down, the dawn of the 15th century brought the beginning of a new stability — even prosperity. There was a trend to build fortified houses and stone towers in every kingdom, (in a total contrast to the neglect of defences in the 14th century) and this suggests that definable kingdoms had become established. Trade with Europe strengthened and many new churches were built by the Gaelic chieftains.

The old English barons, quietly comfortable within the Pale, were by now busily re-inventing their 'Irishness'. They heaped money on their own poets and historians who obligingly assured them that they had as much a stake in national identity as did any Irish king. Surely, it was argued, the early English colonists were no different to the Gaelic traveller of a few centuries earlier. Both were invaders turned settlers. Both engaged in intermarriage and sought private land rights. Therefore it followed that the two peoples had a common heritage. It was simply that the men of the Pale had ended up wealthier! Convenient as this reasoning may have been it was, as we have seen, historically flawed. There was no Gaelic 'invasion' as such. But there was certainly a Norman conquest, however arbitrary.

As the century drew on there became a growing realisation in England that the mere passing of new laws was never going to bring Irish rebels to heel. Apart from anything else there were more important things to consider — continental campaigns and internal English treason to name but two. The Crown adopted a policy of benign neglect. It wanted to rule Ireland but it wasn't going to get embroiled in a vastly expensive military conflict which promised neither economic nor political rewards. It was content to leave things to the Lords of the Pale, the barons whose family roots were in England and whose ancestors were the first Norman colonists. They could always be counted upon to give unquestioned loyalty to the English king.

This of course was true. But the Old English — as historians confusingly call the barons — had their own agenda. They knew they were held in contempt by the native Irish and that old grudges dating back to the days of the Norman invasion were still nurtured. They expected Irish attacks on their outposts and they were by no means disappointed. However, rather than throw themselves at the mercy of a disinterested king across the Irish Sea, they made alliances amongst themselves, turning those more powerful lords into unofficial protectors of the Old English community. It was to these leaders that allegiance was owed, not the Crown, and they fostered intense loyalty among their followers. They maintained well-trained armies, built strong castles and towers and mounted attacks on any Irish chieftain who came too close.

By the early 16th century, the FitzGerald earls of Kildare had emerged above the Butler earls of Ormond as the most dominant Old English force. The advantages of harnessing the FitzGeralds' political and military power was not lost on Henry VII and Henry VIII, who successively appointed them crown agents responsible for raising the king's taxes and ensuring good government. While this seemed to re-assert the authority of the English kings, in fact the reverse was true. The Kildares made clear that should they not be confirmed as Lord Lieutenants, even the 'loyal' Old English areas of Ireland would become ungovernable. On the odd occasions they were sacked, they proved this to be no empty threat.

Opposite: *The city of Kilkenny saw the passing of the 1366 statutes which reinforced English colonial law on an area regarded as an outpost of civilisation.*

K PRODUCE
Fresh Fruit & Vegetables 27
28 JOHN CLEERE 28
Widow

13 Ireland in the Reformation

King Henry VIII's refusal to accept the authority of the Pope put further strain on relations between the Crown and its more loyal Irish subjects. These Old English Catholic families wanted nothing to do with Henry's Reformation, and campaigned actively against his new state church. Many even removed their sons from Oxford and Cambridge colleges for fear that they would become indoctrinated with the heretic Protestant doctrine. The young men were instead sent to continental universities where counter-reformation Catholicism had already taken root.

For months the Old English agonised over a divided loyalty between their god and their king. Eventually, a group of lawyers devised a compromise in which it was suggested that offering political loyalty to the Crown did not necessarily mean an acceptance of its spiritual supremacy. It was a good try — but it was doomed to failure. No Protestant king or queen would agree a deal completely at odds with most other European monarchies. Rulers, not Rome, were to decide the peoples' religion.

The result of all this was that whenever a plum job in the Dublin civil service was up for grabs, the Crown would seek a 'reliable' English-born Protestant to fill it rather than an Old English Catholic. This caused great resentment among Dublin's lawyers, who realised that, despite their genuine loyalty, their ambitions in government were dead in the water. To their credit, they didn't go down without a fight.

When the new breed of Protestant administrators began to introduce aggressive anti-Catholic legislation (such as the confiscation of land and property) it was the Old English who travelled to London to plead for Crown intervention. They argued that the administrators were trying to inflame a revolt in which they themselves would directly benefit. Perhaps surprisingly, these appeals were very often heeded by English rulers (apart from Oliver Cromwell). Many an ambitious Irish governor would suddenly find his master plan for solving the Irish Problem abruptly cancelled.

Yet it would be wrong to imagine that the conflict between Protestant English monarchs and the Catholic Old English was conducted in the manner of a polite, theological debating society. There was some out and out resistance and some brutal responses. The first Irish challenge to a Protestant monarch came in 1534 with a show of military force by Lord Thomas Offaly, son of the 9th earl of Kildare and a leading light in the mighty FitzGerald dynasty. In fact Offaly's motives were political rather than religious — he just wanted King Henry VIII to understand that FitzGerald loyalty to the Crown was conditional on London keeping its nose out of Irish government. There was much support among the Old English for this grandstanding. They saw it as a symbolic show of strength rather than a rebellion. But they soon switched sides when they realised their king was outraged. Henry called Offaly's bluff by sending an army of 2,300 men under Sir William Skeffington to crush him. The king successfully portrayed Offaly as an enemy of the Crown and of its Old English supporters and exacted a terrible revenge by confiscating FitzGerald lands and sentencing all male members of the family, apart from one small child, to death. This uprising, incidentally, saw the only known siege of Dublin Castle during an unsuccessful attempt to wrest it from Crown control.

Henry followed his success by convening an Irish Parliament in 1536 and forcing its members (many of whom had participated in Offaly's revolt) to declare him supreme head of the Irish church. The country was now in exactly the same position as England and indeed a whole weight of new religious laws, already passed by the English Reformation Parliament, was imposed on Ireland.

King Henry knew that he would have to back his new regime with military force and the modest 300-strong garrison in Dublin was, by the middle of the century, reinforced by a further 2,200 men. It was felt in London that the extra cost of maintaining this army could easily be offset by rents wrung from the confiscated monasteries. But the Crown reckoned without the crooked administrators of the Pale, who squirrelled much of the profit away. When Elizabeth I succeeded to the English throne in 1558 a new approach to Irish government was soon well under way.

The first serious attempts to find a non-military solution to the Crown's problems in Ireland were made by successive governors — Thomas, earl of Sussex, and Sir Henry Sidney. These men were ambitious rivals, each seeking a heightened reputation at Elizabeth's court, and each opting for a very different approach. Sussex wanted to negotiate with the native Irish chieftains, restoring previously agreed titles and land rights but subjecting any rebels to instant and decisive military force.

Sidney was far more aggressive, though he presented himself as a peace-maker. His aim was to dispossess any Gaelic leader who fought against the Crown or occupied its lands. These estates would then be handed to English Protestant nobles, on the understanding that English families would be settled on them. Ancient land titles, forgotten since Norman times, were searched out and used as further incentives for the Protestant plantations.

Back in England, fortune-seeking adventurers began rubbing their hands with glee. In fact this first attempt at plantation was a failure. The English incomers, with their headstrong private armies, caused widespread bitterness among the native Irish and

Opposite above: *Among many interesting exhibits at Dublin's Christ Church Cathedral are the mummified remains of a cat and mouse, recovered from the Cathedral crypt.*

Opposite below: *A view of the crypt itself.*

soon a rebellion was in full swing. Sidney responded by drawing up plans to extend the plantations far beyond the lands he'd first proposed. But he judged Queen Elizabeth's response badly. Stung to discover that one of her close friends, Thomas, Earl of Ormond, had three brothers involved in the rebellion, she demanded a full report, ordered mercy for all rebel leaders (except one) and suggested the entire crisis was Sidney's fault. Publicly humiliated, he resumed a more conciliatory policy as governor.

The one rebel who was not pardoned was James Fitz Maurice FitzGerald. He had claimed to be fighting a religious war against his heretic queen and, after a short period in exile on the continent, he returned in 1579 intent on driving her out of Ireland. His modest army managed to attract considerable support in both the Pale and Munster, and won the backing of the Earl of Desmond. The earl's seat — Adare Castle, Co Limerick — was one of the finest garrisons in all Ireland and with him on board, the rebellion assumed altogether more serious proportions. The queen responded by sending a powerful 8,000-strong army under Arthur Lord Grey de Wilton to crush it.

The rebel force's cause was hopeless. Some who had supported it quickly changed sides and begged a royal pardon once they saw the odds against them. Others, undecided about whom to back, suddenly emerged as passionately loyal to the Crown. However, although Elizabeth showed some mercy, she was determined to make an example of the ringleaders. Many of FitzGerald's troops were summarily slaughtered and a witch-hunt followed to root out and execute any Gaelic nobleman who had supported him. In the ensuing weeks the English army went on an orgy of slaughter and destruction in Munster on a scale never seen before in Ireland.

Back east, the Palesmen who had rebelled were hung, drawn and quartered — but not before they had been interrogated by Protestant zealots and urged to renounce the pope. When the bloodshed finally stopped, the government officials running Dublin announced plans for a plantation of 20,000 English people on the lands of the Earl of Desmond. These officials were now hell-bent on passing a raft of anti-Catholic laws, including swingeing fines against any landowner who was not following the 'right' religion. But if the Crown believed its atrocities would end opposition in Ireland, it was hopelessly wrong. By the 1590s a new threat had emerged. Hugh O'Neill, earl of Tyrone and probably Gaelic Ireland's greatest leader, began expelling government officials from Ulster and quickly provoked a confrontation with the Crown. He raised an army, adopted elements of both English and Irish military techniques, and soon had almost every disgruntled nobleman in the country rallying round. O'Neill presented himself as champion of the Papist cause (a dubious claim since he was not exactly a devout Catholic) and convinced King Philip III of Spain that he could smash English colonial rule.

In 1600, after widespread success in Ulster, O'Neill marched south to harry Crown interests. He journeyed down through Westmeath, burned part of Kilkenny and wreaked further havoc in Cork. In February of that year his authority as 'Prince of Ireland' was acknowledged by the Munster chiefs and his declaration of a holy war won over many commoners. When Queen Elizabeth's new Lord Deputy, Lord Mountjoy, landed in Ireland at the head of a 20,000-strong army he soon realised the competence of his enemy.

O'Neill was a clever tactician and early on he dictated the rules of engagement. As Mountjoy advanced, the Gaelic army taunted him by withdrawing to Ulster across the Bog of Allen — a nightmarish prospect for the pursuing English. Elizabethan soldiers hated the impenetrable woods and unyielding marshes and an absence of accurate maps made their progress agonisingly slow. Where Mountjoy encountered rebel forces, the Irish knack for ambush and retreat into the mountains left his men floundering. And when, later, he tried to force his way into Ulster along the Moyry Pass he was hopelessly outmanouvred by Irish skirmishing skills.

But O'Neill's strength was primarily in Ulster, and in the south his rebellion was much more shaky. By 1601 Mountjoy had brought the chiefs of Wicklow and Monaghan into line and his main ally, President of Munster George Carew, had suppressed much of the resistance in the south-west. O'Neill, backed by military support from the king of Spain and strengthened by the forces of another charismatic rebel — 'Red' Hugh O'Donnell, decided the time was ripe for a showdown with the English. It came with the landing of 4,000 Spanish soldiers at Kinsale, Co Cork, in 1601. O'Neill and O'Donnell marched south to join them and reclaim Ireland for the Irish.

Historians have argued for centuries about what went wrong. Certainly many of the cards were stacked in favour of the Irish allies. They were the offensive force. Spanish reinforcements were on the way and the English army was suffering from sickness and desertion. Yet this battle was to be fought on terms which suited Mountjoy. There were no bogs, no woods and no mountains; and unlike his opponents he had a tried and tested military strategy.

O'Neill's tactics were probably his greatest failing and the cause of his downfall. His cumbersome infantry lines were the result of Spanish advice — and they withered before the onslaught of the English cavalry. But there were also worrying divisions within the allied ranks. As the historian Geoffrey Keating later put it: 'It was the fault of the Irish themselves — wrangling over petty, worthless claims — which destroyed them at one stroke, and not the armed might of the foreigners.'

Certainly, the Spanish didn't help matters with their rather timid and indecisive approach to the battle. Mountjoy's cavalry made their decisive charge in the early hours of Christmas Day 1601. Nine days later the besieged rebel force in Kinsale surrendered and O'Neill was defeated.

Mountjoy attempted to rub salt into Irish wounds by symbolically smashing the ancient Stone of Tullahogue, the stone upon which generations of O'Neill kings had been crowned. And yet O'Neill himself salvaged his dignity. In the years following James I accession to the throne (1603) he was confirmed as Earl of Tyrone with all property and land rights intact. In one of those strange twists of history it was O'Neill's old foe Mountjoy, now a senior Crown adviser on Ireland, who fought so hard to ensure he retained his rightful status.

Opposite: *Ruins of a medieval church at Dromineer. The Earl of Ormond became the lord of the manor in 1556 when he took possession of the castle.*

Overleaf: *Christ Church Cathedral as it appears today.*

14 Oliver Cromwell

However well Hugh O'Neill came out of the 1600 rebellion, there was always going to be a Crown backlash. It came in 1607 when James I gave tacit approval for the confiscation of lands and properties owned by rebel Catholics and for new plantations of English Protestants. As ever, Ireland's government officials wasted no time in implementing anti-Catholic laws; laws which they believed would ultimately bring the whole island under the sway of Protestantism. They arranged plantations as far afield as Wexford, Leitrim, Longford, Clare and Tipperary. More significantly, they singled out six of the nine counties of Ulster for Protestant colonization. The religious intolerance which followed (and despite the apologists who say we should not judge past deeds by modern standards, intolerance is the right word) still reverberates today across the island of Ireland.

The rush to join the plantations was unprecedented. In the three decades leading up to 1641 at least 100,000 English, Scottish and Welsh settlers migrated across the Irish Sea. The incomers were handed confiscated land and promptly showed how good they were at confiscating even more. Any patch of territory with an uncertain land title was claimed for the Crown, and therefore for the settler. This phenomena was particularly common in Munster, but not a single Irish county escaped the clutches of some rapacious British landowner.

A fact sometimes forgotten by Irish nationalists however is that native Irish landowners actively assisted this process to feather their own nests. These noblemen wanted to be seen as loyal subjects of the Crown because they saw how wealthy it would make them. By settling English families on their estates they qualified for handsome cash sums and could be assured that their farms would be well maintained and improved. With the money thus acquired, they worked hard to portray themselves for all the world as English gentlemen — building English style manor houses, riding in ornate carriages, commissioning stonemasons to create family vaults and dressing in the latest London fashions.

From 1633 on, the plantation policy moved into overdrive. The new Irish Governor, Thomas Wentworth, made clear that he was looking to begin a new wave of land confiscations and Catholic landowners were tartly informed that they could not expect the king to back them against the more aggressive Protestant incomers. In 1641, believing they faced annihilation, the leading Catholic lords of Ulster began yet another rebellion.

Perhaps they hoped a show of strength would be enough to make their point and sway Crown opinion against the anti-Catholic government regime. If so, they misread the undercurrent of anger and bitterness among ordinary Catholic people. What began as a military uprising turned into a bloody attempt at revolution in which at least 2,000 Protestant settlers were murdered. Thousands more were stripped of their every possession (even their clothes) and terrible atrocities were committed. The slaughter was seized upon and greatly embellished by Protestant zealots back in Britain, to the point where the British believed there had been a general massacre of their people in Ireland. The English and the Scots demanded that Charles I should avenge the deaths, but he had other things on his mind. Civil war was approaching and he would need every last royalist in his realm to counter the Parliamentarian army. The Catholic rebels, led by Hugh O'Neill's nephew Owen Roe O'Neill, knew they had been handed a golden opportunity to destroy Protestant power and drive the Crown out of Ireland. But their goal was not supported by those who stood to lose most, namely the Old English landowners. They refused to help O'Neill engage the Scottish Covenanter army which had landed in Ulster to protect the Protestant plantations. And with the Scots eager for revenge, O'Neill could not risk travelling south to expel Crown interests from Dublin.

As the months passed, the chances of a united Ireland grew ever slimmer. Once it became clear that the Parliamentarians, rather than the Royalists, would emerge victorious from the English civil war, Catholic leaders knew their cause was lost. In January 1649, King Charles I was tried and executed and the Parliamentarians could at last turn their attention to Ireland and revenge for the slaughter of 1641. The army they despatched was the most feared, ruthless and efficient fighting force in Europe. On

Above: *The old walls at Youghal, Co Cork. In the post-Cromwellian era the town became an important port for the export of farming produce.*

Opposite: *St Canice's Cathedral, Kilkenny City.*

15th August 1649, Oliver Cromwell, Lord Protector of England, arrived in Dublin as civil and military Governor of Ireland.

Cromwell's strategy was not particularly original. He planned to crush all military resistance to the English Parliament — whether it be from Catholics or Protestant Royalists — and he intended to confiscate the lands of any clergy or estate owners who could be linked to the 1641 rebellion. Further, he prepared an evangelical crusade aimed at bringing the entire country under the Protestant religion. All of these measures had been tried before to some extent in Ireland. The difference was that Cromwell's army was hell-bent on slaughter to achieve his aims.

This wasn't just because his 20,000 soliders were thirsting for revenge and fired with religious motives, although both sentiments played a part. The English infantrymen were also out to fill their pockets after long years on campaign at home. Ireland offered an opportunity to plunder at will.

The atrocities they carried out rank alongside the worst of any army in history. Entire towns were massacred, women and children slaughtered and senior Catholic churchmen publicly executed. Priests were hunted down like animals and the persecution of the Catholic church was so efficient that within a few years its carefully re-organised structure was unrecognisable. Catholic estates were seized and their owners left to fend for themselves alongside all the other refugees.

Some leniency was shown to landowners who could prove they had played no part in the rebellion, although their treatment was hardly just. Cromwell forced them into the poor-quality agricultural belt west of the River Shannon to scrabble among themselves for land. At a stroke, the power and influence enjoyed by wealthy Catholics over their tenants was ended. In their place, Cromwell installed his favoured soldiers and those people from Britain who had helped finance his military campaign.

And what of that campaign? The first point to make is that Cromwell's army was much smaller than that of the Irish coalition forces facing him. Confusingly, the joint-leader of the coalition was actually an Old English Protestant — James Butler, 12th Earl of Ormond. But a common religious belief mattered little to the two commanders. Ormond was an ardent royalist, and therefore Cromwell's enemy.

Ormond had spent the years after 1641 trying to agree a lasting peace with the Irish Catholic Confederates. By 1648 the imminent arrival of Cromwell had created this uneasy alliance and for the exiled Charles II, whom Ormond now represented as Lord Lieutenant of Ireland, there were hopes that the royal standard could be raised again. But the early omens were not good. A fortnight before Cromwell arrived, Ormond and his new allies were trounced by an advance force of Parliamentarians at the Battle of Rathmines in Ulster. It was not until October 1649 that Ormond finally struck a deal with Owen Roe O'Neill ensuring that the coalition forces had numerical superiority.

Right: *Roscommon Castle, Co Roscommon, was captured by Catholic forces in 1645 but was surrendered to the Cromwellian commander Reynalds in 1652.*

Carlow Castle, Co Carlow. Taken by the Catholics in the 1640s, it was recovered and held by Ireton in 1650.

By then Cromwell's men had already set the barbarous tone of their campaign. On 11 September they stormed the decaying 12th century castle at Drogheda and massacred the townspeople, following this on 11 October with similar horrors in Wexford. Unlike many acts of atrocity in Ireland, which are exaggerated or contested depending on which side of the religious divide you stand, all parties at the time confirmed the unprecedented level of slaughter. Even Cromwell in his later writings seemed uncomfortable with his army's actions, though he never saw the need to make excuses. His supporters simply pointed to similar outrages carried out by Catholics against Protestants in 1641, such as the slaughter of an entire garrison at Augher after it had surrendered (again confirmed by both sides).

There is little doubt that the Wexford and Drogheda bloodbaths inspired terror in other towns, many of which capitulated without a fight. The onset of plague and famine made matters worse and Owen Roe O'Neill's death from an unknown illness in early November was a severe blow to the morale of the Irish allies. When Charles II withdrew his support, the alliance splintered into factions. Its collapse as a serious military force was so rapid that once Cromwell's artillery had battered Kilkenny Castle into submission early in 1650, the Lord Protector began making plans to return home. He finally left in May that year, leaving his trusted commander Henry Ireton in charge of mopping up operations, ably assisted by Edmund Ludlow and Sir Charles Coote.

In the years between 1649 and 1652, Ireland's castles and stronghouses saw more action than at any time in their history. Most of them faced the wrath of Cromwell at some time and to their credit many offered stubborn resistance in the face of hopeless odds. Roscommon Castle in Connacht held out until 1652, but was captured when the Parliamentarian commander Reynalds destroyed much of the northern and southern defences. Athlone, in Co Westmeath, only succumbed after two prolonged attacks by Sir Charles Coote, while Ross Castle, Co Kerry, proved particularly stubborn. This impressive stronghold, which sits on a promontory in Lough Leane, proved intensely frustrating for Ludlow's force of 1,500 infantrymen and 700 horse. It was eventually taken in 1652 after Ludlow's men used floating artillery batteries to bombard it — so fulfilling an ancient prophecy that Ross would remain impregnable until it was attacked by water.

Doe Castle, in Co Donegal, was rather less well prepared, falling victim to Coote's surprise attack in 1650. The castle's owner, Catholic nobleman Colonel Myles MacSweeney, later sent a 1,400 strong detachment to re-capture his family seat. This proved a bad tactical blunder because it weakened his main Catholic army, allowing Coote to rout it in battle.

The years 1650 and 1651 saw garrison after garrison fall to the Cromwellians. Carlow Castle, Co Carlow, and Nenagh Castle, Co Tipperary, both surrendered to Ireton, while Burncourt in Co Tipperary was taken after Cromwell fired the stronghouse and took its owner Sir Richard Everard prisoner (Everard was later hanged). Reynalds and Ireton took Dunamase, Co Laois, the same year. Limerick fell to siege tactics, but Blarney Castle in Cork, claimed to have won a moral victory over the Cromwellians. According to Irish folklore the entire garrison escaped down a tunnel constructed beneath its massive 20m (66ft) tower.

Folk stories abounded in the aftermath of the war. One of the best concerned Leamaneh Castle in Co Clare, owned by Conor O'Brien and his wife Maire Ni Mahon. After O'Brien died in the Battle of Inchicronan in 1651 she apparently saved the family estate from confiscation by marrying a Cromwellian soldier. The marriage did not last long. Legend has it that she pushed him out of an upstairs window after he made some unkind suggestions about her first husband.

At the end of the campaign, Cromwell had good reason to be satisfied. All serious opposition had been crushed. Plans were well underway for a massive new wave of plantations and a framework was in place for the religious 'education' of the Gaelic Irish. This third plank of his political strategy had some success in that Catholics were forced to attend Protestant churches and willing bands of English clergy descended on Ireland as missionairies preaching the 'true faith'. But while this was fine in theory, in many Gaelic-speaking areas worshippers couldn't understand what the new priests were talking about! Ireland's existing Protestant clergy, mindful of Cromwell's excesses, wanted nothing to do with any church run by him. The result was that although Ireland was as Protestant as England in appearance, in reality it remained staunchly Catholic.

Given time, Cromwell might have done something about this; but time was an impossible luxury. The fledgling Parliamentary regime in England was already tottering towards crisis and political stagnation and he needed to devote all his energies to it. The Protestant zealots he'd left behind in Ireland gradually began to drift home, to be replaced by more conciliatory administrators and settlers. Furthermore, many of the Cromwellian military men who had benefited from confiscated Catholic lands soon found themselves homesick. They sold their estates back to the Old English Protestants who had lived in Ireland for generations.

By 1659 Cromwell and his followers were a spent force. Charles II was restored to the throne of England, Scotland and Ireland and many Irishmen — both Protestant and Catholic — believed a new age of peace and prosperity was dawning. Catholic landowners were particularly hopeful of the return of their lands and so when Charles indicated that he would uphold the Cromwellian settlements their despondency was all the harder to bear.

It seemed the only relief offered by the new monarch would be an end to religious persecution and a chance for the Catholic clergy to regroup. Had the Gaelic Irish but known it, their prayers for a true royal saviour would soon be answered. Charles II died (acknowledging his secret adherence to Rome on his deathbed) and on 6th February, 1685 his brother James II — the Catholic duke of York — succeeded the throne.

Opposite: *Another of Ireton's conquests — Nenagh Castle, Co Tipperary — taken by government troops in 1650 following a short siege.*

Above: *The heavily-garrisoned walls of Youghal, Co Cork, a vital trading port in the early 18th century.*

Left: *The courtyard at Dublin Castle. Catholic rebels plotted to take the fortress in 1641 but were betrayed to government forces.*

Opposite above: *The Rock of Dunamase fort, Co Laois was destroyed by Cromwell's troops in 1650.*

Opposite below: *A general view of Roscommon Castle.*

15 William of Orange and the Great Revolution

James II lived up to his billing in Ireland. He quickly appointed one of his court favourites, Richard Talbot, as Lord Lieutenant and Duke of Tyrconnell with the aim of restoring all Catholic land rights. This was worrying enough for the Protestant population but when they discovered that Tyrconnell was also planning to convene an Irish Catholic Parliament and raise a Catholic army under the command of the king, they began to fear the worst. There was talk of a return to the carnage of 1641.

Tyrconnell's bold (some would say politically naïve) proposals also caused uproar in Britain. His plans were seized upon by a powerful Protestant lobby which was already preparing to 'invite' Prince William of Orange to seize the English throne. The convenience of this 'Glorious Revolution' was that William, a staunch Protestant, was married to James II's daughter Mary, maintaining a tenuous link to the line of succession. With powerful military support, William arrived in England on 5 November, 1688. Eight weeks later James fled — first to France to enlist an army and, in March 1689, on to Kinsale. By now all Ireland outside Ulster was being run by a Catholic administration, and Protestants who had not yet fled north found themselves interviewed and disarmed. In Ulster meanwhile, the Protestant fortresses of Derry and Enniskillen were already plotting hard with William.

The biggest problem facing James and Tyrconnell was to raise a good enough army. They knew they could get the men — Tyrconnell claimed to have 40,000 volunteers — but these troops were largely untrained and inexperienced in warfare. Equipping them was also difficult. Most of Ireland's armourers tended to be unsympathetic Protestants and, in any case, large-scale manufacture of weapons would take time. Hopes that King Louis XIV of France would provide a large, well-trained force were dashed when just 3,000 Frenchmen joined James' Irish adventure in April 1689. But there was no more time for preparations — the siege of Derry had begun.

To all Irish Protestants, the endurance of Derry in the face of overwhelming Catholic military superiority was one of the greatest triumphs in their history. There can be no question of the tenacity and determination of the 30,000 who held out, nor is there any dispute over the hardship they suffered. But the city's achievement in resisting the attackers must be put in perspective.

For a start, the encircling army had never been to war before — let alone worked on siege tactics. It also allowed many of the defenders to leave the city, limiting the psychological effect of this kind of warfare. Protestant accounts tell of the 'treachery' of Derry's commander Colonel Robert Lundy, who fled the city before the siege began, and of the uplifting influence of the fire-and-brimstone preacher George Walker, who took over as joint Governor. Certainly the relief of Derry on 28 July, when food supplies finally arrived, was a massive morale boost for the Protestants and enabled the city to outlast the Catholic troops outside. It was the first major encounter of the war and it won William time to get his act together. The following month his commander, Marshal Schomberg, set off for Ireland with orders to engage and destroy the 'Jacobite' army — the name describing James' coalition of Irish, French, German and Walloon troops.

Schomberg's force, made up of Irish, English, Dutch, German, Jacobite turncoats and (later) Danish troops, was a reasonably well trained outfit, although lacking in military hardware. Schomberg showed little desire to get on with the job and spent much of autumn 1689 riding out cold and wet weather and scouting for intelligence. The Jacobites were equally cautious, using the breathing space to re-structure their army and intensify battle-training. The following spring however both sides were reinforced — French troops for King James; Danish for Schomberg — and when William himself joined the Protestant army a few weeks later all the main players were as ready for war as they could ever be. On 1 July came the moment of truth: the Battle of the Boyne.

The Boyne has been described as the turning point of the war. Yet it was neither a decisive nor a one-sided battle. Although the Williamite forces emerged with most of the honours, allowing them to continue their march south, the Irish cavalry marshalled by their charismatic leader Patrick Sarsfield aquitted themselves quite brilliantly. The battlefield action must have been the most dramatic ever seen by those taking part, with innovations such as cavalrymen hurling grenades and toting carbine rockets.

But it was not so much enemy firepower as indiscipline in the ranks that did for the Jacobites. There was argument over strategy and great jealousy about Sarsfield's reputation (his detractors argued that he was too stupid to be a commander). Whether or not this was true, Sarsfield made up for it by ensuring a comparatively orderly retreat and raising morale when it was most needed. The Irish regrouped at their great western fortress, Limerick Castle, and William's campaign ended on a downbeat note when he failed to dislodge them. On the 5th September he left Ireland, handing over leadership of his army to the Utrecht-born commander Godert de Ginkel.

For the Jacobites the decision of James II to cut and run within three days of the Boyne defeat was a far greater blow. Senior Irish commanders later argued that if the king had not comman-

Opposite: *A simple cross marks the Jacobite camp in the hours before the Battle of the Boyne, Co Meath.*

deered French ships waiting in the River Shannon to carry him into exile, the long-term outcome of the war would have been very different. Those self-same frigates, it was said, could easily have cut William's supply lines and left him stranded. As it turned out the Irish were left on the defensive, abandoned by their monarch and with little chance of regaining the initiative. When the Duke of Marlborough, a British general, captured Cork and Kinsale for William, prospects for the Catholics looked ever more bleak. These had been the towns best placed to keep open communication links with the French.

By the end of 1690, there were influential voices on both sides arguing for peace. The Old English Catholics, who had done so well under the post-Cromwell re-distribution of land, were prepared to accept almost any terms from William if it meant they could hang on to their property. The hardline Gaelic Irish on the other hand, believed there was still plenty of fighting to be done. Their highly mobile guerilla groups operating behind Protestant lines — the so-called 'rapparees' — seemed capable of dragging Ginkel's forces into a costly war of attrition. Besides, the Limerick-based Catholic army still numbered around 25,000 men.

Ginkel was well aware of the struggle ahead and he favoured a pardon for all Jacobites who surrendered, plus the return of their lands. In his book, the war had effectively ended when James left. A negotiated peace would save money, rapidly get his troops home and avoid the tricky problem of how to take Limerick.

This all made a lot of sense, but to the Protestant hawks in England and Ireland it was quite unthinkable. They wanted their opponments crushed without mercy and so in the early months of 1691 money was poured into Ginkel's army in readiness for the final push. The Jacobites responded by securing further help from France in the shape of reinforcements led by the legendary Marquis de Saint-Ruth. Saint-Ruth had achieved notoriety in Europe through his ruthless persecution of the French Huguenot Protestants (a minority loathed by Louis XIV). His arrival on 9 May brought a new religious passion to the Jacobite cause, although he provoked disunity by his dismissive attitude towards Patrick Sarsfield, his second-in-command.

In June the Williamites managed to win control of Athlone, from where they seemed dangerously capable of sweeping through the entire west. But Saint-Ruth had galvanised his forces and inspired a mood of confidence. There was a plan to outflank Ginkel by re-crossing the Shannon — even sweeping down to Dublin — but this was forestalled by the last great engagement of the war at Aughrim on 12 July.

Aughrim was an unprecedented disaster for the Irish cause. The cavalry, so well-marshalled at the Boyne, broke formation and fled; Saint-Ruth himself was killed, and both Catholic and Protestant losses were immense. Galway Castle surrendered soon afterwards and the Jacobites, with Sarsfield in command, retreated in disarray to Limerick. Their cause was now totally dependant on further reinforcements from the French, and some of the more hardline Gaelic leaders were prepared to hold the city until this help arrived. This counsel was not as reckless as it seemed. For one thing, winter was drawing on and any protracted siege of Limerick would be as uncomfortable for Ginkel's army as it would the defenders. For another, Sarsfield still had many thousands of men and the supplies to maintain them. With rapparee assistance, he was in the best possible position to resist a lengthy siege.

Above: *The port of Waterford, on the River Suir. In the early months of Cromwell's onslaught it was among the very few major towns to hold out and was a stronghold of Catholic forces during the Glorious Revolution.*

Opposite: *Mummified remains discovered at Dublin's St Michan's Church.*

But such defiance counted for little alongside troop morale. The Irish were battle-weary and increasingly affected by disputes within their leadership. Sarsfield knew that he could hold Limerick, but saw little point, and it was therefore he who approached Ginkel to talk peace. He was clearly not as stupid as his critics claimed, because the deal he wrung from the Williamite General was almost absurdly generous.

Ginkel agreed that Sarsfield's army could be shipped intact over to France, an act tantamount to re-equipping the forces of the enemy. For those Jacobites who stayed behind, however, the constitutional future was as confused as ever. The Treaty of Limerick, signed on 3 October 1691, was so loosely drafted that its terms could be interpreted in any number of different ways. Protestants worried that it was too lenient; Catholics feared it gave no general safeguards for either their property or their religion (although in practice a good proportion of Catholic lands were returned).

In a sense the Treaty was an irrelevance. Protestants felt they had stared into the abyss with events at the Boyne, Aughrim and Limerick and they desperately wanted an end to insecurity. As the 18th century dawned, their power in Ireland would be achieved by a new-wave of sinister laws such as restricting Catholic education, banning priests, denying Catholics the right to bear arms and even preventing them from owning horses worth more than £5.

The single thread that drew this pernicious legislation together was an intent to give Protestants control of the professions, the best government jobs, the best lands and the most political influence. It was the birth of what is now called the Protestant 'Ascendancy'. Today, 200 years on, it remains a key factor in a cruelly-divided nation.

Above: *A quiet stretch of water on the Boyne battlefield site.*

Right: *The grounds of Townley Hall, Co Meath. During and after the battle, the normally tranquil fields in this area would have echoed to the harrowing cries of the dying and wounded.*

Overleaf: *New Ross, on the Barrow River, Co Wexford, was the scene of Confederate Catholic commander Thomas Preston's defeat by Ormond in 1643.*

BARGAIN LINE
WHOLESALE
CASH 'n CARRY

16 Georgian Rule

When James II succeeded the throne of England, Scotland and Ireland in 1685 he was hailed a saviour by Irish Catholics. Lands which had remained confiscated since Cromwell's reign of terror would, it seemed, be recovered from the Protestant ruling classes and handed back. Protestants were nervous enough when James nominated his court favourite Richard Talbot as Lord Lieutenant and Duke of Tyrconnell to oversee this task. But when Tyrconnell announced plans for an Irish Catholic Parliament and Army, their worst fears were realised. News that the King had tried to prosecute the Archbishop of Canterbury and six English bishops for refusing to proclaim religious tolerance convinced many that another massacre of Protestants on the scale of the 1641 Ulster uprising was imminent.

It was a fear shared by a powerful Protestant lobby in England. The birth of James's son (James Edward Stuart) in 1688 was for them the final straw because it meant the prospect of a Roman Catholic succession. The plotters embarked upon the Glorious Revolution, inviting William of Orange to claim the throne as joint sovereign with his wife Mary (James II's daughter). William landed in England on 5 November 1688 heading a formidable force and within eight weeks James had fled to France to raise his own army. He docked at Kinsale in March 1689 with the intention of rallying Catholics and using Ireland as a springboard to reclaim his throne.

In 1689 James's forces began the siege of Derry, one of Ulster's main Protestant strongholds. The story, still celebrated in songs and marches today, tells how the gates of the city were slammed shut in the face of approaching soldiers by 13 apprentice boys. For the next 105 days Derry endured appalling privation, its citizens reduced to eating dogs, rats and even laundry starch. By the time relief arrived in the shape of William's forces, the city was celebrating a moral victory over its enemy.

The importance of the siege from William's point of view was that it bought him time to build up his Ulster-based army. In the Spring of 1690 he arrived in Ireland intent on crushing the Jacobite force and on 1 July the two sides came together in one of the greatest battles ever seen on Irish soil, the Battle of the Boyne. In fact, the Boyne was not a decisive engagement – William would have to wait until Aughrim a year later for that – but it took the initiative away from the Catholic force. James fled to Limerick, from where French frigates carried him into exile.

The Catholic Defeat at Aughrim, with massive losses on both sides, resulted in the Treaty of Limerick – a hopelessly fudged

Right: *Exhibits from the Famine Museum, housed in the stableblock of Strokestown Park House, Co Roscommon, a marvellous Palladian mansion built in the 1730s.*

affair. Protestants thought it too lenient; Catholics feared it gave them no religious or property safeguards. In fact the treaty was so loosely drafted that it could mean all things to all people. Protestants, now back in control, simply got on with securing themselves more stability and security and drafted a raft of pernicious laws designed to deliver overall control of wealth, land and the professions. The Protestant Ascendancy was born and the stage set for centuries of division.

The postwar economic recovery was, however, rapid. Despite fluctuating currency values, a run of bad harvests in the 1720s and 1730s, and a famine in 1740 the country's overall prosperity rose steadily and benefited Catholic and Protestant alike. The popular image of a dispossessed Gaelic underclass living in abject poverty at the behest of foreign landlords is simplistic. For a start, steady growth in agriculture had created a cattle-owning Catholic farming class every bit as ready to exploit working people as land-owning Protestants. The rise of the linen industry and spectacular successes in foreign trade spurred big improvements in bridges, turnpike roads and inland waterways – an infrastructure which helped market towns such as Cork, Limerick and Waterford share the prosperity. Much of Dublin's superb Georgian architecture was built in this period, together with many notable country mansions. As Ireland entered the 19th century economic buoyancy had doubled the population to five million and by 1845 it stood nearer nine million, four-fifths of them Catholic.

The population explosion was mainly among the poor, people for whom there was no corresponding increase in jobs. The result was that everyone needed land to grow food and so even small farms were divided and sub-divided. An 1845 land census showed there were more than 300,000 farms of five acres of less, the vast majority growing potatoes. A carefully-tended acre of this crop could feed a family of five for a year and, especially in the poorer farmland of the west, there was therefore no incentive to diversify. So when potato blight struck in the autumn of 1845, wiping out half the crop, there was an immediate threat of starvation. The poor of England and Scotland suffered hardship from a similar blight, although it was on nothing like the same scale.

The Government set up a Relief Commission which distributed £100,000 worth of maize from Britain, the United States, Canada and India. This lasted until June 1846 but a few months later almost the entire potato crop failed again, causing a devastating famine. Poor health and overcrowding led to malnutrition and disease on a massive scale and the incompetence of Government ministers undoubtedly caused hundreds of thousands of deaths. Politicians in London insisted that food should be imported and sold in the usual way; not grasping that in many parts there were no jobs, shops, food merchants or transport systems and that people survived by growing their own vittals.

Some jobs were created with special road-building schemes, but the work was too hard for people weak with hunger. Even when soup-kitchens were at last set up in March 1847, the government decreed that only 'deserving' cases would qualify. By the time a successful crop was harvested in 1847, around one million people had died and a further 1.5 million had emigrated to Britain, Canada and the United States. Many of these emigrants felt they had been betrayed by Britain; some even believed the famine had been deliberately engineered. Soon they were sending money back to nationalist causes such as the Fenians dedicated to toppling British rule.

Above: *Exhibit from the Famine Museum. The potato blight struck of autumn 1845, wiping out half the potato crop, with an immediate threat of starvation. By the time a successful crop was harvested in 1847, around one million people had died and a further 1.5 million had emigrated to Britain, Canada and the United States.*

Following page: *The New Market and 1798 Catholic Rebellion Memorial in Wexford — the history of a tormented past is never far away in modern Ireland.*

ROYAL LIVER ASSURANCE
WEXFORD CORPORA
NEW MARK
Diana Donnelly
Sale
Sale
1798

T. Furlong & Son Ltd.
MASTER BUTCHER
TELEFÓN
T. FURLONG & SON
INCORP
EST 1852

17 Rebellion and Republic

There is an old saying that England's difficulty is Ireland's opportunity and so it proved for the Easter Rising of 1916. The King's Irish Volunteers, formed in 1913, had turned into a regiment dominated and controlled by members of the Irish Republican Brotherhood. Their rebellion was brutally crushed by the British Army, which shelled the leaders HQ at the General Post Office in O'Connell Street. Yet ironically it was British over-reaction, rather than popular Irish support for the uprising, which fuelled the fire of Nationalism.

In the executions of the Easter Rising leaders, the formation of 'special' forces such as the Black-and-Tans and the Auxiliaries, the night curfews and the military court trials held without juries, the government played into the hands of Sinn Fein and volunteers in what had now become the Irish Republican Army.

Moderates had been turned against Britain and Prime Minister Lloyd George knew he would have to negotiate a settlement with the Irish nationalist leaders Eamon De Valera, Arthur Griffith and Michael Collins. Lloyd George's solution was Home Rule. The catch however was Partition – an imposed 'agreement' by which the six Protestant-dominated counties in Ulster would have their own Parliament running alongside a similar body in Dublin. Both would be subject to the overall control of London. Lloyd George also refused to concede full independence, offering instead an Irish Free State remaining a dominion of the British Commonwealth.

Reluctantly, Griffith and Collins signed the Treaty on 6 December 1921. Collins defended it back home as 'the freedom to achieve freedom', although de Valera and almost half the members of the Dail voted against it. Within months the Irish Civil War had broken out, pitting the Free Staters against de Valera's 'Irregular' Republicans. Men who were once comrades at arms now committed atrocities against each other reminiscent of the worst excesses of British rule. Even possessing an unauthorised gun was considered a capital offence by the Free Staters. Yet De Valera's supporters were in the minority and also facing the condemnation of the Church. In April 1923, the leaders of the IRA irregulars ordered a voluntary ceasefire.

It would be nine years before De Valera, now at the head of his own party Fianna Fail, won control of the Dail. In 1936, angered at continuing terrorist attacks by his natural supporters, he declared the IRA illegal and the following year introduced a new constitution referring to the country for the first time as Eire, the Gaelic word for Ireland. This was taken up by the British media as a convenient way to describe the 26 counties. Eire now had her own Head of State, a position completely at odds with her Commonwealth status, and emphasised independence by remaining neutral throughout World War 2. But Britain still treated the fledgling democracy as a member of the Commonwealth and many Irish citizens lived and worked in the UK. More to the point, many thousands gave their lives in the war against Germany.

In 1948 a coalition government headed by Fine Gael passed the Republic of Ireland Act, formally severing the Commonwealth link. Independence was a reality but only for 26 counties. The British government made clear that the position of Northern Ireland would never be changed without the democratic consent of its people and with the province's huge Protestant majority, unification seemed as distant as ever.

Despite these political uncertainties, the fledgling Republic was quickly into its stride. Thousands of Irish people had spent the war working in British factories and had grown used to a standard of living commensurate with a modern industrial society. During the war De Valera described his countrymen as 'people who valued material wealth only as a basis for right living . . . who, satisfied with frugal comfort, devoted their leisure to the things of the spirit.' In the Ireland of the 1950s and 1960s this was, for the most part, a forgotten ideal. Even the Catholic Church, long used to unquestioning obedience, discovered that its teachings were publicly challenged.

And yet the new nation offered much. Many health and welfare Acts were passed, pensions, unemployment and sickness benefit were introduced at around two-thirds of the British level, free secondary education was provided for all children and more free university places were made available. All this spending had to be matched by an increase in output and the problem for the Dail remained a poor manufacturing base. Better farming techniques tended to make more farmworkers redundant and the population again began to dip as emigrants took advantage of Britain's labour shortage.

The answer was the Economic Development Programme of 1959 in which £53.4 million was earmarked to attract foreign money into Ireland. The policy worked well. There was talk of an 'economic miracle', investment in industry doubled, 350 foreign companies re-located within nine years, exports rose by 50 per cent, emigration fell from 14.8 per thousand to 5.7 per thousand and in the five years to 1966 there was the first population rise

Opposite: *The immense columns of the General Post Office building in O'Connell Street, Dublin, the city's main thoroughfare. This was the scene of heroic action during the Easter Uprising in 1916 and contains a statue of Cuchulainn (see page 156) dedicated to those who died for their part in the rising.*

Right: *The Parnell monument in O'Connell Street, Dublin — in memory of the leader of the Home Rule Party. Charles Stewart Parnell, the 'uncrowned king of Ireland', was one of many Irish leaders who spent time in Kilmainham gaol; his political career was ruined when he was cited in divorce proceedings.*

Above: *Plaque commemorating the site of Morrison's Hotel in Dawson Street, Dublin.*

Following page: *Kinsale, Co Cork, one of the country's prettiest small towns and a popular yachting centre.*

since the Famine (62,000). Business and financial management became far more slick and professional, though it was the new industries, rather than Ireland's traditional manufacturers, which set the pace.

Membership of the European Economic Community was finally achieved on 1 January 1973, 12 years after the first application and with 83% support in a national referendum. There had been an Anglo-Irish free trade agreement since 1965 and the hope was that a potentially huge EEC export market, together with new investment and grants, would further fuel economic expansion. In fact the boom petered out by the mid-1970s and Ireland faced a classic 'slump recipe' of high unemployment, poor agricultural growth, rising inflation, a looming energy crisis and catastrophic foreign borrowing. In fairness, this recessionary cocktail was part of a general downturn in most Western economies and not a direct result of Euro-club membership.

In some ways, the traditional domestic image of Ireland survived this period of change remarkably well. A 1971 survey claimed that 96 per cent of all Catholics attended mass and that the Protestant population had fallen by 24 per cent in 25 years (largely due to a falling birth rate and inter-marriage). Key elements of the old ways were enshrined in law – there were legal bars to contraception for instance and divorce remained illegal right up until 1997. Yet the Irish had become a more outward-looking people, less chained to doctrine and dogma. By 1972 schools and universities were studying new text books challenging many nationalist myths; no longer was it enough to view Irish history purely as a continuing struggle against British military and political oppression. Heroes such as O'Connell and Parnell themselves became fair game for criticism. And the cherished basis of many patriotic songs – namely that Ireland had once been a unified Celtic nation under a single leader – was firmly despatched to the realms of fiction.

Throughout the 1950s and 1960s politics was divided pretty much along civil war lines with De Valera's Fianna Fail holding a tenuous upper hand over Fine Gael. Ireland's system of proportional representation encouraged minority parties in the Dail and Fianna Fail twice had to rely on their support to form governments. Both De Valera and his tough talking successor Sean Lemass managed to present themselves as leaders of a 'national' party transcending issues of class or wealth. This approach was underpinned by Fianna Fail's sub-title 'The Republican Party', emphasising its role in winning independence and its tacit acknowledgement of the part played by the IRA.

For most of this time the Fine Gael Opposition was perceived as a loose bourgeois alliance, even though in class terms there was little to separate its TDs from those of Fianna Fail. Fine Gael had to wait until the 1980s to achieve political dominance – a feat attributable to the emergence of its charismatic leader and Taoiseach, Garret FitzGerald. FitzGerald's rhetoric gave the party a more focused agenda and showed a readiness to dismantle Irish shibboleths. In 1971 he railed against his political opponents for giving the Catholic Church control of vocational schools and later he attacked an 'authoritarian desire to enforce private morality by means of public law'. This, he argued, served only to heighten the Northern Protestants' fear of Irish unity.

In Northern Ireland itself, postwar expansion had been even more pronounced. Having declared the province a part of the United Kingdom, successive British governments needed to pump in the health and welfare investment necessary to make it so. Between 1961 and 1963 the average payment was £60 million, rising to £160 million by 1971. This level of public spending far exceeded that of the Republic, which would have had to double taxes to compete. Yet the policy failed to achieve any closer feeling of unity between Protestant and Catholic communities. For a start, much of the investment in manufacturing was in Belfast, some distance from the Catholic-dominated towns of the west and south. Moreover, Protestant employers liked Protestant workers. Whether by chance or design, the ghost of Ascendancy politics was still abroad.

Between 1963 and 1969 the Northern Ireland prime minister Terence O'Neill recognised the simmering discontent on the streets and passed a series of measures aimed at relieving Catholic hardship and encouraging fairer distribution of wealth. This infuriated many Protestant extremists, who believed they followed the 'right' religion and were therefore entitled to a batter deal. Terrorist organisations such as the Orange Order and the Ulster Volunteer Force were revived intent on cowing Catholics into submission. Even police officers resorted to open attacks on the very people they were supposed to protect.

The story of the recent Troubles in Northern Ireland dates from 15 August 1969 when British Labour Prime Minister Harold Wilson sent troops onto the streets of Londonderry and Belfast, ostensibly to protect Catholics. This book makes no attempt to dissect the hugely complex social, political and military issues involved, nor to assess the long-term ramifications for Irish prosperity. It can be argued that violence in the North has done little to influence opinion in the South and that ordinary people regard matters of unemployment, wages and taxes as more important than unification. And yet the violence has undoubtedly leeched industrial investment. For a country hugely dependent on foreign money, the Troubles have remained both an economic cancer and a human tragedy.

This is not to suggest that the Ireland of the Nineties is a land spiralling towards poverty and recession. Indeed the opposite is true. In 1996 the construction industry was growing at six per cent per year and economic growth at seven per cent (in contrast Britain's economy was expanding by only 2.5 per cent). For the first time a major advertising campaign was launched in England to attract building workers across the Irish Sea – a huge irony given the volume of tired English jokes about Irish navvies – and around 5,000 British labourers answered the call. The advantages were obvious; a booming industry offering wages well above UK rates and, more importantly, secure jobs in a country legendary for its hospitality.

The cranes towering over the Dublin skyline, the gleaming glass-fronted American banks lining the Liffey, the smart new apartment blocks and The Jervis, one of Europe's newest and largest shopping centres, together present the face of a vibrant capital and nation. As Donal Mooney, editor of the London-based weekly newspaper the Irish Post, observed in a 1997 interview with the Times: 'The days of permanent emigration to Britain are largely gone; the Irish will now come here for a few years to gain experience and then go home again. Many who might once have come to Britain will now work in other EU countries. And of those who come here, the unskilled are now only a small proportion. Ireland has become a well-educated country.'

Opposite: *Street scene in Kilkenny, an inland city built out of the local black limestone.*

Above and Right: *Many people wish to trace their ancestry — including those related to the thousands who fled poverty and famine in the 19th century. A good place to start is North Mayo Genealogy and Heritage Centre at Crossmolina, near Lough Conn, Co Mayo.*

Above: *The Irish National War Memorial at Islandbridge, in Dublin.*

Left: *Leinster House, Dublin. Originally built for the Duke of Leinster in 1745 this imposing building now houses the two chambers of the Irish Parliament, the Dail and the Seanad.*

Right: *O'Connell Street and Bridge, Dublin. The construction of the bridge (originally called Carlisle) in 1790, transformed the street into the city's main north-south thoroughfare, lined with imposing and historic buildings.*

Following page: *Sunset over Dunmanus Bay. The Irish countryside has been an inspiration to some of the finest writers in the English language.*

Irish Nationwide
Building Society
IRISH NATIONWIDE BUILDING SOCIETY
BUS STOP
THE WEST
N4-N5-N6
THE SOUTH
N7-N8-N9
LOOK RIGHT

PART 3: THE ARTS

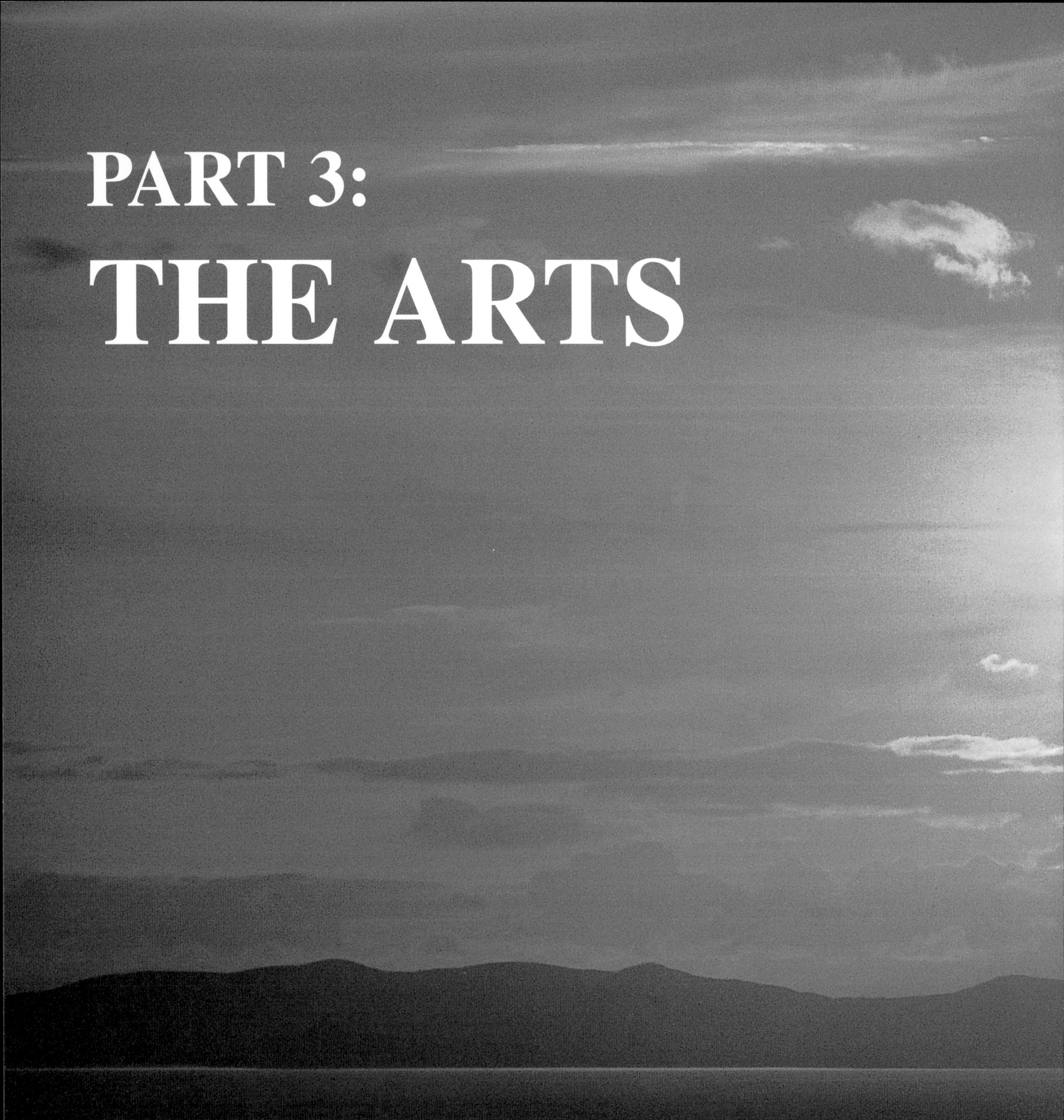

18 The Celtic Legacy

When it comes to myth and magic, fairy stories and folklore, the Irish have cornered the market. No other nation is as romatically immersed in the oft-told stories of heroes, villains, injustice, iniquity, the lucky and the lovelorn.

Mythology formed the seed from which Ireland's healthy tradition of literature eventually bloomed. Staggering though it seems, the tales which delight Ireland's children today were passed down for centuries by word of mouth alone. The Celts did not chronicle poems and stories in the same way as, for example, the Romans and Greeks. The survival of this important Celtic heritage pays tribute to the oratory of the shanachies, men who were skilled in the art to telling stories. It wasn't until the spread of Christianity that the fantastic fables were finally committed to parchment, thanks to painstaking quill work by the early monks. It was not until the 7th century that the majority was captured on paper.

Some fragmented manuscripts containing the mythological sagas remain, including Lebor na huidre (The Book of the Dun Cow), the Book of Leinster, the Yellow Book of Lecan and Egerton. The first two are positively dated in the 12th century while the last two are 14th or 15th century. None are whole.

After the shanachies came the bards, poets or minstrels who were equally adept at weaving tales, in fact, they were tutored in the art. The Bardic College was at Tara. Chief of the poets at the Bardic College was the revered Ard-File. Lady Wilde recalled their role. 'The chief poet was required to know by heart 400 poems and the minor bards two hundred. And they were bound to recite any poem called for by the kings at the festivals.'

The tradition of story-telling in Ireland remains strong. Only in the last century Irish people were heard telling of legends in the same detail yielded in those early manuscripts. Yet these were people who had never seen such manuscripts, indeed, many were illiterate. Stories were handed down with as much pride and feeling as a priceless watch or china bowl.

Although the scope is broad these myths can retrospectively be divided into four different cycles. This classification was not used in the early days of story-telling hence characters travel with ease between one cycle and the next. And it remains difficult to distinguish between gods and mortals, so mirrored are the failings and strengths of the two groups. First comes the Mythological Cycle.

This is placed back in Ireland's pre-history when a divine race called the Tuatha De Danann invaded the country, their arrival on a westerly mountain top shrouded by clouds. Here was a fair-skinned people with astonishing magic powers. With them came the Stone of Destiny which allegedly shrieked when it was touched by a king-in-waiting. The setting for the stories is mainly the Boyne Valley.

One of the most eminent of the Tuatha gods was Aonghus, son of the father of the gods, The Dagda. His mother was the goddess Boinn who already had a partner, Elcmar. The lusty Dagda dispatched Elcmar on a journey that would take a day and a night. Seducing Boinn The Dagda put a spell on the sun which caused it to stand still for nine months. Aonghus was born and immediately taken by his father to train as a champion hurler.

As god of love, Aonghus had a golden harp and his kisses became doves. His palace was at Newgrange on the River Boyne. One night he was visited by a maiden who played a harp and sang to him but disappeared when he tried to embrace her. Aonghus was so besotted with the beauty that he refused to eat the next day. The mysterious maid visited nightly and by day Aonghus continued to pine. After a year the countryside was scoured in order to identify the object of Aonghus' desires. His brother Bodbh the Red finally located her.

But when Aonghus sought to wed her he discovered she was a swan-maiden who assumed her graceful bird form at the end of every summer. At Samhain, now known as Hallowe'en, Aonghus called for his loved one on the shores of Lough Dragan. She appeared, the most gorgeous in a flock of 150 swans. With a word from her, he too changed into a swan and they flew three times around the lake side by side before heading for his home at Brugh na Boinne. At his palace they turned into humans once more and lived happily ever after.

The boundary between life and death is indistinct throughout the Mythological Cycle. Instead of heaven there is the Otherword or Tir na n'Og, the Land of the Ever Young, beyond the horizon in the Atlantic Ocean.

The Tuatha were finally defeated by a Gaelic army. When peace between the two sides broke out it was agreed that the Gaels would inhabit the upper half of the ground while the Tuatha would retire to the ancient burrows and cairns. Afterwards they became the subject of local fairy lore, being known as the Sidhe . (The other popular theory to support the existence of fairies is that they were angels cast out from heaven as unworthy but not bad enough to be dispatched to hell.)

Next comes the Red Branch or Ulster Cycle, revolving around the exploits of the Ulaid, a race of people who lent their name to Ulster. There are a dozen Red Branch heroes, most notably Cuchulainn. The enemies of the Red Branch are the Connachta and included in the cycle is the story of the doomed Deirdre of the Sorrows.

Cuchulainn was born Sedanta mac Sualtamh, son of Lugh, the sun god and Dechtire, the sister of Conchobar, King of Ulster. Dechtire was drinking a glass of wine when a mayfly landed in it. In a dream the god Lugh revealed that he was the mayfly. He lured her into fairyland and transformed her and 50 handmaidens into birds so they could accompany him there.

Both Conchobar and Dechtire's husband Sualtaim searched the countryside until they found the missing maid. When she

Above: *Statue at Glenveagh Castle, Co Donegal.*

returned with them she brought the young son who she had given birth to in fairyland, Sedanta.

Cuchulainn is sometimes remembered as the hound of Culann. As a young lad he impressed the king with his prowess at wrestling and ball games. As the king departed for a feast being given by the smith Culann he invited the boy to come along.
'I have not yet finished playing but I shall follow you later on,' replied the youngster.

When Conchobar arrived for the celebrations Culann asked if anyone else was following. Conchobar, forgetting all about his nephew, said 'no'. To protect the assembled nobility Culann unleashed his ferocious dog. When Sedanta approached the dog sprang at him. Defending himself, the boy fought the dog and finally dashed its head against a stone.

Brought before Conchobar and Culann the boy was welcomed. But he noticed how Culann mourned the loss of his dog which was a trusted guard. 'I shall raise a puppy of the same breed for you and until he is ready to serve you I shall protect you and your cattle myself,' Sedanta pledged. Cathbad the Druid stepped forward to christen him 'the Hound of Culann'.

The wife of Cuchulainn was Emer who was endowed with the six gifts of womanhood; beauty, chastity, eloquence, needlework, sweet-voice and wisdom.

Deirdre of the Sorrows was the daughter of an Ulster chieftan. But the joy at her birth was shattered when a Druid told how she would cause ruin and death to Ulster. Her father wanted to kill her immediately but nobly king Conchobar took responsiblity by promising to wed her when she grew up.

Of course, the adult Deirdre did not want to marry the aged Conchobar. She had fallen in love with Naoise, a Red Branch hero, and together they fled to Scotland. A furious Conchobar lured them back with false promises and on their return Naoise and his brothers were killed by Eoghan MacDuracht. Although she was compelled to marry the Ulster king she did not smile for one whole year. When her angry husband asked who she hated the most, she replied: 'You and Eoghan MacDuracht.' To illicit revenge Conchobar compelled her to become Eoghan's wife for a year. When she was placed in Eoghan's chariot she flung herself out and died when her head struck a rock. It is said a pine tree sprung from her grave and intertwined with another pine growing from Naoise's grave. The unhappy tale formed the basis of plays written later by W.B. Yeats and J.M. Synge.

As the story of the Ulaid continues it becomes clear that this is a society in decline which is ultimately ridiculed by its foes. The third cycle centres on the semi-mythological kings who ruled domains throughout Ireland centuries ago.

Finally comes the Fenian Cycle, dated after the year 1000, which focusses on Fionn MacCumhail, better known as Finn MacCool, and his army, the Fianna or Fenians. His tutor hooked the Salmon of Knowledge. Finn was to cook it and, on touching the flesh of the fish as it lay on the fire, he burned himself. He sucked his wound and thereby absorbed the superhuman knowledge for which he is remembered today. Finn's two hunting hounds were Bran and Sceolan, his bewitched nephews.

Although a masterful soldier he was unlucky in love. He was betrothed to Grainne, daughter of High King Cormac MacArt. However, she loved Diarmuid, foster son of the love god Aonghus and they eloped. For 16 years the couple were pursued by the Fianna until a truce was declared. But when Finn went hunting with Diarmuid on Ben Bulben they encountered an enchanted boar. Diarmuid was killed and Finn failed to use his powers to restore his rival to life. Although Grainne swore to avenge Dairmuid's death she was wooed by Finn and finally became his wife — one of many. Finn died at the age of 230. The story of Finn MacCool was adopted by the Scots who re-christened him Fingal. The romantically moody Fingal's Cave on the Scottish island of Staffa — best known as being the inspiration for an overture by Mendelssohn — is said to be where this fighter based his defences against the marauding norsemen.

Finn's son was Oisin who was lured to the Land of Promise by Niamh of the Golden Hair, a daughter of the sea god Manannan Maclir. After three weeks he discovered three hundred years had passed. Now he longed to return to Ireland so Naimh presented him with a magic horse. However, when he fell from the steed he returned to his true age and was a withered old man. In this form he is said to have met St Patrick.

Fairy lore invokes some other familiar figures. There's the lepracun, traditionally a shoe maker in possession of hidden treasure. That's because he has a 'sporan na sgillinge' or purse of the (recurring) shilling. The only way to hold down a lepracaun is by plough chain or woollen thread. Only the workshy should fear the lepracaun.

The lesser known Geancanach, or love-talker, is less forgiving. With his hands in his pockets and a pipe in his mouth, he will seduce idle girls and fraternise with layabouts across the countryside. To meet him and be in his thrall certainly brought bad luck. Another short, malevolent figure was that of the Clobher-ceann who was closely linked to drinking in excess.

However, if Black Joanna of the Boyne, locally known as Siubhan Dubh na Boinne, appeared on Hallowe'en it brought luck to the household.

Mermaids, goblins, banshees - whose mournful wails foretold a family death - and the churchyard demon of dullaghan, an alarming, headless figure likely to play soccer with his severed topknot, are all crucial characters in Irish folklore. One mythical creatur, the Pooka, was borrowed by Shakespeare and appeared as Puck in 'Midsummer Night's Dream'. Although the oral art so closely associated with the success of Irish mythology may be for the most part lost its core ingredients of love and death means the sagas will continue to endure.

Below: *Fisheye view of the bay and the white beacon at Baltimore, Co Cork. Overlooking the harbour is the ruined 15th century castle of the O'Driscoll clan.*

The Coming of Finn

It was the Eve of Samhain, which we Christians call All Hallows' Eve. The King of Ireland, Conn the Hundred-Fighter, sat at supper in his palace at Tara. All his chiefs and mighty men were with him. On his right hand was his only son, Art the Solitary, so called because he had no brothers. The sons of Morna, who kept the boy Finn out of his rights and were at the time trying to kill him if they could, were here too. Chief amongst them was Gaul mac Morna, a huge and strong warrior and Captain of all the Fians ever since that battle in which Finn's father had been killed.

And Gaul's men were with him. The great long table was spread for suppcr. A thousand wax candles shed their light through the chamber and caused the vessels of gold, silver, and bronze to shine. Yet, though it was a great feast, none of these warriors seemed to care about eating or drinking; every face was sad, and there was little conversation and no music. It seemed as if they were expecting some calamity. Conn's sceptre, which was a plain staff of silver, lay beside him on the table and there was a canopy of bright bronze over his head. Gaul mac Morna sat at the other end of the long table. Every warrior wore a bright banqueting mantle of silk or satin, scarlet crimson, blue, green, or purple, fastened on the breast either with a great brooch or with a pin of gold or silver. Yet, though their raiment was bright and gay, and though all the usual instruments of festivity were there, and a thousand tall candles shed their light over the scene, no one looked happy.

Then was heard a low sound like thunder and the earth seemed to tremble, and after that they distinctly heard a footfall like the slow, deliberate tread of giant. These footfalls sent a chill in every heart, and every face, gloomy before, was now pale. The King leaned past his son, Art the Solitary, and said to a certain Druid who sat beside Art, 'Is this the son Midna come before his time?' 'It is not,' said the Druid, 'but it is the man who is to conquer Midna. One is coming to Tara this night before whose glory all other glory shall wax dim.'

Shortly after that they heard the voices of the doorkeeper raised in contention, as if they would repel from the hall someone who wished to enter, then a slight scuffle, and after that a strange figure entered the chamber. He was dressed in the skins of wild beasts, and wore over his shoulders a huge thick cloak of wild boars' skins, fastened on the breast with a white tusk of the same animal. He wore a shield and two spears.

Though of huge stature, his face was that of a boy, smooth on the cheeks and lips. It was white and ruddy and very handsome. His hair was like refined gold. A light seemed to go out from him, before which the candles burned dim. It was Finn. He stood in the doorway, and cried out in a strong and sonorous, but musical, voice: 'O Conn, the Hundred-Fighter, son of Felimy, the righteous son of Tuthal the legitimate; O King of the Kings of Erin, a wronged and disinherited youth, possessing nowhere one rood of his patrimony, a wanderer and an outlaw, a hunter of the wildernesses and mountains, claims hospitality of thee, illustrious prince, on the eve of the great festival of Samhain.'

'Thou art welcome whoever thou art,' answered the King, 'and doubly welcome because thou art unfortunate. I think, such is thy face and form, that thou art the son of some mighty king on whom disaster has fallen undeserved. The high gods of Erin grant thee speedy restoration and strong vengeance of thy many wrongs. Sit here, O noble youth, between me and my only son, Art, heir to my kingdom.'

An attendant took his weapons from the youth and hung them on the wall with the rest, and Finn sat down between the King of Ireland and his only son. Choice food was set before him, which he ate, and old ale, which he drank. From the moment he entered no one thought of anything but of him. When Finn had made an end of eating and drinking, he said to the King, 'O illustrious prince, though it is not right for a guest to even seem to observe aught that may be awry, or not as it should be, in the hall of his entertainer, yet the sorrow of a kindly host is a sorrow, too, to his guest, and sometimes unawares the man of the house finds succour and help in the stranger. There is sorrow in this chamber of festivity. If anyone who is dear to thee and thy people happens to be dead, I can do nothing. But I say it, and it is not a vain boast, that even if a person is at the point of death, I can restore him to life and health, for there are marvellous powers of life-giving in my two hands.'

Conn the Hundred-Fighter answered, 'Our grief is not such as you suppose; and why should I not tell a cause of shame, which is known far and wide? This, then, is the reason of our being together, and the gloom which is over us. There is a mighty enchanter whose dwelling is in the haunted mountains of Slieve Gullion in the north. His name is Allen, son of Midna, and his enmity to me is as great as his power. Once every year, at this season, it is his pleasure to burn Tara. Descending out of his wizard haunts, he standeth over against the city and shoots balls of fire out of his mouth against it, till it is consumed. Then he goes away mocking and triumphant. This annual building of Tara, only to be annually consumed, is a shame to me, and till this enchanter declared war against me, I have lived without reproach.'

'But,' said Finn, 'how is it that thy young warriors, valiant and swift, do not repel him or kill him? '

'Alas,' said Conn, 'all our valour is in vain against this man. Our hosts encompass Tara on all sides, keeping watch and ward when the fatal night comes. Then the son of Midna plays on his Druidic instrument of music, on his magic pipe and his magic lyre, and as the fairy music falls on our ears, our eyelids grow heavy, and soon all subside upon the grass in deep slumber. So comes this man against the city and shoots his fireballs against it, and utterly consumes it. Nine years he has burnt Tara in that manner, and this is the tenth. At midnight tonight he will come and do the same. Last year (though it was a shame to me that I, who am the High King over all Ireland, should not be able myself to defend Tara) I summoned Gaul mac Morna and all the Fians to my assistance. They came, but the pipe and lyre of the son of Midna prevailed over them too, so that Tara was burned as at other times. Nor have we any reason to believe that the son of Midna will not burn the city again tonight, as he did last year. All the women and children have been sent out of Tara this day. We are only men of war here, waiting for the time. That, O noble youth, is why we are sad. The "Pillars of Tara" are broken, and the might of the Fians is as nought before the power of this man.'

'What shall be my reward if I kill this man and save Tara?' asked Finn. 'Thy inheritance,' answered the King, 'be it great or small, and whether it lies in Ireland or beyond Ireland; and for securities I give you my son Art and Gaul mac Morna, the Chief of the Fians.' Gaul and the captains of the Fianna consented to that arrangement, though reluctantly, for their minds misgave them as to who the great youth might be.

After that all arose and armed themselves and ringed Tara round with horse and foot, and thrice Conn the Hundred-Fighter raised his awful regal voice, enjoining vigilance upon his people, and thrice Gaul mac Morna did the same, addressing the Fians, and after that they filled their ears with wax and wool, and kept a stern and fierce watch, and many of them thrust the points of their swords into their flesh.

Now Finn was alone in the banqueting chamber after the rest had gone out, and he washed his face and his hands in pure water, and he took from the bag that was at his girdle the instruments of divination and magic, which had been his father's, and what use he made of them is not known; but ere long a man stood before him, holding a spear in one hand and a blue mantle in the other. There were twenty nails of gold of Arabia in the spear. The nails glittered like stars, and twinkled with livelight as stars do in a frosty night, and the blade of it quivered like a tongue of white fire. From haft to bladepoint that spear was alive. There were voices in it too, and the war tunes of the enchanted races of Erin, whom they called the Tuatha De Danan, sounded from it. The mantle, too, was a wonder, for innumerable stars twinkled in the blue, and the likeness of clouds passed through it. The man gave these things to Finn, and when he had instructed him in their use, he was not seen.

Then Finn arose and armed himself, and took the magic spear and mantle and went out. There was a ring of flame round Tara that night, for the Fians and the warriors of Conn had torches in their hands, and all the royal buildings of Tara showed clear in the light, and also the dark serpentine course of the Boyne, which flowed past Tara on the north; and there, standing silent and alert, were the innumerable warriors of all Erin, with spear and shield, keeping watch and ward against the son of Midna, also the four Pillars of Tara in four dense divisions around the High King, even Conn the Hundred-Fighter.

Finn stood with his back to the palace, which was called the House-of-the-going-round-of-Mead, between the palace and Conn, and he grasped the magic spear strongly with one hand and the mantle with the other.

As midnight drew nigh, he heard far away in the north, out of the mountains of Slieve Gullion, a fairy tune played, soft, low, and slow, as if on a silver flute; and at the same time the roar of Conn the Hundred-Fighter, and the voice of Gaul like thunder, and the responsive shouts of the captains, and the clamour of the host, for the host shouted all together, and clashed their swords against their shields in fierce defiance, when in spite of all obstructions the fairy music of the enchanter began to steal into their souls. That shout was heard all over Ireland, echoing from sea to sea, and the hollow buildings of Tara reverberated to the uproar. Yet through it all could be heard the low, slow, delicious music that came from Slieve Gullion. Finn put the point of the spear to his forehead. It burned him like fire, yet his stout heart did not fail. Then the roar of the host slowly faded away as in a dream, though the captains were still shouting, and two-thirds of the torches fell to the ground. And now, succeeding the flute music, sounded the music of a stringed instrument exceedingly sweet. Finn pressed the cruel spearhead closer to his forehead, and saw every torch fall, save one which wavered as if held by a drunken man, and beneath it a giant figure that reeled and tottered and strove in vain to keep its feet. It was Conn the Hundred-Fighter. As he fell there was a roar as of many waters; it was the ocean mourning for the High King's fall. Finn passed through the fallen men and stood alone on the dark hillside. He heard the feet of the enchanter splashing through the Boyne, and saw his huge form ascending the slopes of Tara.

When the enchanter saw that all was silent and dark there he laughed and from his mouth blew a red fireball at the Teck-Midcuarta, which he was accustomed first to set in flames. Finn caught the fireball in the magic mantle. The enchanter blew a second and a third, and Finn caught them both. The man saw that his power over Tara was at an end, and that his magic arts had been defeated. On the third occasion he saw Finn's face, and recognised his conqueror. He turned to flee, and though slow was his coming, swifter than the wind was his going, that he might recover the protection of his enchanted palace before the fair-faced youth clad in skins should overtake him.

Finn let fall the mantle as he had been instructed, and pursued him, but in vain. Soon he perceived that he could not possibly overtake the swift enchanter. Then he was aware that the magic spear struggled in his hand like ahound in a leash. 'Go, then, if thou wilt,' he said, and, poising, cast the spear from him. It shot through the dark night hissing and screaming. There was a track of fire behind it. Finn followed, and on the threshold of the enchanted palace, he found the body of Midna. He was quite dead, with the blood pouring through a wound in the middle of his back; but the spear was gone. Finn drew his sword and cut off the enchanter's head, and returned with it to Tara.

When he came to the spot where he had dropped the mantle it was not seen, but smoke and flame issued there from a hole in the ground. That hole was twenty feet deep in the earth, and at the bottom of it there was a fire always from that night, and it was never extinguished. It was called the fire of the son of Midna. It was in a depression on the north side of the hill of Tara, called the Glen of the Mantle, Glen-a-Brat.

Finn, bearing the head, passed through the sleepers into the palace and spiked the head on his own spear, and drove the spear end into the ground at Conn's end of the great hall. Then the sickness and faintness of death came upon Finn, also a great horror and despair overshadowed him, so that he was about to give himself up for utterly lost. Yet he recalled one of his marvellous attributes, and approaching a silver vessel, into which pure water ever flowed and which was always full, he made a cup with his two hands and, lifting it to his mouth, drank, and the blood began to circulate in his veins, and strength returned to his limbs, and the cheerful hue of rosy health to his cheeks.

Having rested himself sufficiently he went forth and shouted to the sleeping host, and called the captains by their names, beginning with Conn. They awoke and rose up, though dazed and stupid, for it was difficult for any man, no matter how he had stopped his ears, to avoid hearing Finn when he sent forth his voice of power. They were astonished to find that Tara was still standing, for though the night was dark, the palaces and temples, all of hewn timber, were brilliantly coloured and of many hues, for in those days men delighted in splendid colours.When the captains came together Finn said, 'I have slain Midna.'

'Where is his head?' they asked, not because they disbelieved him, but because the heads of men slain in battle were always brought away for trophies. 'Come and see,' replied Finn. Conn, his son Art and Gaul mac Morna followed the young hero into the Teck-Midcuarta, where the spear-long waxen candles were still burning, and when they saw the head of Midna impaled there at the end of the hall, the head of the man whom they believed to be immortal and not to be conquered, they were filled with great joy, and praised their deliverer and paid him many compliments. 'Who art thou, O brave youth?' said Conn. 'Surely thou art the son of some great king or champion, for heroic feats like thine are not performed by the sons of inconsiderable and unknown men.'

Then Finn flung back his cloak of wild boars' skins, and holding his father's treasure bag in his hand before them all, cried in a loud voice, 'I am Finn, the son of Cool, the son of Trenmor, the son of Basna; I am he whom the sons of Morna have been seeking to destroy from the time that I was born; and here tonight, O King of the Kings of Erin, I claim the fulfilment of thy promise, and the restoration of my inheritance, which is the Fian leadership of Fail.' Thereupon Gaul mac Morna put his right hand into Finn's, and became his man. Then his brothers and his sons, and the sons of his brothers, did so in succession, and after that all the chief men of the Fians did the same, and that night Finn was solemnly and surely installed in the Fian leadership of Erin, and put in possession of all the woods and forests and waste places, and all the hills and mountains and promontories, and all the streams and rivers of Erin, and the harbours and estuaries and the harbour dues of the merchants, and all ships and boats and galleys with their mariners, and all that pertained of old time to the Fian leadership of Fail.

Below: *Sunset on Clew Bay, Co Mayo.*

The Birth of Cuchulainn

In the long time ago, Conchubar, son of Ness, was King of Ulster, and he held his court in the palace of Emain Macha. And this is the way he came to be king. He was but a young lad, and his father was not living, and Fergus, son of Rogh, who was at that time King of Ulster, asked his mother Ness in marriage. Now Ness, that was at one time the quietest and kindest of the women of Ireland, had got to be unkind and treacherous because of an unkindness that had been done to her, and she planned to get the kingdom away from Fergus for her own son. So she said to Fergus, 'Let Conchubar hold the kingdom for a year, so that his children after him may be called the children of a king; and that is the marriage portion I will ask of you.'

'You may do that,' the men of Ulster said to him; 'for even though Conchubar gets the name of being king, it is yourself that will be our King all the time.' So Fergus agreed to it, and he took Ness as his wife, and her son Conchubar was made King in his place. But all through the year Ness was working to keep the kingdom for him, and she gave great presents to the chief men of Ulster to get them on her side. And though Conchubar was but a young lad at the time, he was wise in his judgments and brave in battle, and good in shape and in form, and they liked him well. And at the end of the year, when Fergus asked to have the kingship back again, they consulted together; and it is what they agreed, that Conchubar was to keep it. And they said, 'It is little Fergus thinks about us, when he was so ready to give up his rule over us for a year; and let Conchubar keep the kingship.' they said, 'and let Fergus keep the wife he has got.'

It happened one day that Conchubar was making a feast at Emain Macha for the marriage of his sister Dechtire with Sualtim, son of Roig. And at the feast Dechtire was thirsty, and they gave her a cup of wine, and as she was drinking it a mayfly flew into the cup, and she drank it down wlth the wine. And presently she went into her sunny parlour, and her fifty maidens along with her, and she fell into a deep sleep. And in her sleep Lugh of the Long Hand appeared to her, and he said, 'It is I myself was the mayfly that came to you in the cup, and it is with me you must come away now, and your fifty maidens along with you.' And he put on them the appearance of a flock of birds, and they went with him southward till they came to Brugh na Boinne, the dwelling place of the Sidhe.

And no one at Emain Macha could get tale or tidings of them, or know where they had gone, or what had happened them. It was about a year after that time there was another feast in Emain, and Conchubar and his chief men were sitting at the feast. And suddenly they saw from the window a great flock of birds, that lit on the ground and began to eat up everything before them, so that not so much as a blade of grass was left. The men of Ulster were vexed when they saw the birds destroying all before them, and they yoked nine of their chariots to follow after them. Conchubar was in his own chariot, and there were following with him Fergus, son of Rogh, and Laegaire Buadach the Battle-Winner, and Celthair, son of Uithecar, and many others, and Bricriu of the bitter tongue was along with them.

They followed after the birds across the whole country southward, across Slieve Fuad, by Ath Lethan, by Ath Garach and Magh Gossa, between Fir Rois and Fir Ardae; and the birds before them always. They were the most beautiful that had ever been seen; nine flocks of them there were, linked together two and two with a chain of silver, and at the head of every flock there were two birds of different colours, linked together with a chain of gold; and there were three birds that flew by themselves, and they all went before the chariots to the far end of the country, until the fall of night, and then there was no more seen of them.

And when the dark night was coming on, Conchubar said to his people, 'It is best for us to unyoke the chariots now, and to look for some place where we can spend the night.' Then Fergus went forward to look for some place, and what he came to was a very small poor looking house. A man and a woman were in it, and when they saw him they said, 'Bring your companions here along with you, and they will be welcome.' Fergus went back to his companions and told them what he had seen. But Bricriu said: 'Where is the use of going into a house like that, with neither room nor provisions nor coverings in it; it is not worth our while to be going there.' Then Bricriu went on himself to the place where the house

Above: *Dusk on the Atlantic.*

was. But when he came to it, what he saw was a grand, new, well lighted house; and at the door there was a young man wearing armour, very tall and handsome and shining. And he said, 'Come into the house, Bricriu; why are you looking about you?' And there was a young woman beside him, fine and noble, and with curled hair, and she said, 'Surely there is a welcome before you from me.' 'Why does she welcome me?' said Bricriu. 'It is on account of her that I myself welcome you,' said the young man. 'And is there no one missing from you at Emain?' he said. 'There is, surely,' said Bricriu. 'We are missing fifty young girls for the length of a year.' 'Would you know them again if you saw them?' said the young man. 'If I would not know them,' said Bricriu, 'it is because a year might make a change in them, so that I would not be sure.'

'Try and know them again,' said the man, 'for the fifty young girls are in this house, and this woman beside me is their mistress, Dechtire. It was they themselves changed into birds, that went to Emain Macha to bring you here.' Then Dechtire gave Bricriu a purple cloak with gold fringes; and he went back to find his companions. But while he was going he thought to himself, 'Conchubar would give great treasure to find these fifty young girls again, and his sister along with them. I will not tell him I have found them. I will only say I have found a house with beautiful women in it, and no more than that.'

When Conchubar saw Bricriu he asked news of him. 'What news do you bring back with you, Bricriu?' he said. 'I came to a fine well lighted house,' said Bricriu; 'I saw a queen, noble, kind, with royal looks, with curled hair; I saw a troop of women, beautiful, well dressed; I saw the man of the house, tall and openhanded and shining.'

'Let us go there for the night,' said Conchubar. So they brought their chariots and their horses and their arms; and they were hardly in the house when every sort of food and of drink, some they knew and some they did not know, was put before them, so that they never spent a better night. And when they had eaten and drunk and began to be satisfied, Conchubar said to the young man, 'Where is the mistress of the house that she does not come to bid us welcome?'

'You cannot see her tonight,' said he, 'for she is in the pains of childbirth.' So they rested there that night, and in the morning Conchubar was the first to rise up; but he saw no more of the man of the house, and what he heard was the cry of a child. And he went to the room it came from, and there he saw Dechtire, and her maidens about her, and a young child beside her. And she bade Conchubar welcome, and she told him all that had happened her, and that she had called him there to bring herself and the child back to Emain Macha. And Conchubar said, 'It is well you have done by me, Dechtire; you gave shelter to me and to my chariots; you kept the cold from my horses; you gave food to me and my people, and now you have given us this good gift. And let our sister, Finchoem, bring up the child,' he said.

'No, it is not for her to bring him up, it is for me,' said Sencha, son of Ailell, chief judge and chief poet of Ulster. 'For I am skilled; I am good in disputes; I am not forgetful; I speak before anyone at all in the presence of the King; I watch over what he says; I give judgment in the quarrels of kings; I am judge of the men of Ulster; no one has a right to dispute my claim, but only Conchubar.'

'If the child is given to me to bring up,' said Blai, the distributor, 'he will not suffer from want of care or from forgetfulness. It is my messages that do the will of Conchubar; I call up the fighting men from all Ireland; I am well able to provide for them for a week, or even for ten days; I settle their business and their disputes; I support their honour; I get satisfaction for their insults.'

'You think too much of yourself,' said Fergus. 'It is I that will bring up the child; I am strong; I have knowledge; I am the King's messenger; no one can stand up against me in honour or riches; I am hardened to war and battles; I am a good craftsman; I am worthy to bring up the child. I am the protector of all the unhappy; thc strong are afraid of me; I am the helper of the weak.'

'If you will listen to me at last, now you are quiet,' said Amergin, 'I am able to bring up a child like a king. The people praise my honour, my bravery, my courage, my wisdom; they praise my good luck, my age, my speaking, my name, my courage, and my race. Though I am a fighter, I am a poet; I am worthy of the King's favour; I overcome all the men who fight from their chariots; I owe thanks to no one except Conchubar; I obey no one but the King.'

Then Sencha said, 'Let Finchoem keep the child until we come to Emain, and Morann, the judge, will settle the question when we are there.' So the men of Ulster set out for Emain, Finchoem having the child with her. And when they came there Morann gave his judgment. 'It is for Conchubar,' he said, 'to help the child to a good name, for he is next of kin to him; let Sencha teach him words and speaking; let Fergus hold him on his knees; let Amergin be his tutor.' And he said, 'This child will be praised by all, by chariot drivers and fighters, by kings and by wise men; he shall be loved by many men; he will avenge all your wrongs; he will defend your fords; he will fight all your battles.' And so it was settled. And the child was left until he should come to sensible years with his mother Dechtire and with her husband Sualtim. And they brought him up upon the plain of Muirthemne, and the name he was known by was Setanta, son of Sualtim.

As soon as Setanta was able to understand the stories and conversation of those around him, he evinced a passion for arms and the martial life, which was so premature and violent as to surprise all who knew him. His thoughts for ever ran on the wars and achievements of the Red Branch. He knew all the knights by name, the appearance and bearing of each, and what deeds of valour they had severally performed. Emain Macha, the capital of the Clanna Rury, was never out of his mind. He saw for ever before his mind its moats and ramparts, its gates and bridges, its streets filled with martial men, its high-raised Duns and Raths, its branching roads, over which came the tributes of wide Ulla to the High King.

He had seen his father's tribute driven thither, and had even longed to be one of the four-footed beasts that he beheld wending their way to the wondrous city. But, above all, he delighted to be told of the great school where the young nobles of Ulster were

Above: *By the headwaters of the River Liffey, Co Wicklow.*

taught martial exercises and the military art, under the superintendence of chosen knights and of the High King himself. Of the several knights he had his own opinion, and had already resolved to accept no one as his instructor save Fergus Mac Roy, tanist of Ulster.

Of his father he saw little. His mind had become impaired, and he was confined in a secluded part of the Dun. But whenever he spoke to his mother of what was nearest his heart, and his desire to enter the military school at Emain Macha, she laughed, and said that he as not yet old enough to endure that rough life. But secretly she was alarmed, and formed plans to detain him at home altogether. Then Setanta concealed his desire, but enquired narrowly concerning the partings of the roads on the way to Emania. At last, when he was ten years old, selecting a favourable night, Setanta stole away from his father's Dun, and before morning had crossed the frontier. He then lay down to rest and sleep in a wood. After this he set out again, travelling quickly, lest he should be met by any of his father's people. On his back was strapped his little wooden shield, and by his side hung a sword of lath. He had brought his ball and hurle of red bronze with him, and ran swiftly along the road, driving the ball before him, or throwing up his javelin into the air, and running to meet it ere it fell.

In the afternoon of that day Fergus Mac Roy and the King sat together in the part that surrounded the King's palace. A chessboard was between them, and their attention was fixed on the game. At a distance the young nobles were at their sports, and the shouts of the boys and the clash of the metal hurles resounded in the evening air.

Suddenly the noise ceased, and Fergus and the King looked up. They saw a strange boy rushing backwards and forwards through the crowd of young nobles, urging the ball in any direction that he pleased, as if in mockery, till none but the very best players attempted to stop him, while the rest stood about the ground in groups. Fergus and the King looked at each other for a moment in silence. After this the boys came together into a group and held a council. Then commenced what seemed to be an attempt to force him out of the ground, followed by a furious fight. The strange boy seemed to be a very demon of war; with his little hurle grasped, like a war mace, in both hands, he laid about him on every side, and the boys were tumbling fast. He sprang at tall youths, like a hound at a stag's throat. He rushed through crowds of his enemies like a hawk through a flock of birds.

The boys, seized with a panic, cried out that it was one of the Tuatha from the fairy hills of the Boyne, and fled right and left to gain the shelter of the trees. Some of them, pursued by the stranger, ran round Conchubar Mac Nessa and his knight. The boy, however, running straight, sprang over the chess table; but Conchubar seized him deftly by the wrist and brought him to a stand, but with dilated eyes and panting. 'Why are you so enraged, my boy?' said the King, 'and why do you so maltreat my nobles?'

'Because they have not treated me with the respect due to a stranger,' replied the boy. 'Who are you yourself?' said Conchubar. 'I am Setanta, the son of Sualtim, and Dectire, your own sister, is my mother; and it is not before my uncle's palace that I should be insulted and dishonoured.'

This was the debut and first martial exploit of the great Cuchulainn, type of Irish chivalry and courage, in the bardic firmament a bright and particular star of strength, daring, and glory, that will not set nor suffer aught but transient obscuration till the extinction of the Irish race; Cuchulainn, bravest of the brave,

post

whose glory aflected even the temperate-minded Tierna, so that his sober pen has inscribed, in the annals of ancient Erin, this testimony: '*Cuculain, filius Sualtim fortissimus heros Scotorum.*'

After this Setanta was regularly received into the military school, where, ere long, he became a favourite both with old and young. He placed himself under the tuition of Fergus Mac Roy, who, each day, grew more and more proud of his pupil, for while still a boy his fame was extending over Ulla. It was not long after this that Setanta received the name by which he is more generally known. Chulainn was chief of the black country of Ulla, and of a people altogether given up to the making of weapons and armour, where the sound of the hammer and husky bellows were for ever heard. One day Conchubar and some of his knights, passing through the park to partake of an entertainment at the house of the armourer, paused awhile, looking at the boys at play. Then, as all were praising his little nephew, Conchubar called to him, and the boy came up, flushed and shy, for there were with the King the chief warriors of the Red Branch. But Conchubar bade him come with them to the feast, and the knights around him laughed, and enumerated the good things which Chulainn had prepared for them. But when Setanta's brow fell, Conchubar bade him finish his game, and after that proceed to Chulainn's house, which was to the west of Emain Macha, and more than a mile distant from the city. Then the King and his knights went on to the feast, and Setanta returned joyfully to his game.

Now, when they were seen afar upon the plain the smith left his workshop and put by his implements, and having washed from him the sweat and smoke, made himself ready to receive his guests; but the evening fell as they were coming into the liss, and all his people came in also, and sat at the lower table, and the bridge was drawn up and the door was shut for the night, and the candles were lit in the high chamber. Then said Chulainn, 'Have all thy retinue come in, O Conchubar?' And when the King said that they were all there, Chulainn bade one of his apprentices go out and let loose the great mastiff that guarded the house. Now, this mastiff was as large as a calf and exceedingly fierce, and he guarded all the smith's property outside the house, and if anyone approached the house without beating on the gong, which was outside the foss and in front of the drawbridge, he was accustomed to rend him. Then the mastiff, having been let loose, careered three times round the liss, baying dreadfully, and after that remained quiet outside his kennel, guarding his master's property. But, inside, they devoted themselves to feasting and merriment, and there were many jests made concerning Chulainn, for he was wont to cause laughter to Conchubar Mac Nessa and his knights, yet he was good to his own people and faithful to the Crave Rue, and very ardent and skilful in the practice of his art.

But as they were amusing themselves in this manner, eating and drinking, a deep growl came from without, as it were a note of warning, and after that one yet more savage; but where he sat in the champion's seat, Fergus Mac Roy struck the table with his hand and rose straightway, crying out, 'It is Setanta.' But ere the door could be opened they heard the boy's voice raised in anger and the fierce yelling of the dog, and a scuffling in the bawn of the liss. Then they rushed to the door in great fear, for they said that the boy was torn in pieces; but when the bolts were drawn back and they sprang forth, eager to save the boy's life, they found the dog dead, and Setanta standing over him with his hurle, for he had sprung over the foss, not fearing the dog. Forthwith, then, his tutor, Fergus Mac Roy, snatched him up on his shoulder, and returned with great joy into the banquet hall, where all were well pleased at the preservation of the boy, except Chulainn himself, who began to lament over the death of his dog and to enumerate all the services which he rendered to him.

'Do not grieve for thy dog, O Chulainn,' said Setanta, from the shoulder of Fergus, 'for I will perform those services for you myself until a dog equally good is procured to take the place of him I slew.' Then one jesting, said, 'Cuchulainn!' (Hound of Chulainn) and thenceforward he went by this name.

Left: *The statue of Cuchulainn at the General Post Office, Dublin. It is dedicated to those who died for their part in the Easter Rising in 1916.*

Right: *Glenlee, Co Donegal.*

A Legend of Knockmany

It so happened that Finn and his gigantic relatives were all working at the Giant's Causeway in order to make a bridge, or, what was still better, a good stout padroad across to Scotland, when Finn, who was very fond of his wife, Oonagh, took it into his head that he would go home and see how the poor woman got on in his absence. So accordingly he pulled up a firtree, and after lopping off the roots and branches, made a walkingstick of it and set out on his way to Oonagh.

Finn lived at this time on Knockmany Hill, which faces Cullamore, that rises up, half hill, half mountain, on the opposite side. The truth is that honest Finn's affection for his wife was by no manner of means the whole cause of his journey home. There was at that time another giant, named Far Rua – some say he was Irish and some say he was Scotch – but whether Scotch or Irish, sorrow doubt of it but he was a targer. No other giant of the day could stand before him; and such was his strength that, when well vexed, he could give a stamp that shook the country about him. The fame and name of him went far and near, and nothing in the shape of a man, it was said, had any chance with him in a fight. Whether the story is true or not I cannot say, but the report went that by one blow of his fist he flattened a thunderbolt, and kept it in his pocket in the shape of a pancake to show to all his enemies when they were about to fight him. Undoubtedly he had given every giant in Ireland a considerable beating, barring Finn M'Cool himself; and he swore that he would never rest night or day, winter or summer, till he could serve Finn with the same sauce, if he could catch him. Finn, however, had a strong disinclination to meet a giant who could make a young earthquake or flatten a thunderbolt when he was angry, so accordingly he kept dodging about from place to place – not much to his credit as a Trojan, to be sure – whenever he happened to get the hard word that Far Rua was on the scent of him. And the long and the short of it was that he heard Far Rua was coming to the Causeway to have a trial of strength with him; and he was, naturally enough, seized in consequence with a very warm and sudden fit of affection for his wife, who was delicate in her health, poor woman, and leading, besides, a very lonely, uncomfortable life of it in his absence.

'God save all here,' said Finn good-humouredly, putting his honest face into his own door. 'Musha, Finn, avick, an' you're welcome to your own Oonagh, you darlin' bully.' Here followed a smack that it is said to have made the waters of the lake curl, as it were, with kindness and sympathy. 'Faith,' said Finn, 'beautiful; and how are you, Oonagh – and how did you sport your figure during my absence, my bilberry?' 'Never a merrier – as bouncing a grass widow as ever there was in sweet Tyrone among the bushes.' Finn gave a short, goodhumoured cough, and laughed most heartily to show her how much he was delighted that she made herself happy in his absence. 'An' what brought you home so soon, Finn?' said she. 'Why,' said Finn, putting his answer in the proper way, 'never the thing but the purest of love and affection for yourself. Sure, you know that's truth, anyhow, Oonagh.'

Finn spent two or three happy days with Oonagh, and felt himself very comfortable considering the dread he had of Far Rua. This, however, grew upon him so much that his wife could not but perceive something lay on his mind which he kept altogether to himself. Let a woman alone in the meantime for ferreting or wheedling a secret out of her good man when she wishes. Finn was a proof of this. 'It's this Far Rua,' said he, 'that's troublin' me. When the fellow gets angry and begins to stamp he'll shake you a whole townland, and it's well known that he can stop a thunderbolt, for he always carries one about with him in the shape of a pancake to show to anyone that might misdoubt it.' As he spoke he clapped his thumb in his mouth, as he always did when he wanted to prophesy or to know anything. 'He's coming,' said Finn; 'I see him below at Dungannon.'

'An' who is it, avick?'

'Far Rua,' replied Finn, 'and how to manage I don't know. If I run away I am disgraced, and I know that sooner or later I must meet him, for my thumb tells me so.'

'When will he be here?' says she.

'Tomorrow, about two o'clock,' replied Finn with a groan.

'Don't be cast down,' said Oonagh; 'depend on me, and, maybe, I'll bring you out of this scrape better than you could bring yourself.'

Above: *Sunset over the Lower Lake, Killarney. A wonderful national park in Co Kerry, Killarney and its lakes are a major tourist attraction.*

This quieted Finn's heart very much, for he knew that Oonagh was hand and glove with the fairies; and, indeed, to tell the truth, she was supposed to be a fairy herself. If she was, however, she must have been a kind hearted one, for by all accounts she never did anything but good in the neighbourhood.

Now, it so happened that Oonagh had a sister named Granua living opposite to them, on the very top of Cullamore, which I have mentioned already, and this Granua was quite as powerful as herself. The beautiful valley that lies between the Granlisses is not more than three or four miles broad, so that of a summer evening Granua and Oonagh were able to hold many an agreeable conversation across it, from one hilltop to the other. Upon this occasion Oonagh resolved to consult her sister as to what was best to be done in the difficulty that surrounded them. 'Granua,' said she, 'are you at home?'

'No,' said the other, 'I'm picking bilberries at Althadhawan (the Devil's Glen).'

'Well,' said Oonagh, 'go up to the top of Cullamore, look about you, and then tell us what you see.'

'Very well,' replied Granua, after a few minutes; 'I am there now.'

'What do you see?' asked the other.

'Goodness be about us!' exclaimed Granua, 'I see the biggest giant that ever was known coming up from Dungannon.'

'Ay,' said Oonagh, 'there's our difficulty. That's Far Rua, and he's comin' up now to leather Finn. What's to be done?'

'I'll call to him,' she replied, 'to come up to Cullamore and refresh himself, and maybe that will give you and Finn time to think of some plan to get yourselves out of the scrape. But,' she proceeded, 'I'm short of butter, having in the house only half a dozen firkins, and as I'm to have a few giants and giantesses to spend the evenin' with me I'd feel thankful, Oonagh, if you'd throw me up fifteen or sixteen tubs, or the largest miscaun you've got, and you'll oblige me very much.'

'I'll do that with a heart and a half,' replied Oonagh; 'and, indeed, Granua, I feel myself under great obligations to you for your kindness in keeping him off us till we see what can be done; for what would become of us all if anything happened to Finn, poor man!' She accordingly got the largest miscaun of butter she had – which might be about the weight of a couple of dozen millstones, so that you can easily judge of its size – and calling up her sister, 'Granua,' says she, 'are you ready? I'm going to throw you up a miscaun, so be prepared to catch it.'

'I will,' said the other. 'A good throw, now, and take care it does not fall short.' Oonagh threw it, but in consequence of her anxiety about Finn and Far Rua she forgot to say the charm that was to send it up, so that instead of reaching Cullamore, as she expected, it fell about halfway between the two hills at the edge of the Broad Bog, near Augher. 'A curse upon you!' she exclaimed, 'you've disgraced me. I now change you into a grey stone. Lie there as a testimony of what has happened, and may evil betide the first living man that will ever attempt to move or injure you!' And, sure enough, there it lies to this day, with the mark of the four fingers and thumb imprinted on it, exactly as it came out of her hand. 'Never mind,' said Granua, 'I must only do the best I can with Far Rua. If all fail, I'll give him a cast of heather broth, or a panada of oak bark. But, above all things, think of some plan to get Finn out of the scrape he's in, or he's a lost man. You know you used to be sharp and readywitted; and my own opinion is, Oonagh, that it will go hard with you, or you'll outdo Far Rua yet.'

She then made a high smoke on the top of the hill, after which she put her finger in her mouth and gave three whistles, and by that Far Rua knew that he was invited to the top of Cullamore – for this was the way that the Irish long ago gave a sign to all strangers and travellers to let them know they are welcome to come and take share of whatever was going. In the meantime Finn was very melancholy, and did not know what to do, or how to act at all. Far Rua was an ugly customer, no doubt, to meet with; and, moreover, the idea of the confounded 'cake' aforesaid flattened the very heart within him. What chance could he have, strong and brave as he was, with a man who could, when put in a passion, walk the country into earthquakes and knock thunderbolts into pancakes? The thing was impossible, and Finn knew not on what hand to turn him. Right or left, backward or forward, where to go: he could form no guess whatever.

'Oonagh,' said he, 'can you do anything for me? Where's all your invention? Am I to be skivered like a rabbit before your eyes and to have my name disgraced for ever in the sight of all my tribe, and me the best man among them? How am I to fight this man-mountain – this huge cross between an earthquake and a thunderbolt – with a pancake in his pocket that was once . . .?'

'Be aisy, Finn,' replied Oonagh. 'Troth, I'm ashamed of you. Keep your toe in your pump, will you? Talking of pancakes, maybe we'll give him as good as any he brings with him – thunderbolts or otherwise. If I don't treat him to as smart feeding as he's got this many a day, don't trust Oonagh again. Leave him to me, and do just as I bid you.' This relieved Finn very much, for, after all, he had great confidence in his wife, knowing, as he did, that she had got him out of many a quandary before. The present, however, was the greatest of all; but, still, he began to get courage and to eat his victuals as usual.

Oonagh then drew the nine woollen threads of different colours, which she always did to find out the best way of succeeding in anything of importance she went about. She then plaited them into three plaits, with three colours in each, putting one on her right arm, one round her heart, and the third round her right ankle, for then she knew that nothing could fail her that she undertook.

Everything now prepared, she sent round to the neighbours and borrowed one and twenty iron griddles, which she took and kneaded into the hearts of one and twenty cakes of bread, and these she baked on the fire in the usual way, setting them aside in the cupboard according as they were done. She then put down a large pot of new milk, which she made into curds and whey, and gave Finn due instructions how to use the curds when Far Rua should come.

Having done all this, she sat down quite contented waiting for his arrival on the next day about two o'clock, that being the hour at which he was expected – for Finn knew as much by the sucking of his thumb. Now, this was a curious property that Finn's thumb had; but notwithstanding all the wisdom and logic he used to suck out of it, it could never have stood to him here were it not for the wit of his wife. In this very thing, moreover, he was very much resembled by his great foe, Far Rua; for it was well known that the huge strength that he possessed all lay in the middle finger of his right hand, and that if he happened by any chance to lose it, he was no more, notwithstanding his bulk, than a common man.

At length the next day he was seen coming across the valley, and Oonagh knew that it was time to commence operations. She immediately made the cradle, and desired Finn to lie down in it and cover himself up with the clothes. 'You must pass for your own child,' said she, 'so just lie there snug and say nothing, but be guided by me.' This, to be sure, was wormwood to Finn – I mean going into the cradle in such a cowardly manner – but he knew Oonagh very well; and finding that he had nothing else for it, with a very rueful face he gathered himself into it and lay snug, as she had desired him.

At about two o'clock, as he had been expected, Far Rua came in. 'God save all here!' said he. 'Is this where the great Finn M'Cool lives?'

'Indeed it is, honest man,' replied Oonagh. 'God save you kindly – won't you be sitting?'

'Thank you, ma'am,' says he, sitting down. 'You're Mrs. M'Cool, I suppose?'

'I am,' says she, 'and I have no reason, I hope, to be ashamed of my husband.'

'No,' said the other; 'he has the name of being the strongest and bravest man in Ireland. But, for all that, there's a man not far from you that's very anxious of taking a shake with him. Is he at home?'

'Why, no, then,' she replied; 'and if ever a man left in a fury he did. It appears that someone told him of a big bosthoon of a giant called Far Rua being down at the Causeway to look for him, and so he set out there to try if he could catch him. Troth, I hope, for the poor giant's sake, he won't meet with him, for if he does Finn will make paste of him at once.'

'Well,' said the other, 'I am Far Rua, and I have been seeking him these twelve months, but he always kept clear of me; and I will never rest day or night till I lay my hands on him.' At this Oonagh set up a loud laugh of great contempt, by the way, and looked at him as if he were only a mere handful of a man. ' Did you ever see Finn?' said she, changing her manner all at once.

'How could I?' said he. 'He always took care to keep his distance.'

'I thought so,' she replied. 'I judged as much; and if you take my advice, you poor looking creature, you'll pray night and day that you may neversee him, for I tell you it will be a black day for you when you do. But, in the meantime, you perceive that the wind's on the door and, as Finn himself is far from home, maybe you'd be civil enough to turn the house, for it's always what Finn does when he's here.'

This was a startler, even to Far Rua; but he got up, however, and after pulling the middle finger of his right hand until it cracked three times, he went outside, and getting his arms about the house, completely turned it as she had wished. When Finn saw this he felt a certain description of moisture, which shall be nameless, oozing out through every pore of his skin; but Oonagh, depending upon her woman's wit, felt not a whit daunted. 'Arrah, then,' said she, 'as you're so civil, maybe you'd do another obliging turn for us, as Finn's not here to do it himself. You see after this long stretch of dry weather that we've had, we feel very badly off for want of water. Now, Finn says there's a fine spring well somewhere under the rocks behind the hill there below, and it was his intention to pull them asunder; but having heard of you he left the place in such a fury that he never thought of it. Now, if you try to find it, troth, I'd feel it a kindness.'

She then brought Far Rua down to see the place, which was then all one solid rock; and after looking at it for some time, he cracked his right middle finger nine times and, stooping down, tore a cleft about four hundred feet deep and a quarter of a mile in length, which has since been christened by the name of Lumford's Glen. This feat nearly threw Oonagh herself off her guard; but what won't a woman's sagacity and presence of mind accomplish? 'You'll now come in,' said she, 'and eat a bit of such humble fare as we can give. Finn, even though you and he were enemies, would scorn not to treat you kindly in his own house; and, indeed, if I did not do it even in his absence, he would not be pleased with me.' She accordingly brought him in, and placing half a dozen of the cakes we spoke of before him, together with a can or two of butter, a side of boiled bacon, and a stack of cabbage, she desired him to help himself – for this, be it known, was long before the invention of potatoes. Far Rua, who, by the way, was a glutton as well as a hero, put one of the cakes in his mouth to take a huge whack out of it, when both Finn and Oonagh were stunned with a noise that resembled something between a growl and a yell. 'Blood and fury!' he shouted out. 'How is this? Here are two of my teeth out! What kind of bread is this you gave me?'

'What's the matter?' said Oonagh coolly.

'Matter!' shouted the other. 'Why, here are two of the best teeth in my head gone.'

'Why,' said she, 'that's Finn's bread – the only bread he ever eats when at home; but, indeed, I forgot to tell you that nobody can eat it but himself and that child in the cradle there. I thought, however, that as you were reported to be rather a stout little fellow of your size you might be able to manage it, and I did not wish to

Above: *Reed patterns in Innesfree, Co Sligo.*

Above: *Reed texture, Lough Derg.*

affront a man that thinks himself able to fight Finn. Here's another cake – maybe it's not so hard as that.'

Far Rua, at the moment, was not only hungry, but ravenous, so he accordingly made a fresh set at the second cake, and immediately another yell was heard twice as loud as the first. 'Thunder and giblets!' he roared, 'take your bread out of this house, or I will not have a tooth in my head; there's another pair gone.'

'Well, honest man,' replied Oonagh, 'if you're not able to eat the bread say so quietly, and don't be awakening the child in the cradle there. There, now, he's awake upon me!' Finn now gave a skirl that frightened the giant, as coming from such a youngster as he was represented to be. 'Mother,' said he, 'I'm hungry – get me something to eat. Oonagh went over, and put into his hand a cake that had no griddle in it. Finn, whose appetite in the meantime was sharpened by what he saw going forward, soon made it disappear. Far Rua was thunderstruck, and secretly thanked his stars that he had the good fortune to miss meeting Finn, for, as he said to himself, I'd have no chance with a man who could eat such bread as that, which even his son that's in the cradle can munch before my eyes. 'I'd like to take a glimpse at the lad in the cradle,' said he to Oonagh, 'for I can tell you that the infant who can manage that nutriment is no joke to look at or to feed of a scarce summer.'

'With all the veins of my heart,' replied Oonagh. 'Get up, acushla, and show this decent little man something that won't be unworthy of your father.' Finn, who was dressed for the occasion as much like a boy as possible, got up, and bringing Far Rua out, 'Are you strong?' said he.

'Thunder and ounze!' exclaimed the other, 'what a voice in so small a chap!'

'Are you strong?' said Finn again. 'Are you able to squeeze water out of that white stone?' he asked, putting one into Far Rua's hand. The latter squeezed and squeezed the stone, but to no purpose; he might pull the rocks of Lumford's Glen asunder, and flatten a thunderbolt, but to squeeze water out of a white stone was beyond his strength. Finn eyed him with great contempt as he kept straining hard squeezing and squeezing and straining till he got black in the face with the efforts. 'Ah, you're a poor creature,' said Finn. 'You a giant! Give me the stone here, and when I'll show what Finn's little son can do you may then judge of what my daddy himself is.' Finn then took the stone, and then, slyly exchanging it for the curds, he squeezed the latter until the whey, as clear as water, oozed out in a little shower from his hand.'

'I'll now go in,' said he, 'to my cradle; for I scorn to lose my time with anyone that's not able to eat my daddy's bread, or squeeze water out of a stone. Bedad, you had better be off out of this before he comes back, for if he catches you, it's in flummery he'd have you in two minutes.'

Far Rua, seeing what he had seen, was of the same opinion himself; his knees knocked together with the terror of Finn's return, and he accordingly hastened in to bid Oonagh farewell, and to assure her that, from that day out, he never wished to hear of, much less to see, her husband. 'I admit fairly that I'm not a match for him,' said he, 'strong as I am. Tell him I will avoid him as I would the plague, and that I will make myself scarce in this part of the country while I live.' Finn, in the meantime, had gone into the cradle, where he lay very quietly, his heart in his mouth with delight that Far Rua was about to take his departure without discovering the tricks that been played off on him. 'It's well for you,' said Oonagh, 'that he doesn't happen to be here, for it's nothing but hawk's meat he'd make of you.'

'I know that,' said Far Rua, 'divel a thing else he'd make of me; but, before I go, will you let me feel what kind of teeth they are that can eat griddlecakes like that?'and he pointed to the cradle as he spoke. 'With all the pleasure in life,' says she; 'only as they're far back in his head you must put your finger a good way in.'

Far Rua was surprised to find so powerful a set of grinders in one so young; but he was still much more so on finding, when he took his hand from Finn's mouth, that he had left the very finger upon which his whole strength depended behind him. He gave one loud groan and fell down at once with terror and weakness. This was all Finn wanted, who now knew that his most powerful and bitterest enemy was completely at his mercy. He instantly started out of the cradle, and in a few minutes the great Far Rua, that was for such a length of time the terror of him and all his followers, was no more.

Daniel O'Rourke

People may have heard of the renowned adventures of Daniel O'Rourke, but how few are there who know that the cause of all his perils, above and below, was neither more nor less than his having slept under the walls of the Pooka's Tower. I knew the man well. He lived at the bottom of Hungry Hill, just at the right hand side of the road as you go towards Bantry.

An old man was he at the time he told me the story, with grey hair and a red nose; and it was on the 25th of June, 1813, that I heard it from his own lips, as he sat smoking his pipe under the old poplar tree, on as fine an evening as ever shone from the sky. I was going to visit the caves in Dursey Island, having spent the morning at Glengariff.

'Often asked to tell it, sir,' said he, 'so that this is not the first time. The master's son, you see, had come from beyond foreign parts in France and Spain, as young gentlemen used to go before Buonaparte or any such was heard of; and, sure enough, there was a dinner given to all the people on the ground, gentle and simple, high and low, rich and poor. The ould gentlemen were the gentlemen, after all, saving your honour's presence. They'd swear at a body a little, to be sure, and, maybe, give one a cut of a whip now and then, but we were no losers by it in the end; and they were so easy and civil, and kept such rattling houses, and thousands of welcomes; and there was no grinding for rent, and there was hardly a tenant on the estate that did not taste of his landlord's bounty often and often in a year; but now it's another thing. No matter for that, sir, for I'd better be telling you my story.'

'Well, we had everything of the best, and plenty of it; and we ate, and we drank, and we danced, and the young master, by the same token, danced with Peggy Barry, from the Bohereen – a lovely young couple they were, though they are both low enough now. To make a long story short, I got, as a body may say, the same thing as tipsy almost, for I can't remember, ever at all, no ways, how it was I left the place; only I did leave it, that's certain. Well, I thought, for all that, in myself, I'd just step to Molly Cronohan's, the fairy woman, to speak a word about the bracket heifer that was bewitched; and so, as I was crossing the steppingstones of the ford of Ballyashenogh, and was looking up at the stars, and blessing myself – for why? it was Ladyday – I missed my foot, and souse I fell into the water. "Death alive!" thought I, "I'll be drowned now!"

'However, I began swimming, swimming, swimming away for dear life, till at last I got ashore, somehow or other, but never the one of me can tell how, upon a dissolute island. I wandered and wandered about there, without knowing where I wandered, until at last I got into a big bog. The moon was shining as bright as day, or your fair lady's eyes, sir (with your pardon for mentioning her), and I looked east and west, north and south, and every way, and nothing did I see but bog, bog, bog. I could never find out how I got into it; and my heart grew cold with fear, for sure and certain I was that it would be my berrin' place.'

'So I sat upon a stone, which, as good luck would have it, was close by me, and I began to scratch my head, and sing the ULLAGONE – when all of a sudden the moon grew black, and I looked up and saw something for all the world as if it was moving down between me and it, and I could not tell what it was. Down it came with a pounce, and looked at me full in the face; and what was it but an eagle? – as fine a one as ever flew from the kingdom of Kerry! So he looked at me in the face, and says he to me,

"Daniel O'Rourke," says he, "how do you do ?"

"Very well, I thank you, sir," says I, "I hope you are well." wondering out of my senses all the time how an eagle came to speak like a Christian.

"What brings you here, Dan?" says he.

"Nothing at all, sir," says I, "only I wish I was safe home again."

"Is it out of the island you want to go, Dan?" says he.

"Tis, sir," says I; so I up and told him how I had taken a drop too much, and fell into the water, how I swam to the island, and how I got into the bog and did not know my way out of it.

"Dan," says he, after a minute's thought, "though it is very improper of you to get drunk on a Ladyday, yet, as you are a decent sober man, who 'tends mass well, and never fling stones at me or mine, nor cries out after one in the field, my life for yours," says he; "so get up on my back, and grip me well for fear you'd fall off, and I'll fly you out of the bog."

"I am afraid," says I, "your honour's making game of me; for whoever heard of riding ahorseback on an eagle before?"

" 'Pon the honour of a gentleman," says he, putting his right foot on his breast, "I am quite in earnest; and so now either take my offer or starve in the bog – besides I see that your weight is sinking the stone."

'It was true enough, as he said, for I found the stone every minute going from under me. I had no choice; so, thinks I to myself, faint heart never won fair lady, and this is fair persuadance.

"I thank your honour," says I, "for the loan of your civility, and I'll take your kind offer."

'I therefore mounted on the back of the eagle, and held him tight enough by the throat, and up he flew in the air like a lark. Little I knew the trick he was going to serve me. Up, up, up – God knows how far he flew.

"Why, then," said I to him – thinking he did not know the right road home – very civilly, because why? I was in his power entirely; "Sir," says I, "please your honour's glory, and with humble submission to your better judgment, if you'd fly down a bit, you're now just over my cabin, and I could be put down there, and many thanks to your worship."

"Dan," says he, "do you think me a fool? Look down in the next field, and don't you see two men and a gun? By my word, it would be no joke to shoot this way, to oblige a drunken blackguard that I picked up off a cold stone in a bog."

"Bother you," says I to myself, but I did not speak out, for where was the use? Well, sir, up he kept flying, flying, and I asking him every minute to fly down, and all to no use. "Where in the world are you going, sir?" says I to him.

"Hold your tongue, Dan," says he, "and mind your own business, and don't be interfering with the business of other people."

"Faith, this is my business, I think," says I.

"Be quiet, Dan!" says he: so I said no more.

'At last, where should we come to but to the moon itself. Now, you can't see it from this, but there is, or there was in my time, a reapinghook sticking out of the side of the moon, this way (drawing the figure thus on the ground with the end of his stick).

"Dan," says the eagle, "I'm tired with this long fly, I had no notion 'twas so far."

"And my lord, sir," says I, "who in the world asked you to fly so far – was it I? Did not I beg and pray and beseech you to stop half an hour ago?"

"There's no use talking, Dan," said he, "I'm tired bad enough, so you must get off, and sit down on the moon until I rest myself."

"Is it sit down on the moon?" said I, "is it upon that little round thing, then? Why, then, sure, I'd fall off in a minute, and be kilt and spilt, and smashed all to bits; you are a vile deceiver– so you are."

"Not at all, Dan," says he, "you can catch fast hold of the reapinghook that's sticking out of the side of the moon, and 'twill keep you up."

"I won't, then," said I.

"Maybe not," said he, quite quiet. "If you don't, my man, I shall just give you a shake, and one slap of my wing, and send you down to the ground, where every bone in your body will be smashed as small as a drop of dew on a cabbage leaf in the morning."

"Why, then, I'm in a fine way," said I to myself, "ever to have come along with the likes of you." And so, giving him a hearty curse in Irish, for fear he'd know what I said, I got off his back with a heavy heart, took hold of the reapinghook and sat down upon the moon, and a mighty cold seat it was, I can tell you that.

'When he had me there fairly landed, he turned about on me, and said, "Good morning to you, Daniel O'Rourke," said he, "I think I've nicked you fairly now. You robbed my nest last year." ('twas true enough for him, but how he found it out is hard enough to say), "and in return you are freely welcome to cool your heels dangling upon the the moon like a cockthrow."

"Is that all, and is this how you leave me, you brute, you," says I. "You ugly unnatural beast, and is this the way you serve me at last? Bad luck to yourself, with your hook'd nose, and to all your breed, you blackguard."

' 'Twas all to no manner of use; he spread out his great big wings, burst out a laughing, and flew away like lightning. I bawled after him to stop, but I might have called and bawled for ever, without his minding me. Away he went, and I never saw him from that day to this – sorrow fly away with him! You may be sure I was in a disconsolate condition, and kept roaring out for the bare grief, when all at once a door opened right in the middle of the moon, creaking on its hinges as if it had not been opened for a month before – I suppose they never thought of greasing them – and out there walks – who do you think but the man in the moon himself? I knew him by his bush.

"Good morrow to you, Daniel O'Rourke," says he, "how do you do?"

"Very well, thank your honour," says I. "I hope your honour's well."

"What brought you here, Dan?" said he. So I told him how I was a little overtaken in liquor at the master's, and how I was cast on a dissolute island, and how I lost my way in the bog, and the thief of an eagle promised to fly me out of it, and how, instead of that, he had fled me up to the moon.

"Dan," said the man in the moon, taking a pinch of snuff, when I was done, "you must not stay here."

"Indeed, sir," says I, "tis much against my will that I'm here at all, but how am I to go back?"

"That's your business," said he. "Dan, mine is to tell you that you must not stay, so be off in less than no time."

"I'm doing no harm," said I, "only holding on hard by the reapinghook lest I fall off."

"That's what you must not do, Dan," says he.

"Pray, sir," says I, "may I ask how many you are in family that you would not give a poor traveller lodging? I'm sure 'tis not often you are troubled with strangers coming to see you, for 'tis a long way."

"I'm by myself, Dan," says he, "but you'd better let go the reapinghook."

"Faith, and with your leave," says I, "I'll not let go the grip, and the more you bids me the more I won't let go – so I will."

"You had better, Dan," says he again.

"Why, then, my little fellow,' says I, taking the whole weight

Above: *From Roundstone toward the Twelve Pins, Co Galway.*

of him with my eye from head to foot, "there are two words to that bargain, and I'll not budge – you may, if you like."

"We'll see how that is to be," says he, and back he went, giving the door such a great bang after him (for it was plain he was huffed, that I thought the moon and all would fall down with it.

'Well, I was preparing myself to try strength with him, when back he comes, with the kitchen cleaver in his hand, and without saying a word he gives two bangs to the handle of the reapinghook that was holding me up, and whap, it came in two.

"Good morning to you, Dan," says the spiteful little blackguard, when he saw me cleanly falling down with a bit of the handle in my hand, "I thank you for your visit, and fair weather after you, Daniel." I had no time to make any answer to him, for I was tumbling over and over, and rolling and rolling, at the rate of a foxhunt.

"God help me!" says I, "but this is a pretty pickle for a decent man to be seen in at this time of the night. I am now sold fairly." The word was not out of my mouth, when, whiz! what should fly by close to my ear but a flock of wild geese, all the way from my own bog of Ballyasheenagh, else how should they know me? The ould gander, who was their general, turning about his head, cried out to me,

"Is that you, Dan?"

"The same," said I, not a bit daunted now at what he said, for I was by this time used to all kinds of bedivilment, and, besides, I knew him of ould.

"Good morrow to you," says he, "Daniel O'Rourke; how are you in health this morning ?"

"Very well, sir," says I, "thank you kindly." Drawing my breath, for I was mightily in want of some. "I hope your honour's the same."

"I think 'tis falling you are, Daniel," says he.

"You may say that, sir," says I.

"And where are you going all the way so fast ?" said the gander. So I told him how I had taken the drop, and how I came on the island, and how I lost my way in the bog, and how the thief of an eagle flew me up to the moon, and how the man in the moon turned me out.

"Dan," said he, "I'll save you, put out your hand and catch me by the leg, and I'll fly you home."

"Sweet is your hand in a pitcher of honey, my jewel," says I, though all the time I thought within myself that I don't much trust you; but there was no help, so I caught the gander by the leg, and away I and the other geese flew after him as fast as hops.

'We flew, and we flew, and we flew, until we came right over

Above: *Tidal pools, Ring of Kerry.*

the wide ocean. I knew it well, for I saw Cape Clear to my right hand, sticking up out of the water.

"Ah, my lord," said I to the goose, for I thought it best to keep a civil tongue in my head anyway, "fly to land, if you please."

"It is impossible, you see, Dan," said he, "for a while, because, you see, we are going to Arabia."

"To Arabia!" said I, "that's surely some place in foreign parts, far away. Oh! Mr Goose, why, then, to be sure, I'm a man to be pitied among you."

"Hold your tongue; I tell you Arabia is a very decent sort of place, as like West Carbery as one egg is like another, only there is a little more sand there."

'Just as we were talking a ship hove in sight, sailing so beautiful before the wind.

"Ah, then sir," said I, "will you drop me on the ship, if you please?"

"We are not fair over it," said he, "if I dropped you now you would go splash into the sea."

"I would not," says I, "I know better than that, for it is just clean under us, so let me drop now at once."

"If you must, you must," said he, "there, take your own way." And he opened his claw, and, faith, he was right – sure enough, I came down plump into the very bottom of the salt sea! Down to the very bottom I went, and I gave myself up, then, for ever, when a whale walked up to me, scratching himself after his night's sleep, and looked me full in the face, and never the word did he say, but, lifting up his tail, he splashed me all over again with the cold salt water till there wasn't a dry stitch upon my whole carcass ! And I heard somebody saying – 'twas a voice I knew too –"Get up, you drunken brute, off o' that"; and with that I woke up, and there was Judy with a tub full of water, which she was splashing all over me – for, rest her soul, though she was a good wife, she could never bear to see me in drink, and had a bitter hand of her own.

"Get up," said she again, "and of all places in the parish, would no place sarve your turn to lie down upon but under the ould walls of Carrigapooka? An uneasy resting I am sure you had of it."

'And, sure enough, I had, for I was fairly bothered out of my senses with eagles, and men of the moons, and flying ganders, and whales, driving me through bogs and up to the moon, and down to the bottom of the green ocean. If I was in drink ten times over, long would it be before I'd lie down in the same spot again, I know that!'

The Demon Cat

There was a woman in Connemara, the wife of a fisherman; as he had always good luck, she had plenty of fish at all times stored away in the house ready for market. But, to her great annoyance, she found that a great cat used to come in at night and devour all the best and finest fish. So she kept a big stick by her, and determined to watch. One day, as she and a woman were spinning together, the house suddenly became quite dark; and the door was burst open as if by the blast of the tempest, when a huge black cat, who went straight up to the fire, then turned round and growled at them. 'Why, surely this is the devil,' said a young girl who was by, sorting fish.

'I'll teach you to call me names,' said the cat; and, jumping at her, he scratched her arm till the blood came. 'There, now,' he said, 'you will be more civil another time when a gentleman comes to see you.' And, with that, he walked over to the door, and shut it close to prevent any of them going out, for the poor young girl, while crying loudly from fright and pain, had made a desperate rush to get away. Just then a man was going by, and, hearing the cries, he pushed open the door, and tried to get in; but the cat stood on the threshold and would let no one pass. On this the man attacked him with a stick, and gave him a sound blow; the cat, however, was more than a match in the fight, for it flew at him, and tore his face and hands so badly that the man at last took to his heels, and ran away as fast as he could.

'Now, it's time for my dinner,' said the cat, going up to examine the fish that was laid out on the tables. 'I hope the fish is good today. Now, don't disturb me, or make a fuss; I can help myself.' With that, he jumped up, and began to devour all the best fish, while he growled at the woman.

'Away out of this, you wicked beast!' she cried, giving it a blow with the tongs that would have broken its back, only it was a devil; 'out of this; no fish shall you have today!'

But the cat only grinned at her, and went on tearing and despoiling and devouring the fish, evidently not a bit the worse for the blows. On this both the women attacked it with sticks, and struck hard blows enough to kill it, on which the cat glared at them and spit fire; then, making a leap, it tore their heads and arms till the blood came, and the frightened women rushed shrieking from the house.

But presently the mistress of the house returned, carrying with her a bottle of holy water; and, looking in, she saw the cat still devouring the fish, and not minding. So she crept over quietly, and threw holy water on it without a word. No sooner was this done than a dense, black smoke filled the place, through which nothing was seen but the two red eyes of the cat burning like coals of fire. Then the smoke gradually cleared away, and she saw the body of the creature burning slowly, till it became shrivelled and black like a cinder, and finally disappeared. And from that time the fish remained untouched and safe from harm, for the power of the Evil One was broken, and the Demon Cat was seen no more.

The Kildare Pooka

A friend of mine, when he was alive, used to live a good deal in Dublin, and he was once a great while out of the country on account of the 'ninety-eight' business. But the servants kept on in the big house at Rath all the same as if the family was at home. Well, they used to be frightened out of their lives, after going to their beds, with the banging of the kitchen door and the clattering of fireirons and the pots and plates and dishes. One evening they sat up ever so long keeping one another in heart with stories about ghosts and that, when – what would you have of it? – the little scullery boy that used to be sleeping over the horses, and could not get room at the fire, crept into the hot hearth, and when he got tired listening to the stories, sorra fear him, but he fell dead asleep.

Well and good. After they were all gone, and the kitchen raked up, he was woke with the noise of the kitchen door opening, and the trampling of an ass on the kitchen floor. He peeped out, and what should he see but a big ass, sure enough, sitting on his curabingo and yawning before the fire. After a little he looked about him, and began scratching his ears as if he was quite tired, and says he, 'I may as well begin first as last.' The poor boy's teeth began to chatter in his head, for, says he, 'Now he's going to ate me'; but the fellow with the long ears and tail on him had something else to do. He stirred the fire, and then he brought in a pail of water from the pump, and filled a big pot that he put on the fire before he went out. He then put in his hand – foot, I mean – into the hearth, and pulled out the little boy. He let a roar out of him with the fright; but the pooka only looked at him, and thrust out his lower lip to show how little he valued him, and then he pitched him into his pew again.

Well, he then lay down before the fire till he heard the boil coming on the water, and maybe there wasn't a plate, or a dish, or a spoon on the dresser that he didn't fetch and put in the pot, and wash and dry the whole bilin' of 'em as well as e'er a kitchen maid from that to Dublin town. He then put all of them up on their places on the shelves; and if he didn't give a good sweepin' to the kitchen. Then he comes and sits next to the boy, let down one of his ears, and cocked up the other, and gave a grin. The poor fellow strove to roar out, but not a dheeg 'ud come out of his throat. The last thing the pooka done was to rake up the fire and walk out, giving such a slap o' the door that the boy thought the house couldn't help tumbling down.

Well, to be sure, if there wasn't a hullabuloo next morning when the poor fellow told his story! They could talk of nothing else the whole day. One said one thing, another said another, but a fat, lazy scullery girl said the wittiest thing of all. 'Musha!' says she, 'if the pooka does be cleaning up everything that way when we are asleep, what should we be slaving ourselves for doing his work?'

'*Sha gu dheine*,' says another, 'them's the wisest words you ever said, Kauth; it's meeself won't contradict you.'

So said, so done. Not a bit of a plate or dish saw a drop of water that evening, and not a besom was laid on the floor, and everyone went to bed soon after sundown. Next morning everything was as fine as fine in the kitchen, and the lord mayor might eat his dinner off the flags. It was great ease to the lazy servants, you may depend, and everything went on well till a foolhardy gag of a boy said he would stay up one night and have a chat with the pooka. He was a little daunted when the door was thrown open and the ass marched up to the fire.

'And then, sir,' says he at last, picking up courage, 'if it isn't taking a liberty, might I ask who you are, and why you are so kind as to do half of the day's work for the girls every night?'

'No liberty at all,' says the pooka, says he: 'I'll tell you, and welcome. I was a servant in the time of Squire R's father, and was the laziest rogue that ever was clothed and fed, and done nothing for it. When my time came for the other world, this is the punishment was laid on me: to come here and do all this labour every night, and then go out in the cold. It isn't so bad in the fine weather; but if you only knew what it is to stand with your head between your legs, facing the storm from midnight to sunrise, on a bleak winter night.'

'And could we do anything for your comfort, my poor fellow?' says the boy. 'Musha, I don't know,' says the pooka; 'but I think a good quilted frieze coat would help me to keep the life in me them long nights.'

'Why, then, in troth, we'd be the ungratefullest of people if we didn't feel for you.'

To make a long story short, the next night the boy was there again; and if he didn't delight the poor pooka, holding a fine warm coat before him, it's no mather! Between the pooka and the man, his legs was got into the four arms of it, and it was buttoned down the breast and the belly, and he was so pleased he walked up to the glass to see how it looked. 'Well,' says he, 'it's a long lane that has no turning. I am much obliged to you and your fellow servants. You have made me happy at last. Good night to you.'

So he was walking out, but the other cried, 'Och! sure you're going too soon. What about the washing and sweeping?'

'Ah, you may tell the girls that they must now get their turn. My punishment was to last till I was thought worthy of a reward for the way I done my duty. You'll see me no more.' And no more they did, and right sorry they were for having been in such a hurry to reward the ungrateful pooka.

Opposite: *The Twelve Bens, Co Galway.*

Below: *Full moon rising.*

19 The Religious Influence

No one knows for sure when the first Christian missionaries set foot in Ireland, but it was probably around the 4th or 5th century AD. The first mention of an Irish Church was recorded by Prosper Tiro, one of Europe's leading opponents of a 'heretic' version of Christianity called Pelagianism. Its founder, Pelagius, who lived at the end of the 4th century, rejected the idea of man's original sin and convinced his followers that everyone had an in-built desire to do good. Pelagian heresy had spread through Ireland by the time Pope Celestine sent his French deacon Palladius to stamp it out in 431AD. Prosper writes that Palladius was sent as bishop to 'the Irish who believe in Christ', a reference to all who followed the orthodox teaching.

The conversion of Ireland to Christianity was a slow process and many people still regard St Patrick, a Briton, as the man who takes most of the credit. In fact, there were many Christian settlements in the country before his mission took place sometime around the middle of the 5th century. Patrick's legacy was that he probably endured more hardship and danger than any previous Irish missionary and took his faith into areas which had remained firmly pagan. The fact that it was a time of great change — the Western Roman Empire was falling apart — perhaps helped him. His teachings seemed to offer certainty in an uncertain world.

Sadly, very little is known about Patrick himself, apart from the few snippets gleaned from his own writings. He seems to have been born in western Britain and was called either Magonus, Succetus or, later on, by the Roman name Patricius. His father was a church deacon who doubled as a local government official and the family was therefore relatively wealthy. It was most likely their country estate which singled them out as a target for the Irish raiders who at that time were pillaging Britain's western seaboard. The 16-year-old Patrick was captured and taken to Ireland as a slave. For six years he lived in the north Connacht area herding sheep but eventually escaped, walked 320km (200 miles) begging what food he could, and obtained passage back to Britain aboard a pagan-crewed ship. A love of the Irish was clearly instilled in him however for he returned later to preach the gospel. Patrick emphasises that he was by then a bishop, although it is unlikely he was sent with the Church's blessing. He seems to have been criticised by his peers as unsuitable to tackle the heathen Irish.

Patrick's stronghold became Armagh, where his local followers worked hard to foster his emergence as a saint. The town established itself as one of the most important Christian outposts of western Europe and by the 7th century Patrick's teachings had spread throughout the north-east of Ireland and into Munster.

However, the organisation of the early church was haphazard, so the organised church evolved through a number of different branches. When the first great monasteries began to spring up in the 6th century they did not claim any link to St Patrick. Instead monastic leaders such as Columba, Finian of Clonard, Ciarán of Clonmacnoise, and Brendan of Clonfert were heavily influenced by the British church. From humble beginnings as places of retreat and personal discipline they soon attracted the interest of wealthy noblemen and became influential in their own right. This form of patronage allowed literacy and the arts to flourish. A new form of art — called Hiberno-Saxon — blended the styles of the Irish, the Anglo-Saxons and the Picts and among the best-known examples is the magnificent 'Tara' brooch, dug up at Bettystown, Co Meath. Dating from the 8th century it was fashioned from gold, silver. copper, glass, enamel and amber.

The earliest Irish writing is thought to be Ogham, a system in which straight lines were cut along the edge of wood or stone. Ogham probably began to appear around the 4th century AD as Irish scholars became more familiar with Latin and Roman numerals. Ogham stones were raised across southern Ireland and the extreme west of Britain (where the Irish settled). But by the late 7th century literacy had become rather more refined as a result of monasteries turning out many Latin-trained scholars. These were men with a thorough grounding in Biblical doctrine. They used Christian tenets as a basis for common law and so began to construct the first building blocks of a civilised society.

Above: *A masonry arch at the Rock of Cashel. The fortress was handed over to the Church in 1101.*

Opposite: *The early Christian stonemasons afforded lavish attention to detail, as seen on Kells High Cross, Co Meath.*

Within the Church and the Christian land-owning classes this task was fairly straightforward. The Collectio Canonum Hibernensis of around 700AD set out the principles of internal church law, property ownership, wills, government, marriage and right of sanctuary. But among the wider population, where a belief in paganism and 'earth magic' was still rife, the church faced a much tougher mission. They got round the problem by assuring the masses that both the laws of nature and the Word of God were compatible, although it was made clear that God's law counted above all others. According to an ancient Irish legal poem:

'The law of the church is as a sea compared with streams, the law of the church is most wonderful law . . . It is known that fenechas (inherited common law) is vain in comparison with the words of God, where neither man is defrauded nor God neglected, as a result of which prosperity increases... the law of the church is founded on rocks of truth... it speaks for all conditions of persons...every grade, every kind... It binds, it is not bound; it restrains, it is not restrained; it is appealed to, it does not appeal; it overswears all, it is not oversworn; each one is ignoble compared to it, it is noble compared to all; it is a sea compared with streams.'

The Old Testament was used as a basis for Irish law but it was by no means the sole source. The monks knew that to be effective the law had to relate to people's everyday lives. For instance, Biblical doctrine on the theft of livestock was expanded to include animals that were extremely valuable to ordinary people at the time, namely the horse and the pig. Paganism was of course heresy. But where a seemingly unshakeable belief persisted in pagan gods such as Brigid and Anu, the monks performed the religious equivalent of a corporate takeover by renaming them St Brigid and St Ann and relaunching them as Christian martyrs.

The early church also took careful note of experiences elsewhere in Europe — information which flooded in from the many foreign students who travelled to Ireland in search of learning. The monks, too, set out to discover Britain and the great European powers, further spreading the image of Ireland as the cultural haven of the West. As they roamed they took note of laws tried and tested as fair in other countries. Many ideas were seized upon by the fledgling legislators at home and adapted to Irish circumstances.

Monasteries in 8th and 9th century Ireland had a very different structure to those operating today. They tended to be Christian centres which drew together a number of different churches and churchmen, plus assorted nuns, monks, priests, bishops, virgins and the plain devout. But monasteries also served as political centres for regional kings and a somewhat less holy concoction of soldiers, courtiers, royal favourites, mistresses and, probably, even prostitutes.

The abbots nominally in control of these monastic centres often became extremely rich with massive estates throughout the land. They would live the lives of kings, mixing with society names of the day and patronisng the arts. It was their taste for the trappings of wealth that so encouraged the superb metalwork, artwork and calligraphy that marks Irish culture between the 7th and 10th centuries. In churches the chalices and books shone with ornate gold and silver, the vestments of the priests glittered with minute specks of gold and no self-respecting worshipper would arrive in church without some fancy brooch or bracelet to show off. No wonder the Viking pillagers, once they discovered Ireland's treasures, kept coming back for more.

At this time the Irish Church had two main power bases. The first was Iona, an island off the Scottish coast, where Columba founded a monastery. Iona headed a large group of churches in both Ireland and Scotland and also had influence in Northumbria. Perhaps its greatest leader was the 9th abbot Adomnán (d. 704) who drew up his Law Of The Innocents. This was a religious order banning women and children from fighting in wars and protecting women from violent men.

The second great centre was Patrick's church in Armagh; here there was no monastic structure but a succession of bishops who used their links with one of the most powerful families in all Ireland, the Úi Néills, to cement their authority. By the 7th century, so sure was Armagh of its position, that it proclaimed itself the country's principal church and its bishop the primate over all other clergy. What seems clear is that each region had a bishop whose responsibility was for the pastoral care of every type of church in his domain. He would make sure buildings, altars and churchyards were well maintained and he had the power to inflict fines on elders who disobeyed his orders.

This was generally accepted, although it would be wrong to think that the churches had a clear pecking order.There were many different types; those that were 'free' — ie, owned their own lands — and those that were tenants belonging to kings, monasteries or well-off families. There were hundreds of what amounted to parish churches, the humblest of which were no more than crude buildings circled by small graveyards on some nobleman's estate. The local priest would turn up whenever he was available, although there was very often a shortage of clerics whose services were very unreliable.

The church survived, much as it does to this day, by accepting donations from the people. The Irish priests regarded this support as a duty of the laity — part of an unsigned agreement in which the clergy would provide spiritual guidance, conduct birth, marriage and death services, preach God's word, hold mass on Sundays and preside over the major religious festivals. In return worshippers were required to hand over firstlings (the first pick of a crop or harvest) and a tenth of their income, as well as pay for burials. Unsurprisingly, the priests did not always get their dues.

Previous page: *Bective Abbey from across the River Boyne, Co Meath, famous for its cloister and carvings.*

Opposite: *The beautiful Cross of the Scriptures stands in the ruins of Clonmacnoise Monastery, near the River Shannon.*

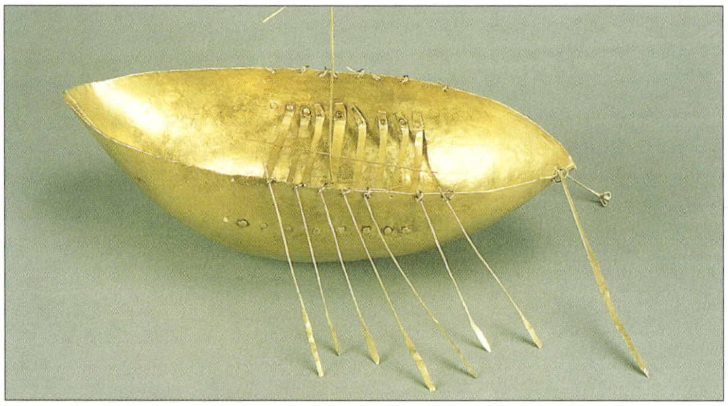

Top: *The Cross of the Scriptures, Clonmacnoise.*

Left: *A golden torc excavated at Clonmacnoise and dating from around the 3rd century BC. Great Christian centres were often founded on earlier, pagan sites.*

Above: *This 1st century AD golden boat, part of the Broighter hoard, had 15 oars, nine seats and a mast with yard arm.*

Opposite: *The Rock of Cashel was the seat of Brian Boru, self-proclaimed king of Ireland. He was crowned in 977.*

Above: *The Irish church was headed in the early years by Iona. Here the cathedral founded by St Columba in AD563 seen from the summit of Dun I, Iona's highest point, with the Isle of Mull beyond the Sound.*

Left: *Little is known about St Patrick — the patron saint of Ireland, although he was probably not the first missionary. Most stories have Patrick being kidnapped from Britain to Ireland by pirates. From here he escaped to France to study Christianity, and from there he returned in 432 to begin converting the Irish.*
Here he stands in a grotto at Faha on the Pilgrim's Route up Mount Brandon in Co Kerry.

Opposite: *St Patrick's grave in the precincts of the Protestant cathedral at Downpatrick Co Down.*

The Rock of Cashel, the seat of Brian Boru.

Ireland's rich religious heritage has produced some of the most beautiful small churches to be seen anywhere in the world.

Above: *St Dolough's, Kinsealy, Co Dublin.*

Right: *The Church of the Assumption, Ballyporeen, Co Tipperary.*

Above: *The stark outline of Baldongan Church, Co Dublin, is a landmark for walkers.*

Opposite: *The supremely elegant St Mary's Cathedral at Kilkenny, one of Ireland's oldest towns.*

20 Literature

Small though the population of Ireland might be, it has been nonetheless prolific. No self-respecting bookshelf in the English-speaking world is without a play, novel or some poetry penned by an Irish author. The tradition for weaving words is both rich and ritual and the land of leprechauns has spawned some literary giants. Consider the quality and quantity of Ireland's greatest writers: Jonathan Swift, Oliver Goldsmith, Richard Brinsley Sheridan, Oscar Wilde, George Bernard Shaw, W. B. Yeats, James Joyce and Samuel Beckett, to name but the high-flying few.

From them and the rest of an army of Irish writers came some of the most eloquent, emotive, witty and whimsical lines of the age. There was Wilde's glib quip to American customs officials: 'I have nothing to declare but my genius.' Jonathan Swift made the pointed observation that: 'Satire is a sort of glass wherein beholders do generally discover everybody's face but their own.' In an altogether more passionate mood Yeats rouses the soul when he tells how 'a terrible beauty is born'.

The tenor of Irish literature is perhaps set by the *Book of Kells*, a stunningly illuminated manuscript of the Gospels produced in the 8th century. Disciples of St Columba began the epic work on the Scottish isle of Iona but, harassed by Viking raiders, they headed for the monastery begun by their patron saint at the town of Kells in County Meath. It is there that the inspiring manuscript was allegedly completed. Although a copy resides in Kells, the original is now housed in Trinity College, Dublin, where it remains a worthy lure to tourists.

Irish mythology and folklore dominated the country's culture for centuries. But it was when English became the first language of Irish writers that international acclaim was assured, for the works reached a broader audience.

Jonathan Swift was born in Dublin in 1667. After becoming an Anglican priest in 1695 he moved to London where he became secretary to eminent diplomat Sir William Temple. Although he remained in England for 20 years he finally returned to his homeland. Back in Dublin he was dean of St Patrick's where he was buried after his death in 1745. His most remarkable work was *Gulliver's Travels* which was both a children's fantasy and a biting satire aimed at the English.

Like Swift, playwright Oliver Goldsmith was born in Dublin but moved to London via Edinburgh where he was sent to study medicine. His best known works, all written in England, are the poem 'The Deserted Village', the novel *The Vicar of Wakefield* and the play *She Stoops to Conquer*. Plagued by poverty, Goldsmith wrote ballads for the street singers of Dublin while he was a student at Trinity College. At night he would slip out of his quarters to hear them sung in the moonlight. Goldsmith was a curious dichotomy. While his flair with language was undeniable he was nevertheless inarticulate in conversation and, though artistically sensitive, he was a bullheaded, compulsive gambler. He died in 1774 aged 46.

In the same generation was playwright Richard Brinsley Sheridan. Irish-born but English raised, he carved his niche as the author of hilarious comedies of manners. In *The Rivals* in 1775 he created Mrs Malaprop, who went on to lend her name to a comical misuse of language. His other best-remembered piece is *School for Scandal*. Sheridan's impetuous youth, in which he eloped with a fashionable singer, gave way to a far more serious career in politics. As a Whig MP he was saluted as a fine orator but his early promise amounted to little which soured his outlook prior to his death in 1816.

The last half of the 19th century saw a wealth of Irish talent emerge to take the literary limelight. Oscar Wilde and George Bernard Shaw were born in the same year, 1856, with William Butler Yeats entering the world less than a decade afterwards. Before the turn of the century playwright John Millington Synge, dramatist Sean O'Casey and one of the greatest Irish writers, James Joyce, were beginning their careers. C. S. Lewis, famous as the writer of the Narnia books, was born in Belfast in 1898. This magnificent tradition was continued in the 20th century by playwright Samuel Beckett and the poets Patrick Kavanagh, Flann O'Brien and Brendan Behan. While novelist J. P. Donleavy was born in Brooklyn, New York, his parents were Irish and he was educated at Trinity College, Dublin, before becoming an Irish citizen in 1967. Oscar Wilde is perhaps the best remembered of the Irish writers – and for all the wrong reasons. When his career peaked he was embroiled in a homosexual scandal which resulted in a two year jail term and ultimately brought about his premature death.

Wilde was the son of a rogue physician, Sir William Wilde, who once was said to have a child in every farmhouse. A clinch between Sir William and a Miss Mary Josephine Travers, the daughter of a Trinity College professor, resulted in the latter accusing him of rape. When Oscar's mother, Lady Jane, wrote a letter charging Travers with blackmail a storm was unleashed. Travers decided to sue Lady Jane for libel but it was Sir William who was effectively in the dock. Details of his scandalous liaisons came pouring forth in the court. The case achieved little other than to severely besmirch the reputations of all the parties involved. Although Lady Jane's letter was deemed libellous Travers was

Opposite: *James Joyce Tower, Sandycove, Dublin. One of the many Martello towers built along the coast to defend Ireland from Napoleonic attack, it now houses a unique collection of Joyce memorabilia.*

awarded only one farthing in damages. The Wildes were compelled to meet the considerable costs of the case.

Although Oscar was only 10 when the courtroom debacle occurred, he would have done well to learn just how messy such events can be. Clearly he did not heed the lessons of history for he himself instigated the proceedings which ultimately brought about his downfall.

Wilde went to Trinity College, Dublin, and later attended Oxford where his fluid mind revealed much brilliance but little application. In a letter to a friend he spelled out his aims. 'I'll be famous, and if not famous, I'll be notorious.'

He embarked on his ambition after he moved to London to be with his mother after the death of his father. When his first poems failed to attract significant publicity, Wilde shook up Victorian fashion by donning some lavish clothes. His foppish tendencies attracted critics but Wilde revelled in the attention.

Lecture tours in America and Scotland followed as did marriage in 1894 with the graceful and elegant Constance Lloyd, the daughter of an Irish barrister. Although Wilde was already intrigued by the possibilities of sexual antics with young boys – a subject that stirred him during his study of the classics – he was deeply in love with Constance. Together they had two sons and the marriage was apparently happy.

However, two years later Wilde discovered the syphilitic infection he had contracted at Oxford had reared again. In deference to his beloved Constance he abandoned the marital bed and gave vent to the homosexual side of his nature. An attractive teenager, Robert Ross, who struck up a friendship with Wilde at about this time later claimed he was the first male partner the writer had bedded.

The change in his sexual predilections was to some extent reflected in his novel *The Picture of Dorian Gray* published in 1891. The outrageous sentiments of the hedonist Gray were closely associated with Wilde's own confessed priorities. It prompted Phillippe Jullian to remark that 'the name of Wilde became a synonym for all that was most unhealthy'. Still, his play *Lady Windermere's Fan* produced the following year was a resounding hit and brought Wilde some of the fortune that he craved.

It was Wilde's relationship with Lord Alfred Douglas that triggered his downward spiral. Douglas was the son of the Marquess of Queensberry, creator of boxing's Queensberry Rules and a Scottish eccentric. When the Marquess received a copy of a love letter written by Wilde to Douglas he went berserk. There followed a campaign of harassment by the Marquess which included haunting Wilde's house, attempting to sabotage the first night of *The Importance of Being Earnest* and sending veiled threats. On 18 February 1895 the Marquess left a card at the Abermarle, Wilde's club. Written on it were the words: 'To Oscar Wilde, posing as a somdomite (sic).'

Opposite: *Foley's 1864 statue of the famous 18th century playwright, Oliver Goldsmith, outside Trinity College, Dublin. Goldsmith, Beckett and Burke were but three Irish writers to attend Ireland's premier seat of learning.*

Wilde freely admitted that his sexual pleasure in men and boys rarely if ever involved sodomy. He consulted a solicitor and consequently decided to sue. Although Wilde performed well in the witness box it was not great chore for the defence to produce numerous young males who were ex-partners of the writer. The Marquess won the day and Wilde had laid himself open to charges of homosexuality, the practise of which was still against the law. The same day that the Marquess was acquitted a warrant was issued for Wilde's arrest on indecency charges. After a first trial the jury failed to reach agreement. However, a second trial which began on 20 May 1895 ended with a guilty verdict. Wilde was sentenced to two years' hard labour at Reading jail.

Wilde served the sentence in full. The experience nearly broke him. By the time of his release in 1897 Wilde was a shadow of the sharp-tongued bon viveur who had charmed and shocked society. 'Something is killed in me,' Wilde wrote to Robbie Ross. While he claimed the ability to write had deserted him he nevertheless produced 'The Ballad of Reading Gaol'. In it are the lines by which many still remember Wilde best:

Yet each man kills the thing he loves,
By each let this be heard,
Some do it with a bitter look,
Some with a flattering word,
The coward does it with a kiss,
The brave man with a sword!

He moved to France where he died on 30 November 1900 in cheap lodgings on the West Bank. Even in death he showed characteristic flashes of genius when he told a friend: 'I am dying beyond my means'.

Fellow playwright and author George Bernard Shaw lived more than twice as long as Wilde. When he died on 2 November 1950 at his home in Ayot St Lawrence, Hertfordshire, he was 94 years old. Like Wilde, fame and fortune did not find him out quickly. He was well into his forties before plays like *Candida* and the comedy *Man and Superman* brought him the acclaim of critics. And he was 57 years old before *Pygmalion*, his most enduring work and the inspiration for the musical *My Fair Lady*, was penned. He won the Nobel Prize for Literature in 1925 at the age of 69. Until his works attained a degree of success GBS, as he is called, was best known as a music and drama critic and a founder of the socialist Fabian Society which helped to lay the foundations of the Labour Party.

GBS was born in Dublin, the youngest of three children. His father, George Carr Shaw was a mill-owner but not a wealthy one. Any profits from the venture were drunk away by the elder Shaw and his behaviour left the family as social outcasts. GBS later recalled: 'If you asked him to a dinner or to a party he was not always quite sober when he arrived; and he was invariably scandalously drunk when he left.' Asserting that his father was a miserable drunk, he went on: 'We were finally dropped socially . . . If my mother and father had dined out or gone to a party their children would have been much more astonished than if the house had caught fire . . .'

After a spell working in a firm of land agents, GBS departed Ireland for England and drew only limited inspiration from his homeland thereafter.

William Butler Yeats was another Nobel Prize winner, beating GBS to the accolade by two years. However, Yeats was as devoted to Ireland as much as GBS was divorced from it. Yeats had started out aiming to become a painter but abandoned the canvas in favour of the written word and his first poem was published in the *Dublin University Review* in 1885. His younger brother Jack carried the mantel of family artist thereafter.

Irish nationalism was a perpetual feature of his work alongside the occult which fascinated him. The lure of magic led him to embrace the Hermetic Order of the Golden Dawn, a short-lived but influential occultist group in England. He helped to expel its ambitious leader, Aleister Crowley, also dubbed 'the beast' whose personal excesses were later laid bare in a shattering court case. Also in London he helped to fund the Rhymers Club for aspiring poets. At home in Dublin his contribution to the cause of Irish nationalism was not that of a terrorist but of a cultural guru. Along with Lady Gregory he established the Abbey Theatre which was a showcase for Irish works. He became a senator of the Irish Free State between 1922 and 1928. The third sphere of influence in his life was that of the folklore of Sligo where he spent many contemplative hours as the guest of Lady Gregory.

In his private life, Yeats was in love with the republican and actress Maud Gonne but the passion was unrequited. Although he ultimately found a relationship of mutual love much of his love poetry was inspired by Gonne.

Yeats died in the south of France in January 1939. However, in 1948 his body was brought back to Ireland for burial at Drumcliff in Sligo.

The fourth cornerstone of Irish literature at the time was James Joyce, author of *Dubliners*, the biographical *A Portrait of the Artist as a Young Man*, *Ulysses* and *Finnegan's Wake*. The last two pieces of work in particular have perplexed critics, and have a reputation for being virtually unfathomable!

James Augustine Aloysius Joyce was born in 1882 in Dublin, the eldest of 13 children. From the age of six he attended a Jesuit boarding school and, while he was there, the fortunes of his middle class family slumped. Nevertheless he continued on to University College where he grew increasingly disillusioned with the confines of the Catholic Church. While he was at university he marked out his own literary heroes – Henrik Ibsen, William Blake, Dante and Aristotle.

In 1902 he left Ireland for Paris, a pre-emptive parting for what would ultimately be a permanent exile. Although his intention was to attend medical school he in fact devoted himself to writing. He began to pen the inward-looking story of his life in the guise of a novel with the principal character, Stephen Hero. This was later re-worked into *A Portrait of the Artist as a Young Man*. During a later visit to Ireland following the death of his mother he met Nora Barnacle who, much later, would become his wife.

In 1904, the year they first met, James and Nora eloped, first visiting Austria and then Italy. Nora went on to give birth to a daughter and son, with Joyce taking poorly rewarded tutoring work to help support his family. The visits to his homeland were increasingly spasmodic. His last trip was in 1912.

When Italy joined the ranks of countries fighting against Germany during World War I Joyce moved to neutral Switzerland. He returned to Paris after the war in order to have *Ulysses*, the masterpiece he had been working on since 1914, published. It finally emerged on the day he celebrated his 40th birthday although legal complications prevented its release in England and America for a further 12 years. In the process of writing *Finnegan's Wake* Joyce was tormented by the lapse into mental illness of his daughter Lucia and his own deteriorating eyesight. The exacting epic *Finnegan's Wake* was published in the same week as the outbreak of World War 2. Its reception varied from lukewarm to hostile. To Joyce, the united voice of opposition was a body blow. If that torment was not enough, Hitler's troops began flooding into France. Joyce went first to the unoccupied south and then to Zurich where he died in January 1941, aged 58. His death came almost 30 years after he last stepped foot on Irish soil yet his work was inextricably bound up with that country, its people and vibrant atmosphere.

As we've already seen, there was a host of writers continuing to wave the flag for Ireland, among them Brendan Behan. The young Behan was undoubtedly cultured by the love of music, poetry and Ireland displayed by his parents, Stephen and Kathleen. Alas, he was also influenced by his grandmother, an eccentric drinker. She began feeding her beloved grandson on whiskey when he was just eight years old, telling his concerned mother that it would cure him of worms. Behan was regularly drunk even before he reached his teens.

Behan's biographer, Ulick O'Connor, describes the poet was affected in his work by Ireland and the Irish. 'Even their swearing was more than mere cursing; it was an orchestration of words, used musically with sense of the rhythm of language to improve the effect of their sentences. Words choicely chosen gave them the same pleasure that other might get from food or drink.'

Although a breathtakingly able pupil, Behan left school at 14 to be an apprentice painter. He took on board the hatred his Catholic family felt for the English and joined the Fianna, youth wing of the Irish Republican Army, at eight years old. He was expelled, however, apparently for being drunk on parade. Still, he spent much of his late teens and early twenties in prison on account of the rebel cause. His love of Ireland and of drink were two enormous parallels in his life. His devotion to the second killed him. Behan died in 1964 with his liver in shreds. One obituary, commenting on the 'sad waste of an enormous talent', likened his fate to that of American writer F. Scott Fitzgerald. Another alcoholic writer, Flann O'Brien, observed: 'He is in fact much more a player than a playwright, or, to use a Dublin saying, "He was as good as a play".'

Today the international emphasis remains on the English language writings of the Irish. However, there was also a crucial revival of Gaelic literature which found a vent in the Abbey Theatre under the direction of W. B. Yeats, Lady Gregory and patriotic playwright John Millington Synge.

And Irish writers still turn to their homeland for inspiration. Irish-born Roddy Doyle wrote *The Commitments*, *The Snapper* and *The Van*, all featuring remarkable reproductions of Dublin-speak. His fourth novel *Paddy Clarke Ha Ha Ha* won the 1993 Booker Prize. Maeve Binchy has also found international fame as the writer of heart-warming stories usually based in Ireland's lush countryside.

Still critics ponder about the lyrical powers of the Irish. Perhaps George Bernard Shaw came closest to explaining the phenomena when he wrote: 'An Irishman's heart is nothing but his imagination.'

Left: *Statue of W. B. Yeats in Sligo Town where he was born in 1865.*

Top: *Kerry's Poets Monument, Killarney, Co Kerry, home of authentic Irish culture.*

Above: *Bram Stoker Plaque in Kildare Street, Dublin. As all aficionados of horror will know, Bram Stoker is the author of* Dracula.

Left and Below: *On 26 July 1856 Number 33 Synge Street became the birthplace of George Bernard Shaw. Open to the public, it is an authentic recreation of a Victorian middle class home.*

Opposite: *Statue of George Bernard Shaw at the National Gallery, Dublin. One of its greatest benefactors, Shaw left a third of his estate to the gallery.*

Above and Opposite: *The Writers' Museum, Parnell Square, Dublin. An 18th century townhouse opened as a museum in 1991, it houses rare editions and mementoes of many of Ireland's finest authors.*

Left: *Bloomsday Pavement Plaque, Dublin. Named after the main character in Joyce's magnum opus —* Ulysses *— the Bloomsday festival is held annually on 16 June to celebrate the writer's extraordinary talent.*

PARNELL SQUARE

Above: *Lough Tay, Wicklow.*

Prelude

Still south I went and west and south again,
Through Wicklow from the morning till the night,
And far from cities, and the sights of men,
Lived with the sunshine, and the moon's delight.

I knew the stars, the flowers, and the birds,
The grey and wintry sides of many glens,
And did but half remember human words,
In converse with the mountains, moors, and fens.

J.M.Synge
1871-1909

Waxies Dargle

Says my aul' one to your aul' one
Will yeh come to the Waxies Dargle
Says your aul' one to my aul' one
Shure I haven't got a farthin'
I've just been down to Monto Town
To see young Kill McArdle
But he wouldn't lend me half a crown
To go to the Waxies Dargle

Chorus
What are you havin'
Will you have a pint
Yes I'll have a pint
With you sir
And if one of ye doesn't order soon
We'll be thrown out of the boozer

Says my aul' one to your aul' one
Will you come to the Galway Races
Says your aul' one to my aul' one
With the price of my aul' lad's braces
I went down to Capel Street
To the Jew man money lenders
But they wouldn't give me a
couple of bob on
My aul' lad's red suspenders

Chorus

Says my aul' one to your aul' one
We have no beef or mutton
But if we go down to Monto Town
We might get a drink for nuttin
Here's a piece of fine advice
I got from an aul' fishmonger
When food is scarce
And you see the hearse
You'll know you have died of hunger

Chorus

Anonymous

Above: *Ross Castle, Killarney.*

I Am Ireland

I am Ireland:
I am older than the Old Woman of Beare.

Great my glory:
I that bore Cuchulainn the valiant.

Great my shame:
My own children that sold their mother.

I am Ireland:
I am lonelier than the Old Woman of Beare.

Patrick Pearse
1879-1916

Above: *Celtic fertility figure on Boa Island, Lough Erne.*

Above: *Newgrange passage grave, Boyne Valley*

Deidrê's Lament for the Sons of Usnach

The lions of the hill are gone,
And I am left alone – alone –
Dig the grave both wide and deep,
For I am sick, and fain would sleep!

The falcons of the wood are flown,
And I am left alone – alone –
Dig the grave both deep and wide,
And let us slumber side by side.

The dragons of the rock are sleeping,
Sleep that wakes not for our weeping –
Dig the grave, and make it ready,
Lay me on my true-love's body.

Lay their spears and bucklers bright
By the warriors' sides aright;
Many a day the three before me
On their linkèd bucklers bore me.

Lay upon the low grave floor,
'Neath each head, the blue claymore;
Many a time the noble three
Reddened their blue blades for me.

Lay the collars, as is meet,
Of the greyhounds at their feet;
Many a time for me have they
Brought the tall red deer to bay.

In the falcon's jesses throw,
Hook and arrow, line and bow;
Never again, by stream or plain,
Shall the gentle woodsmen go.

Sweet companions, were ye ever –
Harsh to me, your sister, never;
Woods and wilds, and misty valleys,
Were with you as good's a palace.

O, to hear my true-love singing,
Sweet as sounds of trumpets ringing;
Like the sway of ocean swelling
Rolled his deep voice round our dwelling.

O! to hear the echos pealing
Round our green and fairy shealing
When the three, with soaring chorus,
Passed the silent skylark o'er us

Echo now, sleep morn and even –
Lark alone enchant the heaven!
Ardan's lips are scant of breath,
Neesa's tongue is cold in death.

Stag, exult on glen and mountain –
Salmon, leap from loch to fountain –
Heron, in the free air warm ye –
Usnach's sons no more will harm ye!

Erin's stay no more you are,
Rulers of the ridge of war;
Never more 'twill be your fate
To keep the beam of battle straight.

Woe is me! by fraud and wrong,
Traitors false and tyrants strong,
Fell Clan Usnach, bought and sold,
For Barach's feast and Conor's gold!

Woe to Eman, roof and wall!
Woe to Red Branch, hearth and hall! –
Tenfold woe and black dishonour
To the foul and false Clan Conor!

Dig the grave both wide and deep,
Sick I am, and fain would sleep!
Dig the grave and make it ready,
Lay me on my true-loves's body

Samuel Ferguson
1810-1886
His translation from ancient Erse

Herring is King

Let all the fish that swim the sea,
  Salmon and turbot, cod and ling,
Bow down the head and bend the knee
  To herring, their king! to herring, their king!

    Sing, Hugamar féin and sowra lin',
    'Tis we have brought the summer in.[1]

The sun sank down so round and red
  Upon the bay, upon the bay;
The sails shook idly overhead,
  Becalmed we lay; becalmed we lay;

    Sing, Hugamar féin and sowra lin',
    'Tis we have brought the summer in.

Till Shawn the eagle dropped on deck,
  The bright-eyed boy, the bright-eyed boy;
'Tis he has spied your silver track,
  Herring, our joy, herring, our joy;

    Sing, Hugamar féin and sowra lin',
    'Tis we have brought the summer in.

Above: *Ballyvaghan, Co Clare.*

Above: *Ballyvaghan, Co Clare.*

It is in with the sails and away to shore,
With the rise and swing, the rise and swing
Of two stout lads at each smoking oar,
After herring, our king! herring, our king.

Sing, Hugamar féin an sowra lin'
'Ti we have brought the summer in!

The Manx and Cornish raised the shout,
And joined the chase, and joined the chase ;
But their fleets they fouled as they went about,
And we won the race, we won the race;

Sing, Hugamar féin an sowra lin'
'Tis we have brought the summer in!

For we turned and faced you full to land,
Down the góleen long, the góleen long,
And after you slipped from strand to strand
Our nets so strong, our nets so strong;

Sing, Hugamar féin an sowra lin'
'Tis we have brought the summer in!

Then we called to our sweethearts and our wives,
'Come welcome us home, welcome us home,'
Till they ran to meet us for their lives
Into the foam, into the foam;

Sing, Hugamar féin an sowra lin'
'Tis we have brought the summer in!

O kissing of hands and waving of caps
From girl and boy, from girl and boy,
While you leapt by scores in the lasses' laps,
Herring our joy, herring our joy!

Sing, Hugamar féin an sowra lin'
'Tis we have brought the summer in!

Alfred Percival Graves
1846-1931

Above: *Ballyvaghan, Co Clare.*

I Saw From the Beach

I saw from the beach, when the morning was shining,
  A bark o'er the waters move gloriously on;
I came when the sun from that beach was declining,
  The bark was still there, but the waters were gone.

And such is the fate of our life's early promise,
  So passing the spring-tide of joy we have known;
Each wave, that we danc'd on at morning, ebbs from us,
  And leaves us, at eve, on the bleak shore alone.

Ne'er tell me of glories, serenely adorning
  The close of our day, the calm eve of our night; –
Give me back, give me back the wild freshness of Morning,
  Her clouds and her tears are worth Evening's best light.

Thomas Moore
1779-1852

Above: *Statue of St Brendan, Bantry harbour.*

Above: *The north coast of Clare.*

Phil the Fluther's Ball

Have you heard of Phil the Fluther, of the town of Ballymuck?
The times were going hard with him, in fact the man was bruk',
So he just sent out a notice to his neighbours, one and all,
As how he'd like their company that ev'ning at a ball.
And when writin' out he was careful to suggest to them,
That if they found a hat of his convaniant to the dure,
The more they put in, whenever he requested them,
'The better would the music be for battherin' the flure.'

Chorus
With the toot of the flute,
And the twiddle of the fiddle, O'
Hopping in the middle, like a herrin' on a griddle, O'
Up, down, hands a-rown'
Crossin' to the wall,
Oh! hadn't we the gaiety at Phil the Fluther's Ball!

There was Misther Denis Dogherty, who kep' 'The Runnin' Dog'
There was little crooked Paddy from the Tiraloughett bog:
There were boys from every Barony, and girls from every 'art,'
And the beautiful Miss Bradys, in a private ass an' cart.
And along with them came bouncing Mrs. Cafferty,
Little Micky Mulligan was also to the fore,
Rose, Suzanne, and Margaret O'Rafferty,
The flower of Ardmagullion, and the Pride of Pethravore.

Chorus

First little Micky Mulligan got up to show them how,
And then the widda' Cafferty steps out and makes her bow.
'I could dance you off your legs,' sez she, 'as sure as you are born,
If ye'll only make the piper play "the hare was in the corn".'
So, Phil plays up to the best of his ability,
The lady and the gentleman begin to do their share;
Faith, then Mick, it's you that has agility!
Begorra! Mrs. Cafferty, yer leppin' like a hare!

Chorus

Then Phil the Fluther tipped a wink to little crooked Pat,
'I think it's nearly time,' sez he, 'for passin' round the hat.'
So Paddy passed the caubeen round, and looking mighty cute,
Sez, 'Ye've got to pay the piper when he toothers on the flute.'
Then all joined in wid the greatest joviality,
Covering the buckle and the shuffle, and the cut;
Jigs were danced, of very finest quality,
But the Widda bet the company at 'handeling the fut.'

Percy French
1854-1920

Under the Round Tower

'Although I'd lie lapped up in linen
A deal I'd sweat and little earn
If I should live as live the neighbours,'
Cried the beggar, Billy Byrne;
'Stretch bones till the daylight come
On great-grandfather's battered tomb.'

Upon a grey old battered tombstone
In Glendalough beside the stream,
Where the O'Byrnes and Byrnes are buried,
He stretched his bones and fell in a dream
Of sun and moon that a good hour
Bellowed and pranced in the round tower;

Of golden king and silver lady,
Bellowing up and bellowing round,
Till toes mastered a sweet measure,
Mouth mastered a sweet sound,
Prancing round and prancing up
Until they pranced upon the top.

That golden king and that wild lady
Sang till stars began to fade,
Hands gripped in hands, toes close together,
Hair spread on the wind they made;
That lady and that golden king
Could like a brace of blackbirds sing.

'It's certain that my luck is broken,'
That rambling jailbird Billy said;
'Before nightfall I'll pick a pocket
And snug it in a feather-bed.
I cannot find the peace of home
On great-grandfather's battered tomb.'

W.B. Yeats
1865-1939

Above: *The Round Tower, Glendalough, Co Wicklow.*

Right: *View from the Wicklow Way down onto the ancient monastic city at Glendalough.*

The Celts

Long, long ago, beyond the misty space
  Of twice a thousand years,
In Erin old there dwelt a mighty race,
  Taller than Roman spears;
Like oaks and towers they had a giant grace,
  Were fleet as deers,
With wind and waves they made their 'biding place,
  These western shepherd seers.

Their Ocean-God was Manannan MacLir,
  Whose angry lips,
In their white foam, full often would inter
  Whole fleets of ships;
Cromah their Day-God, and their Thunderer
  Made morning and eclipse;
Bride was their Queen of Song, and unto her
  They prayed with fire-touched lips.

Great were their deeds, their passions and their sports;
  With clay and stone
They piled on strath and shore those mystic forts,
  Not yet o'erthrown;
On cairn-crowned hills they held their council-courts;
  While youths alone,
With giant dogs, explored the elk resorts,
  And bought them down.

Of these was Finn, the father of the Bard
  Whose ancient song
Over the clamor of all change is heard,
  Sweet-voiced and strong.
Finn once o'ertook Grania, the golden-haired,
  The fleet and young;
From her the lovely, and from him the feared,
  The primal poet sprung.

Ossian! two thousand years of mist and change
  Surround thy name –
Thy Fenian heroes now no longer range
  The hills of fame.
The very names of Finn and Gaul sound strange –
  Yet thine the same –
By miscalled lake and desecrated grange –
  Remains, and shall remain!

The Druid's altar and the Druid's creed
  We scarce can trace,
There is not left an undisputed deed
  Of all your race,
Save your majestic song, which hath their speed,
  And strength and grace
In that sole song, they live and love, and bleed –
  It bears them on through space.

O, inspired giant! shall we e'er behold,
  In our own time,
One fit to speak your spirit on the wold,
  Or seize your rhyme?
One pupil of the past, as mighty-souled
  As in the prime,
Were the fond, fair, and beautiful, and bold –
  They of your song sublime!

Thomas D'Arcy McGee
1825-1868

Above: *The prehistoric fortress of Grianan of Aileach by the River Foyle, Donegal.*

Above: *Roscommon Castle, Co Roscommon.*

The Harp That Once Through Tara's Halls

The harp that once through Tara's halls
The soul of music shed,
Now hangs as mute on Tara's walls
As if that soul were fled.
So sleeps the pride of former days,
So glory's thrill is o'er,
And hearts that once beat high for praise,
Now feel that pulse no more!

No more to chiefs and ladies bright
The harp of Tara swells;
The chord alone that breaks at night,
Its tale of ruin tells.
Thus Freedom now so seldom wakes,
The only throb she gives
Is when some heart indignant breaks,
To show that still she lives.

Thomas Moore
1779-1852

Dark Rosaleen

O my Dark Rosaleen,
  Do not sigh, do not weep!
The priests are on the ocean green,
  They march along the Deep.
There's wine. . . from the royal Pope
  Upon the ocean green;
And Spanish ale shall give you hope,
  My Dark Rosaleen!
  My own Rosaleen!
Shall glad your heart, shall give you hope,
Shall give you health, and help, and hope,
  My Dark Rosaleen.

Over hills and through dales
  Have I roamed for your sake;
All yesterday I sailed with sails
  On river and on lake.
The Erne. . . at its highest flood
  I dashed across unseen,
For there was lightening in my blood,
  My Dark Rosaleen!
  My own Rosaleen!
Oh! there was lightening in my blood,
Red lightning lightened through my blood,
  My Dark Rosaleen!

All day long in unrest
  To and fro do I move,
The very soul within my breast
  Is wasted for you, love!
The heart . . . in my bosom faints
  To think of you, my Queen,
My life of life, my saint of saints,
  My Dark Rosaleen!
  My own Rosaleen!
To hear your sweet and sad complaints,
My life, my love, my saint of saints,
  My Dark Rosaleen!

Woe and pain, pain and woe,
  Are my lot night and noon,
To see your bright face clouded so,
  Like to the mournful moon.
But yet . . .will I rear your throne
  Again in golden sheen;
'Tis you shall reign, shall reign alone,
  My Dark Rosaleen!
  My own Rosaleen!
'Tis you shall have the golden throne,
'Tis you shall reign, and reign alone,
  My Dark Rosaleen!

Over dews, over sands
  Will I fly for your weal;
Your holy delicate white hands
  Shall girdle me with steel.
At home . . .in your emerald bowers,
  From morning's dawn till e'en,
You'll pray for me, my flower of flowers,
  My Dark Rosaleen!
  My fond Rosaleen!
You'll think of me through Daylight's hours,
My virgin flower, my flower of flowers,
  My Dark Rosaleen!

I could scale the blue air,
  I could plough the high hills,
Oh, I could kneel all night in prayer,
  To heal your many ills!
And one . . . beamy smile from you
  Would float like light between
My toils and me, my own, my true,
  My Dark Rosaleen!
  My fond Rosaleen!
Would give me life and soul anew,
A second life, a soul anew,
  My Dark Rosaleen!

O! the Erne shall run red
  With redundance of blood,
The earth shall rock beneath our tread,
  And flames wrap hill and wood,
And gun-peal, and slogan cry,
  Wake many a glen serene,
Ere you shall fade, ere you shall die,
  My Dark Rosaleen!
  My own Rosaleen!
The Judgement Hour must first be nigh,
Ere you can fade, ere you can die,
  My Dark Rosaleen!

James Clarence Mangan
1803-1849

The Dark Man

Rose o' the world,she came to my bed
And changed the dreams of my heart and head:
For joy of mine she left grief of hers
And garlanded me with the prickly furze.

Rose o' the world, they go out and in,
And watch me dream and my mother spin:
And they pity the tears on my sleeping face
While my soul's away in a fairy place.

Rose o' the world, they have words galore,
For wide's the swing of my mother's door:
And soft they speak of my darkened brain,
But what do they know of my heart's dear pain?

Rose o' the world, the grief you give
Is worth all days that a man may live :
Is worth all prayers that the colleens say
On the night that darkens the wedding-day.

Rose o' the world, what man would wed
When he might remember your face instead?
Might go to his grave with the blessed pain
Of hungering after your face again?

Rose o' the world, they may talk their fill,
But dreams are good, and my life stands still
While the neighbours talk by their fires astir:
But my fiddle knows: and *I* talk to her.

Nora Hopper

Above: *Keem Strand, Achill Island.*

Opposite: *Near the meeting of the Waters, Killarney.*

On Behalf of Some Irishmen Not Followers of Tradition

They call us aliens, we are told,
Because our wayward visions stray
From that dim banner they unfold,
The dreams of worn-out yesterday.
The sum of all the past is theirs,
The creeds, the deeds, the fame, the name,
Whose death-created glory flares
And dims the spark of living flame.
They weave the necromancer's spell,
And burst the graves where martyrs slept,
Their ancient story to retell,
Renewing tears the dead have wept.
And they would have us join their dirge,
This worship of an extinct fire
In which they drift beyond the verge
Where races all outworn expire.
The worship of the dead is not
A worship that our hearts allow,
Though every famous shade were wrought
With woven thorns above the brow.
We fling our answer back in scorn:
'We are less children of this clime
Than of some nation yet unborn
Or empire in the womb of time.
We hold the Ireland in the heart
More than the land our eyes have seen,
And love the goal for which we start
More than the tale of what has been.'

The generations as they rise
May live the life men lived before,
Still hold the thought once held as wise,
Go in and out by the same door.
We leave the easy peace it brings:
The few we are shall still unite
In fealty to unseen kings
Or unimaginable light.
We would no Irish sign efface,
But yet our lips would gladlier hail
The firstborn of the Coming Race
Than the last splendour of the Gael.
No blazoned banner we unfold -
One charge alone we give to youth,
Against the sceptred myth to hold
The golden heresy of truth.

George Russell ('AE')
1867-1935

Above: *Derryclare Lough, Connemara.*

Above: *Turf cutting, Connemara.*

Ireland

'Twas the dream of a God,
        And the mould of His hand,
That you shook 'neath His stroke,
        That you trembled and broke
To this beautiful land.

Here He loosed from His hold
        A brown tumult of wings,
Till the wind on the sea
        Bore the strange melody
Of an island that sings.

He made you all fair,
        You in purple and gold,
You in silver and green,
        Till no eye that has seen
Without love can behold.

I have left you behind
        In the path of the past,
With the white breath of flowers,
        With the best of God's hours,
I have left you at last.

Dora Sigerson
1866-1918

The Stolen Child

Where dips the rocky highland
  Of Sleuth Wood in the lake,
There lies a leafy island
  Where flapping herons wake
The drowsy water-rats.
There we've hid our fairy vats
Full of berries,
And of reddest stolen cherries.
Come away, O, human child!
To the woods and waters wild
With a fairy hand in hand,
For the world's more full of weeping than you can understand.

Where the wave of moonlight glosses
  The dim grey sands with light,
Far off by farthest Rosses
  We foot it all the night,
Weaving olden dances,
Mingling hands, and mingling glances,
  Till the moon has taken flight;

To and fro we leap,
  And chase the frothy bubbles,
  While the world is full of troubles.
And is anxious in its sleep.
Come away! O, human child!
To the woods and waters wild,
With a fairy hand in hand,
For the world's more full of weeping than you can understand.

Where the wandering water gushes
  From the hills above Glen-Car,
In pools among the rushes,
  That scarce could bathe a star,
We seek for slumbering trout,
  And whispering in their ears;
    We give them evil dreams,
Leaning softly out
  From ferns that drop their tears
    Of dew on the young streams.
Come! O, human child!
To the woods and waters wild,
With a fairy hand in hand,
For the world's more full of weeping than you can understand.

Away with us, he's going,
  The solemn-eyed;
He'll hear no more the lowing
  Of the calves on the warm hill-side.
Or the kettle on the hob
  Sing peace into his breast;
Or see the brown mice bob
  Round and round the oatmeal chest.
For he comes, the human child,
To the woods and waters wild,
With a fairy hand in hand,
For the world's more full of weeping than he can understand.

W.B.Yeats
1865-1939

Above: *Lough Tay, Co Wicklow.*

Above: *O'Brian's Tower, Cliffs of Moher, Co Clare.*

Under the Moon

I have no happiness in dreaming of Brycelinde,
Nor Avalon the grass-green hollow, nor Joyous Isle,
Where one found Lancelot crazed and hid him for a while;
Nor Ulad, when Naoise had thrown a sail upon the wind;
Nor lands that seem too dim to be burdens on the heart:
Land-under-Wave, where out of the moon's light and the sun's
Seven old sisters wind the threads of the long-lived ones,
Land-of-the-Tower, where Aengus has thrown the gates apart,
And Wood-of-Wonders, where one kills an ox at dawn,
To find it when night falls laid on a golden bier.
Therein are many queens like Branwen and Guinevere;
And Niamh and Laban and Fand, who could change to an otter or fawn,
And the wood-woman, whose lover was changed to a blue-eyed hawk;
And whether I go in my dreams by woodland, or dun, or shore,
Or on the unpeopled waves with kings to pull at the oar,
I hear the harp-string praise them, or hear their mournful talk.
Because of something told under the famished horn
Of the hunter's moon, that hung between the night and the day,
To dream of women whose beauty was folded in dismay,
Even in an old story, is a burden not to be borne.

W.B.Yeats
1865-1939

The Northern Coast

The fields of home for me as a child were the dairy pastures of an Irish farm. A river of salmon and trout ran to the north and my window looked north over the whiskey distillery of Bushmills to the stepped headlands of the Giant's Causeway and beyond to the grey Atlantic. On still September evenings the river mist filled the valley above the church and carried the tumble of water from where a mill race turned a wheel. In the old tongue the river name meant 'the stream of the bursting torrents'. On its banks dwelt the poet Amergin, favourite of the high kings of Ireland, who sang of heroes and listened to the salmon.

These small things I learned as a child.

On sharp winter nights I had my father's work tending cattle in must-sweet byres. Barley straw for bedding. (Some of the neighbours grew barley for the distillery. Some, more mindful of mortal sin, thought that wasn't right.) Outside, the cold constellations astride the vast sky held me in thrall.

One winter a neighbour's tractor wheel split the capstone of a buried cist. A grave untended for 3,000 years opened to the sky. My grandfather led me to where rings of ancient trees hid neglected dolmens twenty times as old as the trees.

At school they taught us victors' names and dates, the profits of empires in tonnes of bananas, and the dry balancing of mathematical equations empty on either side. A mile down the road from he classroom, the seamen's cottages lined the shore. They were strangers who talked with foreign-sounding words like 'glashen' and 'gurnet'. Farmers eat salt fish no more than fishermen gather potatoes. Two miles from the sea, I never learned to swim, but I could stand for hours in the dark theatre of sea cliffs watching the grey swell breathing under a heavy moon.

I asked my teacher why the sea was blue. She told me it reflected the sky. I asked her why the sky is blue. I think I first left my home and my fields to find out why the sky was blue.

In all our lives we grow to recognise ourselves more certainly year by year. We learn what simple things give us pleasure and how their absence leads to illness, pain or anger. Our forefathers, neighbour by neighbour, also knew these simple things, the essentials of contentment, knew them through necessity for without them they quite literally could not live.

They understood their seasons, they understood their soils, their crops, and they understood that their lives were inseparably connected with them. Their own daily lives were made their songs, and their dances weaved through harvest sheaves where young-blood feuds and romances were encompassed within a village hall. Their first ancestors marked the spoor of deer they hunted and knew the woodland glades where elderberry, blackberry and hazelnuts grew, and measured the days until each returned in their different seasons. In the memories of our own families often our lives have been lived in different fields again where the soil has been hidden by concrete and we have measured our days and sold them by the hours of a factory clock.

Now, from my window, on the steady land the plough returns each time to the headrig and turns. Shallow scratches approved by their straightness each harvest erased with cutting bars and threshers with the sweet smell of tea in the tin can. Bleak runnels in cold November rain seep to sheughs that swell and flood the river meadows. The people of this place, we dip our mills in the river and grind from the stone what we can. Running up the headland the blast from the dangerous sea holds me braced above the cliff while below the edge of the vast ocean plunders the basalt rock. Between the black cliffs and the white cliffs, the glorious, plunging waves drown the wails of Cuchulainn over his slain son, dead by his own red hand; drown the saintly prayers of Patrick on high Dunseverick's rock; drown the splintering of the Armada treasure on the black dykes of Port na Spaniagh; drown the shrieks from grand Dunluce as the banqueting hall slides below the air; drown the cries from Casement's soul, still lost in Murlough Bay; drown the rantings and ravings and the bullet cracks and all giants and the little men are tangled, thrashed upon the shore. And as I count toward the seventh wave the quiet deep salmon move home across the cold Atlantic toward the mouth of the River Bush and, amongst the fields we know, four white swans alight on the water meadow and we wait for them to sing.

Above: *Dunluce Castle, Co Antrim.*

Above: *The Giant's Causeway, Co Antrim.*

The Fairy Thorn (an Ulster Ballad)

'Get up, our Anna dear, from the weary spinning-wheel;
For your father's on the hill, and your mother is asleep:
Come up above the crags, and we'll dance a highland reel
Around the fairy thorn on the steep.'

At Anna Grace's door 'twas thus the maidens cried,
Three merry maidens fair in kirtles of the green;
And Anna laid the rock and the weary wheel aside,
The fairest of the four, I ween.

They're glancing through the glimmer of the quiet eve,
Away in milky wavings of neck and ankle bare;
The heavy-sliding stream in its sleepy song they leave,
And the crags in the ghostly air:

And linking hand and hand, and singing as they go,
The maids along the hill-side have ta'en their fearless way,
Till they come to where the rowan trees in lonely beauty grow
Beside the Fairy Hawthorn grey.

The Hawthorn stands between the ashes tall and slim,
Like matron with her twin grand-daughters at her knee;
The rowan berries cluster o'er her low head grey and dim
In ruddy kisses sweet to see.

The merry maidens four have ranged them in a row,
Between each lovely couple a stately rowan stem,
And away in mazes wavy, like skimming birds they go,
Oh, never caroll'd bird like them!

But solemn is the silence of the silvery haze
That drinks away their voices in echoless repose,
And dreamily the evening has still'd the haunted braes,
And dreamier the gloaming grows.

And sinking one by one, like lark-notes from the sky
When the falcon's shadow saileth across the open shaw,
Are hush'd the maidens' voices, as cowering down they lie
In the flutter of their sudden awe.

Above: *Glenariff, Co Antrim.*

Above: *Glenariff, Co Antrim.*

For, from the air above, and the grassy ground beneath,
And from the mountain-ashes and the old whitethorn between,
A Power of faint enchantment doth through their beings breathe,
And they sink down together on the green.

They sink together silent, and stealing side to side,
They fling their lovely arms o'er their drooping necks so fair,
Then vainly strive again their naked arms to hide,
For their shrinking necks again are bare.

Thus clasp'd and prostrate all, with their heads together bow'd,
Soft o'er their bosoms' beating - the only human sound -
They hear the silky footsteps of the silent fairy crowd,
Like a river in the air, gliding round.

No scream can any raise, nor prayer can any say,
But wild, wild, the terror of the speechless three-
For they feel fair Anna Grace drawn silently away,
By whom they dare not look to see.

They feel their tresses twine with her parting locks of gold,
And the curls elastic falling, as her head withdraws;
They feel her sliding arms from their tranced arms unfold,
But they may not look to see the cause:

For heavy on their senses the faint enchantment lies
Through all that night of anguish and perilous amaze;
And neither fear nor wonder can ope their quivering eyes
Or their limbs from the cold ground raise,

Till out of night the earth has roll'd her dewy side,
With every haunted mountain and streamy vale below;
When, as the mist dissolves in the yellow morning tide,
The maidens' trance dissolveth so.

Then fly the ghastly three as swiftly as they may,
And tell their tale of sorrow to anxious friends in vain -
They pined away and died within the year and day,
And ne'er was Anna Grace seen again.

Samuel Ferguson
1810-1886

Cuchullin in his Chariot

'What is the cause of thy journey or thy story?'

The cause of my journey and my story
The men of Erin, yonder, as we see them,
Coming towards you on the plain.
The chariot on which is the fold, figured and cerulean,
Which is made strongly, handy, solid;
Where were active, and where were vigorous;
And where were full-wise, the noble hearted folk;
In the prolific, faithful city; –
Fine, hard, stone-bedecked, well-shafted;
Four large-chested horses in that splendid chariot;
Comely, frolicsome.

'What do we see in that chariot?'

The white-bellied, white-haired, small-eared,
Thin-sided, thin-hoofed, horse-large, steed-large horses;
With fine, shining, polished bridles;
Like a gem; or like red sparkling fire; –
Like the motion of a fawn, wounded;
Like the rustling of a loud wind in winter; –
Coming to you in that chariot. –

'What do we see in that chariot?'

We see in that chariot,
The strong, broad-chested, nimble, gray horses, –
So mighty, so broad-chested, so fleet, so choice; –
Which would wrench the sea skerries from the rocks. –
The lively, shielded, powerful horses; –
So mettlesome, so active, so clear-shining; –
Like the talon of an eagle 'gainst a fierce beast;
Which are called the beautiful Large-Gray –
The fond, large Meactroigh.

'What do we see in that chariot?'

We see in that chariot,
The horses; which are white-headed, white-hoofed, slender-legged,
Fine-haired, sturdy, imperious;
Satin-bannered, wide chested;
Small-aged, small-haired, small-eared;
Large-hearted, large-shaped, large-nostriled;
Slender-waisted, long-bodied, – and they are foal-like;
Handsome, playful, brilliant, wild-leaping;
Which are called the Dubh-Seimhlinn.

'Who sits in that chariot?'

He who sits in that chariot,
Is the warrior, able, powerful, well-worded,
Polished, brilliant, very graceful. –
There are seven sights on his eye;
And we think that that is good vision to him;
There are six bony, fat fingers,
On each hand that comes from his shoulder;
There are seven kinds of fair hair on his head; –
Brown hair next his head's skin,
And smooth red hair over that;
And fair-yellow hair, of the colour of gold;
And clasps on the top, holding it fast; –
Whose name is Cuchullin, Seimh-suailte,
Son of Aodh, son of Agh, son of other Aodh. –
His face is like red sparkles; –
Fast-moving on the plain like mountain fleet-mist;
Or like the speed of a hill hind;
Or like a hare on rented level ground. –
It was a frequent step – a fast step – a joyful step; –
The horses coming towards us:
Like snow hewing the slopes; –
The panting and the snorting,
Of the horses coming towards thee.

Ancient Erse

Above: *White Park Bay, Co Antrim.*

Above: *The Cliffs of Moher, Co Clare.*

Ossian Sang

Sweet is the voice in the land of gold,
And sweeter the music of birds that soar,
When the cry of the heron is heard on the wold,
And the waves break softly on Bundatrore.

Down floats on the murmuring of the breeze
The call of the cuckoo from Cossahun,
The blackbird is warbling among the trees,
And soft is the kiss of the warming sun.

The cry of the eagle of Assaroe
O'er the court of Mac Morne to me is sweet,
And sweet is the cry of the bird below
Where the wave and the wind and the tall cliff meet.

Finn mac Cool is the father of me,
Whom seven battalions of Fenians fear:
When he launches his hounds on the open lea
Grand is their cry as they rouse the deer.

Old Gaelic

The Death-Song of Ossian

Such were the words of the bards in the days of song; when the king heard the music of harps, the tales of other times! The chiefs gathered from all their hills, and heard the lovely sound. They praised the Voice of Cona! The first among a thousand bards! But age is now on my tongue; my soul has failed! I hear, at times, the ghosts of the bards, and learn their pleasant song. But memory fails on my mind. I hear the call of years! They say, as they pass along, why does Ossian sing? Soon shall he lie in the narrow house, and no bard shall raise his fame! Roll on, ye dark-brown years; ye bring no joy on your course! Let the tomb open to Ossian, for his strength has failed. The sons of song are gone to rest. My voice remains, like a blast, that roars, lonely, on a sea-surrounded rock, after the winds are laid. The dark moss whistles there; the distant mariner sees the waving trees!

Ossian
Old Gaelic

Above: *Ossian's Grave, Glennan, Co Antrim.*

Above: *Pub musicians, Bantry, Co Cork.*

Ode

We are the music-makers
And we are the dreamers of dreams,
Wandering by lone sea-breakers,
And sitting by desolate streams; –
World-losers and world-forsakers,
On whom the pale moon gleams:
Yet we are the movers and shakers
Of the world for ever, it seems.

With wonderful deathless ditties
We build up the world's great cities,
And out of a fabulous story
We fashion an empire's glory:
One man with a dream, at pleasure,
Shall go forth and conquer a crown;
And three with a new song's measure
Can trample an empire down.

We, in the ages lying
In the buried past of the earth
Built Nineveh with our sighing,
And Babel itself with our mirth;
And o'erthrew them with prophesying,
To the old of the new world's worth;
For each age is a dream that is dying,
Or one that is coming to birth

Arthur O'Shaughnessy
1844-1881

Above: *Slea Head, Co Kerry.*

The Fiddler of Dooney

When I play on my fiddle in Dooney,
Folk dance like a wave of the sea;
My cousin is priest in Kilvarnet,
My brother in Mocharabuiee.

I passed my brother and cousin:
They read in their books of prayer;
I read in my book of songs
I bought at the Sligo fair.

When we come at the end of time
To Peter sitting in state,
He will smile on the three old spirits,
But call me first through the gate;

For the good are always the merry,
Save by an evil chance,
And the merry love the fiddle,
And the merry love to dance:

And when the folk there spy me,
They will all come up to me,
With 'Here is the fiddler of Dooney!'
And dance like a wave of the sea.

W.B.Yeats
1865-1939

Columcille Cecenit

O, Son of my God, what a pride, what a pleasure
To plough the blue sea!
The waves of the fountain of deluge to measure
Dear Eiré to thee.

We are rounding Moy-n-Olurg, we sweep by its head, and
We plunge through Loch Foyle,
Whose swans could enchant with their music the dead, and
Make pleasure of toil.

The host of the gulls come with joyous commotion
And screaming and sport,
I welcome my own 'Dewy-Red' * from the ocean
Arriving in port.

O Eiré, were wealth my desire, what a wealth were
To gain far from thee,
In the land of the stranger, but there even health were
A sickness to me!

Alas for the voyage O high King of Heaven
Enjoined upon me,
For that I on the red plain of bloody Cooldrevin
Was present to see.

How happy the son is of Dima ; no sorrow
For him is designed,
He is having, this hour, round his own hill in Durrow
The wish of his mind.

The sounds of the winds in the elms, like the strings of
A harp being played,
The note of the blackbird that claps with the wings of
Delight in the glade.

With him in Ros-Grencha the cattle are lowing
At earliest dawn,
On the brink of the summer the pigeons are cooing
And doves in the lawn

Three things am I leaving behind me, the very
Most dear that I know,
Tir-Leedach I'm leaving, and Durrow and Derry,
Alas I must go!

Yet my visit and feasting with Comgall have eased me
At Cainneach's right hand,
All but thy government, Eiré, has pleased me,
Thou waterfall land.

* Dearg-dreúchtach, 'Dewy-Red' - was the name of St Columba's boat.

St Columcille

Above: *The Mussenden Temple over Magilligan Strand to Inishowen.*

Above: *Belfarsad, Co Mayo.*

By the Margin of the Great Deep

When the breath of twilight blows to flame the misty skies,
All its vaporous sapphire, violet glow and silver gleam,
With their magic flood me through the gateway of the eyes;
    I am one with the twilight's dream.

When the trees and skies and fields are one in dusky mood,
Every heart of man is rapt within the mother's breast:
Full of peace and sleep and dreams in the vasty quietude,
    I am one with their hearts at rest.

From our immemorial joys of hearth and home and love
Strayed away along the margin of the unknown tide,
All its reach of soundless calm can thrill me far above
    Word or touch from the lips beside.

Aye, and deep and deep and deeper let me drink and draw
From the olden fountain more than light or peace or dream,
Such primeval being as o'erfills the heart with awe,
    Growing one with its silent stream.

George Russell ('AE')
1867-1935

The Fair Hills of Ireland

A plenteous place is Ireland for hospitable cheer,
Uileacan dubh O!
Where the wholesome fruit is bursting from the yellow barley ear;
Uileacan dubh O!
There is honey in the trees where her misty vales expand,
And her forest paths, in summer, are by falling waters fann'd,
There is dew at high noontide there, and springs i'the yellow sand,
On the fair hills of holy Ireland.

Curl'd he is and ringletted, and plaited to the knee,
Uileacan dubh O!
Each captain who comes sailing across the Irish sea;
Uileacan dubh O!
And I will make my journey, if life and health but stand,
Unto that pleasant country, that fresh and fragrant strand,
And leave your boasted braveries, your wealth and high command,
For the fair hills of holy Ireland.

Large and profitable are the stacks upon the ground,
Uileacan dubh O!
The butter and the cream do wondrously abound,
Uileacan dubh O!
The cresses on the water and the sorrels are at hand,
And the cuckoo's calling daily his note of mimic bland,
And the bold thrush sings so bravely his song i'the forests grand,
On the fair hills of holy Ireland.

Samuel Ferguson
1810-1886
(Old Irish Song)

Above: *Glengariff Harbour and the Caha Mountains, Co Cork.*

21 Music and Dance

Think of Irish music and the image of a frantic fiddler, chin down, skipping across the strings with bow and dexterous fingers looms large in the mind.

The audience are torn between listening in wonder at the skill and speed of the musician and jumping around to this compulsive rhythm. To those who have seen the stage sensation Riverdance the picture is a familiar one.

Riverdance was born out of a seven-minute stage routine to while away the interval of the 1994 Eurovision Song Contest. Michael Flatley and Jean Butler were the dancers who would soon be propelled to stardom while the music was by choral singers known as Anuna. Courageous investors were persuaded that this celebration of Irish dance and music was worthy of a full-length show. With breathtaking speed the show moved from the Point Theatre, Dublin via London's Hammersmith Odeon to triumph at Radio City Music Hall on Broadway on St Patrick's Day 1996. The single Riverdance stayed at the top of the Irish charts for 18 weeks. By the end of 1996 it had been seen by more than 1.2 million people and had taken some £25 million at the box office. The album *Riverdance - Music from the Show* won a Grammy Award in 1997. Boys and girls forced into Irish dancing lessons by patriot parents were no longer saddled with a 'nerd' image. They could skip and kick with pride.

The top half of Irish dancers remains virtually motionless while their legs and feet move nimbly with the beat. It became the habit to keep arms uniformly pinned to the side of the body because rooms were always so packed with dancers that there was no space left in which to fling limbs about. Emphasising the beat knocked out by fast-moving feet today are the 'treble' shoes worn by dancers. The unmistakeable sound of dancers at work peppers the music which is itself inevitably led by the fiddler.

Yet the fiddle has become entrenched in the tradition of Irish music within just 200 years. Before that came a glorious musical heritage which has survived at least in part to this day. The harp was probably the most widely played instrument across the country before the sweeping popularity of the fiddle, or violin, but it was by no means the first.

The earliest instruments known to have been played on Irish soil date from the Bronze Age. They were variously shaped horns, some 800 years old, with a hole in the side by which, with some effort, two or maybe three notes could be sounded. These horns, called Lurer, are closely related to similar instruments found across Scandanavia. Hardly music but it was a start.

We must skip more than a dozen centuries before we next pick up the musical lineage of Ireland. It is now that we come across the harp, Ireland's national symbol for the past five centuries. The shrine of St Mogue in the National Museum is embellished with a harp while the Welsh king Gruffydd ap Cynan, who died in 1137, is thought to have introduced the harp from his native Ireland into Wales. Although it is not clear how, the Celtic harp probably hailed from Asia. That's where archaeologists have unearthed similar instruments on ancient sites. Like England, the music of Ireland was shaped in early times by visitors, invaders and soldiers who never returned home, all contributing a technique, sound or flourish which melded into one.

Today the oldest example of an Irish harp is housed at Trinity College, Dublin. The Great Harp may be only a modest 70cm high but it is so-called because it dates from the 14th century. It is this very harp which is illustrated on Irish coins. Although it is popularly called Brian Boru's harp there's actually little to link it with the folkhero who died in 1014 defeating a Danish invasion at the Battle of Clontarf. With its soundbox crafted from a solid piece of willow and 29 brass strings, the harp emits a delicate chime quite unlike that of the modern harp.

Harpists of the Middle Ages had a secure place in society, ranking somewhere alongside judges in the accepted order of social merit. Not only did they perform songs and poems at the court of kings they were trusted advisors. Their advice was sought about the wisdom of going to war or the treatment to be handed down to a felon. The titles and honours bestowed on them in life were transferred not to their sons but to the most able harpist remaining.

Gaelic harps were often encrusted with carvings and crystals, gold ornaments and jewels. The players used long, curly finger nails to pluck the strings rather than fingertips.

It is thought the characteristically small instruments were held against the left shoulder with the left hand playing the upper strings and the right hand the lower strings. Today harps are on placed against the right shoulder and playing positions are reversed.

Evidently, the musicians of the era showed a light touch. Cleric Gerald Barry, who visited the courts of England, France and Ireland, generally felt the latter country was found wanting. However, in 1185 he wrote: 'I find among these people commendable diligence only on musical instruments, on which they are incomparably more skilled than any other nation I have seen. Their style is not, as on British instruments to which we are accustomed, deliberate and solemn, but quick and lively; nevertheless the sound is smooth and pleasant.

Opposite: *The traditional components of Irish dance: a dancer accompanied by pipes — the main source of musical accompaniment before the fiddle displaced them. Note the Celtic embroidery on the dancer's clothing and the style of dancing, with the top half of the body virtually motionless while the legs and feet are moving nimbly with the beat, the arms uniformly pinned to the side of the body.*

'It is remarkable that, with such rapid fingerwork, the musical rhythm is maintained and that, by unfailingly disciplined art, the intergrity of the tune is full preserved . . . '

His opinions were echoed later by Polydore Virgil who lived in England during first half of the 16th century. He wrote: '. . . that the Irish practice music, and are eminently skilled in it. Their performance, both vocal and instrumental, is exquisite but so bold and impassioned that it is amazing how they can observe the rules of their art amidst such rapid evolutions of the fingers and vibrations of the voice and yet they do observe them to perfection.'

Part of the harpists role was to lead troops into battle. Irish harpists provided the music on at least one of the crusades of the era while composer Vincenzo Galilei, father of astronomer Gallileo, complimented the Irish on their skills with the instruments, presumably while the musicians were en route through Italy to the east. Just what the harpists of the day played remains a mystery.

Records of Irish folk music only date back to the 17th century. Among the earliest are the compositions of the great Carolan. Harpist Turlough O'Carolan (Toirdhealbhach O Cearbhallain in Gaelic) was born in County Meath in 1670. At the age of 18 he was blinded by an attack of small pox. Like many in his predicament, he turned musician to make a living. He found a patron-teacher, Mrs Ann MacDermott Roe, who tutored him on the instrument and secured him a horse and a reliable guide. Thereafter Carolan embarked on a successful career as a wandering minstrel. Carolan was a crowd-pulling entertainer and poet until his death in 1738. About 200 of Carolan's compositions have survived him, giving us a major clue to the tenor of Irish music of the day.

It is even said that the German composer George Frederick Handel borrowed a tune of Carolan's. The claim is not as outlandish as it may at first appear. Handel had by 1712 deserted Germany in favour of England. Clearly, he visited Dublin in his capacity as director of the newly-formed Royal Academy of Music and was impressed by the genteel drawing room society that the city fostered. And he favoured Ireland when he later fell on hard times.

Consequently it was at the unlikely venue of Mr Neal's New Musick Hall in Fishamble Street, Dublin, that Handel staged the premiere of his masterpiece Messiah in 1742.

Carolan surely considered himself lucky to escape the repression of harpists by the occupying English. Upright Englishman were horrified to find mere musicians dining at the same table as the aristocracy. Harpists were effectively banished from the right hand of the rulers they had served for centuries before.

Elizabeth I, although enjoying such music in her own court, issued the following order for Ireland: 'Hang harpers, wherever found, and destroy their instruments.'

Cromwell ordered the confiscation and burning of harps at a time when it was a clearly identifiable symbol of Ireland. So concerted was the oppression that patronage of harpists virtually died out.

Opposite: *An Irish traditional musician with the harp, a symbol of Celtic culture, and played in Ireland since the 10th century.*

A cultural renaissance at the end of the 18th century demanded the revival of the old harpist tradition. Yet in 1790 at the Belfast Harp Meeting only 10 players showed up. And Dennis Hempson, one of the few ever to have lived in three centuries, was the only harper to play in the old style with his talon finger-nails. Hempson, born in 1695, was 95 years old at the time. He used a harp crafted in 1702 and now preserved at the Guiness Brewery. When he died in 1807 he had reached the incredible age of 112.

At the festival teenager Edward Bunting endeavoured to commit the songs he heard there to paper. Unfortunately, in doing so, he standardised the works and consequently lost much of the original verve. Later Thomas Moore collected and published the old songs on the basis of Bunting's work. The resulting 'Irish Melodies' was a charming bunch of minor classics which made him famous all over the world.

However, the purists were horrified. The prettied-up versions which earned great acclaim owed little to the raw traditional music. It would be 150 years before genuine Irish traditional music would be in the limelight again.

By the 1890s psuedo Irish harps were made but woefully poor workmanship consigned the notion of a revival to failure. It was only a decade ago that authentic Celtic harps with wire strings were reproduced on a meaningful scale. Possibly the most familiar percussion instrument to emerge from Ireland is the bodhran, a primitive drum. Its purpose was little more than to hammer out a rhythm. Bizarrely, it was re-introduced into the performance of traditional music only 30 years ago. One of the key Irish bands to promote the bodhran is the Chieftans, modern players of traditional music.

Originally, bodhrans were made from goatskin or sheepskin which had been buried in lime for six to eight weeks then soaked them in a river to wash away the hairs. The hide was stretched over a crosspiece. Modern drum makers use the skins of donkeys, reindeer, calf, elk, deer and buffalo. Another recent improvement are six or twelve tuning screws which quickly alter the pitch of the instrument. It is played with a double-headed stick called a cipin, tipper or beater.

Another typically Celtic instrument is the flute. Originally the flutes were wooden with six holes and up to eight keys and they produced hollow airy tones. It is these basic models which are style favoured in Ireland today.

For those who had no flute there was the tin whistle or pennywhistle, a metal tube with six holes and a mouthpiece. Although primitive it had a two octave range and lent a distinctive sound to folk music. Excavations in Dublin have unearthed a whistle made of bone with two finger holes dating from the 12th century.

Irish Warpipes are similar to their more famous cousins, the Scottish bagpipes, except they possess one tenor drone instead of two or three. The Warpipes had all but vanished from Ireland by the end of the 19th century. When the nationalists sought to adopt them during the troubles they were forced to borrow a Scottish design.

The softer and more familiar Uilleann pipe has probably been around since the time of Shakespeare. It has a chanter with a range of two octaves in the key of D, three to four drones and regulators producing independent harmonies. Another name for the instrument is na piopai.

Traditionally the bag is made of soft, cured sheepskin. African hardwoods and ebony are used for the body of the pipes and the fittings are of silver and brass where once there might have been ivory. There are startling similarities between Uilleann pipes and those native to Northumberland. It was pipes that provided most of the dance music in Ireland before the fiddle emerged as favourite.

Some notable composers, musicians and singers have emerged from Ireland. Michael Kelly, born in Dublin in 1762, was a friend of Amadeus Mozart. He was even instrumental in the writing of Mozart's masterpiece *The Marriage of Figaro*, the details of his contribution are revealed in his autobiography.

Felllow Dubliner John Field, born in 1782, moved to London and then Russia as a pianoist. In Moscow there's a monument dedicated to him, paying tribute to his talents.

William Balfe, author of *The Bohemian Girl*, grew up in Wexford and it was there that his opera *The Rose of Castile* was premiered.

William Wallace was known in his native Ireland was a fine violinist and organ-player. The genteel existence of this Dublin musician in the 19th century was turned on its head after he travelled to the Australian bush, survived a mutiny in the south seas, was rescued from tribal sacrifice by a Maori chief's daughter in New Zealand, and had adventures in India, Mexico and the United States, where he lost his fortune.

Other important Irish composers and musicians include Victor Herbet, born in Dublin in 1859, who went on to make his mark on American musicals. Sir Charles Villiers Stanford, who emigrated to Britain in 1870, aged 18, went on to become an eminent composer and a teacher whose pupils include the great Vaughan Williams.

Sir Hamilton Harty, best known as the conductor of the Halle Orchestra, was born in Hillsborough, County Down in 1879. Singer John McCormack, born in Athlone in 1884, became an American citizen and was heaped with accolades, particularly for his charitable works. He died in Dublin in 1945.

Although she worked mostly in Italy, Margaret Sheridan was born in Castlebar, County Mayo in 1889. She was described by Puccini, composer of the operas *La Bohème* and *Madame Butterfly*, as 'the ideal Mimi and the only Butterfly'. Co-incidentally, the Irish are recognised world-wide as a nation of opera-buffs.

Irish music is today familiar worldwide. While the protest song has left its mark the best-loved ingredient of Irish folk music is its sentimentality. This has undoubtedly been acclerated because it has been written not only by the Irish at home but by the Irish overseas who are reknown for their enduring passion for the 'old country'. Irish navvies working in hideous conditions in England, emigrants travelling steerage to a new life in the States and those who likewise departed in poverty for Australia have all contributed to an enormous sense of longing for the deserted homeland.

The well-known lament 'Galway Bay' which begins 'If you ever go across the sea to Ireland . . .' talks of the breezes blowing from the beloved country being perfumed by heather. It ends: 'And if there's going to be a life hereafter, And faith, I am sure there's going to be, I will ask my God to let me make my heaven, In that dear land across the Irish sea.'

Three tunes which are closely related to the love of Ireland, 'Cockles and Mussels', 'Dublin in the Rare Ould Times' and 'Danny Boy' are unashamedly sentimental. They belong to a sector of Irish music which was notoriously dewey.

Another facet of Irish music, however, is hard-edged and rousing. The unsung modern father of this particular Gaelic tradition is Sean O'Riada, who was born in Cork in 1931. Even while he was the assistant director of music at the national broadcasting service the traditional melodies were his inspiration.

Then he exiled himself to a remote western corner of Ireland, learned the Irish language and studied Irish songs. Thanks to him the largely solo music of old Ireland was translated into material for bands, without losing its fundamental spirit. The Chieftains were a byproduct of his labours, as was the London-based band The Pogues.

His legendary status was compounded by his early death in 1971. At his funeral on a rain-lashed day at Ballyvourney he was mourned by thousands.

Just five years afterwards a band that has become synonymous with Ireland gave its first concert. The gymnasium at Mount Temple school in Dublin was packed as the performers stepped out on to a stage made of tables. If 15-year old lead singer Paul Hewson was surprised by the adulation of the crowd comprising his fellow pupils he didn't let it show.

The group, called Feedback, was later known as the Hype and finally emerged as U2. Paul Hewson became better known by his nickname of Bono. His schoolmates Dave Evans, otherwise known as The Edge, Larry Mullen and Adam Clayton have remained with him in the band. The only change from that starting line-up is the departure of Dave's older brother Dick.

Their debut album in 1981 was called *Boy*. Before the release of their 10th album *Pop* in 1997 they had sold some 70 million records and were veterans of the biggest venues in the world.

Later Bono spoke about that first schooldays concert. 'There was, from the very start, the evidence of a spark. When I heard that D-chord I got some kick. It was like starting up a motorbike. And the audience went wild!

'That was a very special concert, that was one of the best concerts of our lives . . . And we built ourselves around that spark.' U2 have always marked themselves out from other supergroups. They have remained loyal to Ireland, keeping a home there despite their international travels.

Bono is still married to his childhood sweetheart Alison Stuart, the mother of his two children. He, The Edge and Larry Mullen are devoutly Christian. But, above all, they have remained together when other groups subject to the same pressures when international stardom strikes have parted ways.

Opposite: *Irish music at Brian Boru Heritage Centre, Cashel, Co Tipperary. Named after Brian Boru, the 10th century king of Munster and mythical High-King of Ireland, the Centre offers folk theatre and traditional music and culture.*

RICE
SELF
FLOUR

PART 4: FOOD

Left: *Baking is an important part of Irish life and Ireland boasts a wonderful variety of breads (often called cakes), baked both on and in the stove.*

22 The Irish Table

For centuries Irish feasts were imbued with almost mystical quality. Ancient Celtic chieftains regarded a plentiful table as a mark of wealth and authority and seating plans were considered as carefully as in any Presidential or Crown function today. The position of a nobleman relative to his host was a political gesture designed to establish a clear pecking order. Those near the head of the table would be favoured warriors or influential allies; those at the foot perhaps untested men or even potential enemies. Feasting could continue for hours, enlivened with the presence of a 'praise poet' whose job was to relate songs and stories extolling the bravery and power of certain diners. Often, there would be a satirist who balanced this sycophancy by poking fun at a few puffed-up egos. The curious balance appears to have been the Irish Celts approach to after-dinner speeches, although for some it must have been anything but relaxing. In a culture geared to pride and status, the satirist was a figure to be endured and feared.

There used to be a persistent school of thought that Irish cooking was plain and predictable, that the long years of poverty in rural areas had robbed the country of much 'traditional' cuisine and that, aside from thousands of potato bread and cake recipes, imaginative dishes were a rare jewel. Meat was served up in standard steaks, roasts or stews; fish was a Friday 'penance' food to be eaten and forgotten and green vegetables (aside from cabbage) were strangers to a plate. There are still parts of Ireland where, it was said, locals would shake heads in disbelief at foreigners enthusing over fat oysters, fresh wild salmon and Dublin Bay prawns. Frozen meats and tasteless tinned vegetables were considered more the order of the day.

There is probably a lingering truth in this assessment of the Irish palate and yet, like all generalisations, the reality is very different. Poor or not, good cooks learned to make the most of their ingredients and recipes were faithfully handed down the generations in the oral tradition of the Celts. Irish hospitality – enshrined in the culture since the Brehon Laws of the 8th century – has always ensured that any dinner gathering is treated as a special event. Moreover, the arrival of better economic conditions has allowed Irish cooks to refine and experiment with the old dishes. At its best, the cuisine now rates among the finest in Europe. Anyone who doubts this has never been to the Kinsale Gourmet Festival.

The food industry for which Ireland can justly claim world renown is dairying. Superb cream, butter and cheese are the products of at least two thousand years experience and from the time of the early Christians, right through to the Middle Ages, they were seen as necessities rather than luxuries. Farms in the west were centred mostly on livestock (the moors and bogland were unsuited to crops) and just as meat was the staple food of the upper classes dairy products would sustain the poor. The plenty of summer would be preserved in the form of heavily-salted bacon, beef, butter and cheeses, along with dried fish where possible.

Grain-growing was also important, especially in the drier east. Because of their versatility, oats were the most common crop, providing porridge, gruel and coarse bread for the masses. They could also be mixed with milk or herbed butter and were even mashed into blood taken from live animals. Unappetising as it may sound, blood pudding would have been a great delicacy for poor families unused to the luxury of meat.

Barley (for ale and bread-making), wheat and rye were also produced and corn was harvested along narrow ridges. Wheaten bread however tended to be the exclusive food of kings and noblemen and vegetables were tended in such small quantities that they were inevitably beyond the purchasing power of ordinary people. In early Christian times only Welsh onions, leeks, chives, garlic, parsley, a few root crops such as parsnips, and kale were widely grown. Apart from apples there was no fruit production; children would instead be sent to gather wild berries and nuts – an important part of the diet. Honey was a cheap and plentiful as a sweetening agent but potatoes, destined to be the country's staple food, were not cultivated on any scale until the late 16th century.

Since then the face of Irish culinary history has changed little. It is essentially a peasant tradition into which few new or foreign influences have ever permeated. Although the Romans did make it to Ireland (contrary to the assertions of countless old school text books) they never populated the land in any numbers. The Vikings came from a similar cultural background, the Normans had enough to do keeping the Anglo-Saxon English in their place and the Crusaders never bothered to export the exotic spices and Oriental delicacies they had discovered in the East. Yet while the overall base of Irish ingredients remained comparatively small, the quality was always superlative.

The simplicity of the Irish approach to food is best seen in their soups, dishes common to rich and poor alike. In times of hardship these were nourishing meals, albeit consisting of little more than water, bacon and potatoes. Sometimes, perhaps to give the illusion of plenty, the meat would be removed and kept warm to be served as a separate meal. Bacon was the only meat to be had in most households and for those who kept a pig it was vital that nothing was wasted. Dishes such as Crubins or Crubeens, a soup made from pigs' trotters and dried peas, were popular while around the coast clams, cockles and mussels would be harvested and boiled up with potatoes and vegetables to make a rich broth.

A bowl of soup is still the most common way to start an Irish dinner or high tea. Traditionally though, food was never served in the clearly-separated courses common in the rest of Europe and many restaurants have now taken to presenting a fish or offal appetiser as well. The magnificent Galway oyster is a favourite; served simply with lemon juice and black pepper or occasionally whipped into a soufflé. Smoked trout and salmon, kippers and prawns are also popular.

The Dublin Bay prawn is, naturally enough in Ireland, not a prawn at all. It is actually a Norway lobster, a cousin of the Adriatic scampi, and got its name after being caught accidentally by fishermen and sold to Dublin street vendors of the kind immortalised in the song 'Molly Malone'. It is best eaten boiled or grilled within hours of landing, dressed only with a little parsley or chopped garlic. Grilled Dublin prawns with savoury rice, or stewed in a light fish consommé, make excellent supper dishes.

As mentioned earlier, fish was long considered a poor man's meal to be eaten only in unavoidable circumstances on Fridays. This hasn't prevented it becoming a key part of modern Irish cuisine and the combination of a long coastline and countless inland streams and rivers allows fresh fish to be easily obtained. Herrings (fresh or pickled), mackerel and perch appear in many dishes though rarely accompanied by strongly-flavoured sauces. The finest oysters come from the beds around Galway and are best eaten with the minimum of tinkering – salt, pepper and lemon juice are all you need. Galway's much-loved oyster festival at Clarinbridge is now a major tourist attraction at which the world's fastest oyster-openers gather to compete in a challenge match.

One reason fish has taken a while to become established on menus is because of the Irish love affair with meat. A brief walk around any city or town will reveal a disproportionately large number of butchers, meat wholesalers and slaughterhouses. From the mouth-watering steaks of the south-west to the cholesterol-packed Ulster Fry breakfast, Ireland remains one of the last bastions of unashamed meat eating in a world increasingly obsessed with 'healthy' food. The range of dishes are massive and, even though Ireland is now probably richer than it has ever been – there is still a bias towards using every scrap of a carcass.

Consequently there remains a great tradition of tasty offal dishes, although few restaurants have the nerve to promote them heavily to diners. Perhaps it's because too many Irish people remember stories of how their grandfathers would be paid partly in money; partly in tripe for a week's labouring. Even so, you can still find the odd offal treasure on a menu – tripe and trotters, tripe hot-pot, brawn (boiled pig's head), faggots, stuffed pig's ears, pickled tongue and stuffed roast heart.

The all-time national classic – Irish Stew – was originally made with mutton (lamb would have been an undreamed of luxury) potatoes (to give bulk) and onions (for flavouring). Traditionally, no other vegetables were added and the stew would sometimes simmer on a hearth for days with stock, meat and veg tipped in occasionally. This may not have provided diners with huge variety but it would have been a hot, tasty and wholesome meal in winters where food was a premium.

Regional and festive meat dishes are one of the country's culinary delights. Dublin Coddle, a much-loved Saturday supper dish, combines sausages, bacon and potatoes in a rich stew. Irish pig haggis (popular in the west) comprises mashed potatoes, sage and onions stuffed into a pig's stomach and boiled. It is delicious served piping hit with apple sauce and gravy. The king of pork delicacies is Limerick Ham, pickled and smoked over a low fire of oak shavings, straw and juniper berries, while spiced meats are popular at Christmas; many butchers will display their best cuts decked with a sprig of holly. Beef cooked in Guinness has become an internationally-acclaimed dish and is popular in France as Ragout à l'Irelandaise. Even the ubiquitous boiled bacon and cabbage, despised by schoolchildren down the years, has come into its own as a mainstream dish.

Poultry and game were, for many families, a cheap alternative to meat. Sadly, the strong flavour of a young, free-range backyard chicken is almost impossible to replicate using the modern battery-hen techniques to which Ireland like every other European nation has succumbed. Chicken casseroled with cabbage is a flavoursome farmhouse dish, while traditional game recipes include rabbit hot-pot and hare and bacon stew.

Irish breads and cakes are as varied and mouth-watering as any in the world. They have the genuine stamp of imagination which sets classical regional cooking apart, even though this was born more out of necessity than a desire to impress (the addition of potatoes helped eke out a household's meagre supplies of flour). Boxty bread, which incorporates grated and mashed potatoes, is sublime spread with melted butter while the simplicity of soda bread – flour, salt, bicarbonate of soda and sour milk – belies its mouthwatering taste. Then there are delights such as potato scones, potato apple bread, potato farls and treacle bread, all of which were once cooked using a griddle or pot above an open turf fire. For many Irish people still alive today, the smell of smouldering turf and freshly baked bread conjures up evocative scenes of childhood.

One final word in praise of Ireland's cheesemakers, who are fast acquiring a European-wide reputation. It is impossible to do justice to them all except to point out the large number of new varieties coming onto the market, all of which are worth trying. One of the absolute best is Milleens, made in the far west. And of course the legendary creaminess of Irish cheddar is superb in any cheese recipe.

Whether you are Irish or not, keen amateur cook or experienced professional, the recipes which follow will make any dinner gathering special. And remember, if you're cooking for an Irishman or woman the most heinous crime of all is to serve up paltry portions. As many a still-hungry diner has darkly observed on leaving the table: 'It was like a daisy in a bull's mouth'.

Potato Scones

Makes about 8-10

50 g/2 oz butter or margarine
225 g/8 oz plain flour
2.5 ml/½ tsp salt
5 ml/1 tsp baking powder
15 ml/1 tbsp sugar
50 g/2 oz mashed cooked potato
1 egg
a little milk

METHOD

1 Preheat the oven to 200°C/400°F/GAS MARK 6. Grease a baking sheet.

2 Rub the butter into the flour, then stir in the salt, baking powder, sugar and mashed potato. Mix in enough egg and milk to make a very soft dough.

3 Knead lightly, then roll out to 12 mm-1 cm/½-¾ in thick. Using a glass, pastry cutter or knife, cut out eight to ten scones.

4 Place the scones on the baking sheet and brush with egg or milk. Bake for 20-30 minutes.

Oven Soda Bread

Serves 4

700 g/1½ lb plain flour
10 ml/2 tsp sugar
7.5 ml/1½ tsp bicarbonate of soda (baking soda)
7.5 ml/1 ½ tsp cream of tartar
5 ml/1 tsp salt
450 ml/15 fl oz buttermilk

METHOD

1 Preheat the oven to 200°C/400°F/GAS MARK 6. Lightly flour a baking sheet.

2 Sift the dry ingredients together and mix in just enough buttermilk to make a fairly stiff dough.

3 Turn the dough out onto a floured surface and knead lightly until the dough has a smooth texture. Shape into a round.

4 Place on the baking sheet and cut a slash or a cross in the top.

5 Bake for 50-60 minutes. Leave to cool wrapped in a clean tea towel.

Soda Farls

Makes 4

450 g/1 lb plain flour
10 ml/2 tsp sugar
5 ml/1 tsp bicarbonate of soda (baking soda)
5 ml/1 tsp cream of tartar
2.5 ml/½ tsp salt
300 ml/10 fl oz buttermilk

METHOD

1 Sift the dry ingredients into a bowl, make a well in the centre and mix in half the buttermilk. Using a knife, draw in the flour from the sides of the bowl, adding more buttermilk as the batter thickens. The mixing should be done with as little working as possible until the mixture leaves the sides of the bowl fairly cleanly.

2 Turn out onto a floured surface and knead lightly, turning the corners into the centre and turning the round as you do so. When smooth underneath, turn it upside down .

3 Lightly roll out to a round 12 mm/½ in thick. Cut into four quarters (farls).

4 Heat a griddle over low heat (see Note). Place the farls on the griddle and cook for 5-6 minutes, until they have risen and there is a white skin on top.

5 Increase the heat and continue cooking until the farls are brown on the bottom. Turn them over and cook on the other side -- it takes about 15 minutes from the time the farls are put on the griddle.

Note: The griddle should be just hot enough to prevent the farls sticking: if a sprinkling of flour browns when it is thrown on the griddle, it is too hot.

Variation: Add finely chopped herbs to the mixture. Serve the farls with cheese.

Potato and Oat Farls

Makes 4

6 medium-sized potatoes, cooked
5 ml/1 tsp salt
knob of butter
oatmeal

METHOD

1 Mash the potatoes and stir in the salt and butter. Work in enough oatmeal to form a soft dough.

2 Turn onto a surface scattered with oatmeal and form into a round or square. Cut into quarters (farls) or squares.

3 Heat a griddle. Cook the farls on the hot griddle until browned on both sides. Eat hot or cold with plenty of butter.

Variation: These farls are very good served with bacon. If preferred, cook the bacon and keep it warm while frying the farls in the bacon fat.

BOOK POST VIEW SOUVENIR
BAKING SOD
HOME
sweet Home

Irish Stew

Serves 4-6

900 g/2 lb potatoes,thinly sliced
900 g/2 lb best end of neck lamb chops
450 g/1 lb onions, thinly sliced
4 carrots, thinly sliced
2 parsnips, halved and thinly sliced
salt and pepper
15 ml/1 tbsp chopped fresh parsley
15 ml/1 tbsp chopped fresh thyme
25 g/1 oz butter
thyme sprigs, to garnish

METHOD

1 Preheat the oven to 190°C/3375°F/GAS MARK 5.
2 Arrange one third of the sliced potatoes in a casserole and add half the chops, onions, carrots and parsnips. Season well with salt and pepper and sprinkle with half the chopped herbs.
3 Repeat these layers once more and finish with a layer of potatoes. Pour over 600 ml/1 pint water, cover with buttered greaseproof paper (using a little of the butter) and a lid.
4 Bake for 1½ hours, then remove the lid and the greaseproof paper. Dot the potatoes with the remaining butter and cook, uncovered, for a further 10-15 minutes. Garnish with thyme sprigs and serve hot with soda bread.

Note: While an authentic Irish stew is made with just lamb, potatoes and onions, the extra vegetables in this version give added colour. For a juicier stew, add 750 ml/1¼ pints water instead of 600 ml/1 pint.

Champ

Serves 6

1.8 kg/4 lb potatoes (new floury ones are best), halved
salt and pepper
75 g/3 oz butter
approximately 175 ml/6 fl oz milk
6 spring onions (scallions), finely chopped
chopped chives, to garnish

METHOD

1 Cook the potatoes in boiling salted water until tender. Drain well, then put them back on a very low heat, covering the pan with a clean tea towel, to dry out the potatoes.
2 When dry, mash the potatoes with some of the butter.
3 Put the milk in a pan with the spring onions and bring to the boil. Pour the mixture onto the mashed potato and mix in. Do not make the potato too sloppy: if this does happen, dry it out a little over low heat.
4 Spoon the potato into individual bowls, make a small well in the centre and add the remaining butter. Serve garnished with chopped chives.

Note: This buttery potato dish makes a tasty accompaniment to serve with hearty casseroles, joints of meat or fish dishes.

GUINNESS'S EXTRA STOUT
GORINGS
DUBLIN AND LONDON

Coffee Cake

75 g/3 oz butter or margarine
50 g/2 oz caster sugar
30 ml/2 tbsp golden syrup (pouring treacle)
2 eggs, beaten
175 g/6 oz plain flour
5 ml/1 tsp baking powder
10 ml/2 tsp coffee essence
45-60 ml/3-4 tbsp buttermilk, to mix

For the buttercream filling and topping:
175 g/6 oz icing sugar
75 g/3 oz butter
10 ml/2 tsp coffee essence
a little milk, to mix
icing sugar for dusting

METHOD

1 Preheat the oven to 180°C/350°F/GAS MARK 4. Grease two 18 cm/7 in sandwich tins (alternatively, use two fluted flan tins).
2 Cream the butter, sugar and syrup. Beat in half the beaten egg with the flour and baking powder, then beat in the rest of the egg.
3 Add the coffee essence and enough buttermilk to beat to a soft dropping consistency. Pour the mixture into the tins and level the surface. Bake for 20-25 minutes, until risen and firm to the touch. Cool on a wire rack.
4 To make the buttercream, beat together the 175 g/6 oz icing sugar, butter, coffee essence and enough milk to make it spreadable. Sandwich the cakes together with half the buttercream and pipe the rest around the top edge of the cake. Dust the centre with icing sugar.

Variations: Omit the coffee essence and add 15 ml/1 tbsp cocoa powder to the mixture, or the finely grated rind of 1 lemon or 1 orange.

Irish Whiskey Cake

350 g/12 oz mixed dried fruit
60 ml/4 tbsp whiskey
175 g/6 oz butter
175 g/6 oz soft brown sugar
grated zest of 1 orange
3 eggs, beaten
225 g/8 oz plain flour
5 ml/1 tsp baking powder
pinch of salt
ml/1 tsp mixed spice
50 g/2 oz ground almonds

METHOD

1 Soak the mixed fruit in the whiskey overnight.
2 Preheat the oven to 170°C/325°F/GAS MARK 3. Grease and base line a 20 cm/8 in cake tin.
3 Cream the butter and sugar until fluffy. Add the orange zest. Gradually beat in the eggs.
4 Sift the flour, baking powder, salt and mixed spice and add to the egg mixture with the fruit and whiskey and the ground almonds.
5 Turn the mixture into the cake tin and bake for 1½-2 hours.

Variation: Cover the top of the mixture with halved glacé cherries and sprinkle with demerara sugar before baking, to give an attractive crunchy topping.

WHISKY
Killarney House, Killarney.

IRISHMAN'S OMELETTE

Serves 2

25 g/1 oz butter
100 g/4 oz streaky bacon rashers, rinded and chopped
1 small onion, chopped
1 large potato, cooked and diced
50 g/2 oz cabbage, shredded
3-4 eggs
15 ml/1 tbsp chopped fresh herbs
salt and pepper

METHOD

1 Heat the butter in a large non-stick frying pan. Add the bacon, onion, potato and cabbage and fry, stirring from time, for 8-10 minutes, until the bacon and onion are cooked.

2 In a bowl, beat the eggs just enough to break them down. Add the herbs and season with salt and pepper.

3 Stir the eggs into the pan and cook over a gentle heat until the eggs set.

4 Place the pan under a preheated grill until the omelette is golden brown on top. Serve with crusty bread, new or jacket potatoes and grilled or sliced tomatoes.

IRISH COFFEE

Serves 1

15 ml/1 tbsp Irish whiskey
5 ml/1 tsp sugar
strong black coffee
15-30 ml/1-2 tbsp double cream

METHOD

1 Pour the whiskey into a small warmed goblet and add the sugar.

2 Fill to within 12 mm/½ in of the top with black coffee and stir quickly to dissolve the sugar.

3 Top with a 6mm/¼ in layer of double cream. The best way to do this is to hold a spoon over the coffee and gently pour the cream over the back of the spoon so that the cream floats on the top of the coffee.
Do not stir the cream into the coffee.

Arranmore Island , Co. Donegal, looking back towards the mainland.

PART 5:
AN IRISH CHRONOLOGY

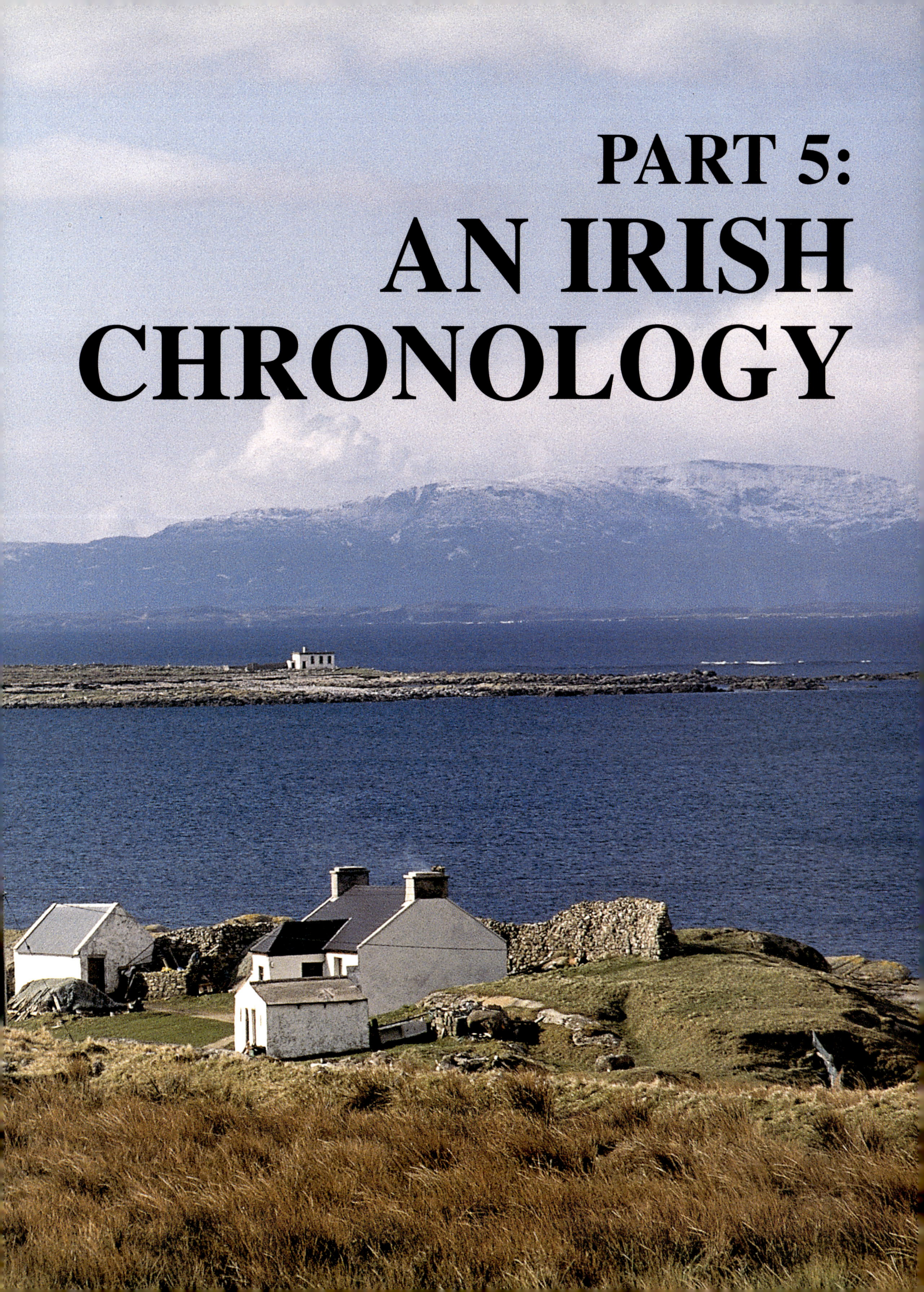

23 AN IRISH CHRONOLOGY

c1.5 million BC Ireland is linked to the European continent, most of which is predominantly ice-covered. As the climate warms up the ice melts and sea levels rise, gradually beginning to cut Ireland off from the rest of the land mass.

c8,000BC The first inhabitants, Mesolithic peoples, arrive over the land-bridges from Britain. Ireland at this time is covered in dense forest.

c4,000BC Arrival of Neolithic people. First real expansions and land-clearances. High-quality stone-axe factories lead to exports.

c2,000BC The Bronze Age flowering of native Irish culture, with distinctive masterful goldwork traded far across Europe. Much building of stone circles and tombs.

c1,500BC – 1,180BC The zenith of the indigenous Irish culture; an important factor of which is extensive copper mining.

c100BC Arrival of Gaels, who intermix and marry peacefully with the native population.

79BC–138AD A recent discovery (1996) has revealed a considerably greater Roman presence in Ireland than was first thought. At Drumanagh (24 km/15 miles north of Dublin) a massive Roman town has been discovered.

130-80AD Ptolemy's account of Ireland.

367AD Major attacks on coastal Britain by the Irish; also by the Picts and Saxons.

431AD Palladius sent as bishop to Ireland by Pope Celestine I.

432AD Arrival of St Patrick and his mission to convert the pagan Gaels to Christianity.

433–4AD Prosper of Aquitaine attributes the conversion of Ireland to Christianity to Pope Celestine I.

550–650AD Growth and flowering of monasticism in Ireland.

563AD Foundation of Iona by Columba.

575AD Convention of Druim Ceat.

590AD Colombanus begins his mission to the continent.

597AD Death of Columba.

615AD Death of Columbanus at Bobbio.

650–670AD Irish canon and vernacular law is developed and entabulated.

663AD Death of Guaire Aidni, Úi Fiachrach king of Connacht.

670-700AD Tirechán and Muirchú produce hagiographical works about St Patrick.

697AD Synod of Birr. Proclamation of the Law of the Innocents.

700AD The eastern Eóganacht become dominant in Munster. Writing of the law tract on status, the *Crith Gablach*.

700 - 800AD Christian-Gaelic golden age. *The Book of Kells*. Durrow, Ardagh chalice, monastries, superb goldwork.

704AD Death of Adomnán, ninth abbot of Iona.

721–42AD Cathal mac Finguine king of Munster.

725AD The Úi Briúin dynasty rules in Connacht.

735AD Abdication of Flaithbertach mac Loingsig. Cenél Conaill is excluded from Úi Néill overkingship.

743AD Clann Cholmáin first holds the overkingship of the Úi Néill.

750-850AD Armagh comes under Úi Néill control.

793AD Vikings raid Lindisfarne on the north-east coast of England. Artrí mac Cathail is crowned king of Munster.

795AD Earliest known Viking assaults on Ireland, the burning of Rathlin marks the start of a wave of Viking pillaging, including attacks on Iona, Inishmurray and Inishbofin.

800AD The Úi Néill clan dominate north Leinster.

802AD Iona is raided and burned by the Vikings.

804AD Áed Oirnide is crowned overking of the Úi Néill.

806AD 68 people belonging to Iona monastery are killed in a devastating Viking raid.

807AD Building starts on Kells monastery.

820–7AD Feidlimid mac Crimthainn becomes king of Munster.

836AD Viking raids start to cut deeply into the Irish countryside bringing terror and bloodshed.

837AD Viking fleets raid along the rivers Boyne and Liffey.

840AD A Viking fleet overwinters on Lough Neagh.

841AD A Viking fleet spends the winter in Dublin.

842AD The first Viking-Irish alliance.

845AD Abbot Forannán of Armagh is captured by Vikings.

846-62AD Mael Sechnaill I rules as overking of the Úi Néill.

866AD Áed Finnliath clears the Vikings out from their settlements along the northern Irish coastline.

914AD A large Viking fleet raids Waterford, marking the beginning of the second wave of Viking incursions.

919AD Niall Glúndub, overking of the Úi Néill, is killed in the battle of Dublin.

950AD The second wave of Viking invasion stops.

956-80AD Domnall ua Néill rules as overking of the Úi Néill.

980AD Mael Sechnaill II becomes overking of the Uí Néill.

975–1014AD Brian Boru rules as king of Munster, until eventually crowned High King of Ireland.

997AD Brian Boru and Mael Sechnaill agree equably on an division of Ireland.

999AD Brian Boru defeats the Leinstermen and Ostmen at the battle of Glen Máma. Sitric Silkenbeard, king of the Ostmen of Dublin, submits to him.

1002–1014AD Brian Boru reigns as king of Ireland.

1014AD Death of the High King Brian Boru after victory over the Norsemen and their Irish allies at the battle of Clontarf.

1022AD Death of Mael Sechnaill II.

1086–1119AD Muirchertach O'Brien king of Munster and chief claimant to the Irish High Kingship.

1101AD Synod of Cashel. Muirchertach O'Brien grants Cashel to the church as the seat of a metropolitan.

1106–56AD Turlough O'Connor king of Connacht and another claimant to the Irish High Kingship.

1111AD Synod of Ráth Breasail, where the Ireland is divided into territorial dioceses under two metropolitans.

1134AD Consecration of Cormac's Chapel at Cashel.

1142AD Foundation of first Cistercian moanastery, at Mellifont.

1152AD Synod of Kells-Mellifont. Armagh becomes the seat of the primate and the national church is organised into four metropolitans,

1166AD Death of Muirchertach Mac Lochlainn, High King of Ireland. Dermot MacMurrough, king of Leinster, is driven into exile overseas where he seeks help from Henry II of England, and recruits Norman mercenaries.

1169AD Arrival of FitzStephen, FitzGerald and other Normans. Wexford is taken. Dermot MacMurrough is restored to the throne of Leinster.

1170AD Arrival of the Earl of Pembroke, known as Strongbow, who marries MacMurrough's daughter, Aoife. Siege and capture of Dublin. Invasion of Meath.

1171AD Macmurrough dies, Strongbow becomes king of Leinster. Arrival of Henry II intent on controlling his unruly barons. Submission of Irish clergy, plus most of the Irish kings.

1172AD Second Synod of Cashel. Meath granted to Hugh de Lacy. Henry II returns to England.

1175AD Treaty of Windsor between Henry II and Rory O'Connor, High King of Ireland, who agrees to rule all unoccupied Irish lands as a vassal of the English monarch.

1176AD Death of Strongbow.

1177AD Conquest of Ulaid by John de Courcy. Council of Oxford, at which Prince John made Lord of Ireland, and various speculative land-grants, of the kingdoms of Cork and Limerick are made to Norman vassals.

1185AD Prince John's first visit to Ireland. Occupation of lands in Limerick begun.

1200AD Beginning of the Classic Period of Irish literarature.

1210AD Second visit by John, now king of England. Appropriation of Ulster and Limerick. Submission of Irish kings.

1235AD Final conquest of Connacht by Richard de Burgh. Five King's Cantreds left for O'Connor.

1257AD Sligo ravaged by Godfrey O'Donell after the death of FitzGerald. Normans defeated in Thomond by Conor O'Brien and his son, Tadhg.

1258AD Meeting at Caol-Uisce on the Erne. Attended by Aodh son of O'Connor, Tadhg, son of O'Brien, and Brian O'Neill, pretender to the High Kingship.

1260AD Battle of Down. Defeat and death of Brian O'Neill.

1261AD Battle of Callan. John fitz Thomas of Desmond and his heir killed by Finghin MacCarthy. Death of MacCarthy.

1263AD Walter de Burgh, lord of Connacht, gains the earldom of Ulster.

1276AD Hereditary lordship of Thomond granted to Thomas de Clare.

1292AD Thomas fitz Maurice of Desmond gains custody of all Crown rents and services in the Decies. Desmond granted to Thomas fitz Maurice of Desmond.

1315AD Invasion of Ireland by Edward Bruce, calling himself king of Ireland.

1316AD Battle of Athenry at which the rebellious Irish chiefs of Connacht are killed.

1318AD Battle of Dysert O'Dea. Defeat and death of Richard de Clare by O'Brien. Battle of Faughart. Edward Bruce is killed.

1333AD Murder of the Earl of Ulster, William de Burgh. Loss of Crown control of Anglo-Norman Connacht.

1361AD English military expedition lead by Prince Lionel of Clarence and the Earl of Ulster arrives to revive the colony.

1366AD Statutes of Kilkenny, drawn up to prevent the Norman settlers from becoming too Irish, by prohibiting the adoption of the native language.

1394–5AD Richard II's first expedition to Ireland. Defeat of the Leinster Irish under Art MacMurrough. Submission of most rebel Irish and English chiefs.

1398AD Death of Roger Mortimer in war against the Leinster Irish.

1399AD Richard II second expedition to Ireland.

1414–47AD Struggle for control of royal government in Ireland breaks out, between the factions of James Butler, earl of Ormond, and John Talbot, earl of Shrewsbury.

1449–50AD Richard Duke of York in Ireland, serving as the King's Lieutenant. Submission of Irish and English rebel chiefs.

1459–60AD Duke of York's second visit. Parliament meets at Drogheda, and upholds his authority against Henry VI.

1467–8AD Tiptoft, earl of Worcester appointed Lord Deputy of Ireland by Edward IV, in place of Thomas FitzGerald, earl of Desmond, who is subsequently executed for treason. Rebellion in Munster.

1478–9AD Edward IV frustrated in his attempts to replace Gerald Mór FitzGerald as Lord Deputy with Lord Grey.

1487AD FitzGerald has the crown pretender Lambert Simnel crowned as Edward VI in Christchurch cathedral, Dublin.

1494AD Sir Edward Poynings appointed Lord Deputy, who makes all legislation passed in the English Parliament applicable to Ireland, and makes all future summons and legislation of the Anglo-Irish Parliament dependent on the King's approval.

1496AD FitzGerald, earl of Kildare, reappointed as Lord-Deputy. Line of the Pale at Clongowes.

1504AD Battle of Knocktoe. FitzGerald completes his dominance of Ireland with the defeat of Burke, O'Brien, and the Irish of Ormond.

1509AD Accession of Henry VIII to the throne of England.

1513AD Death of Lord Deputy FitzGerald. Succeeded by his son Gerald, the ninth earl of Kildare.

1520AD Thomas Howard, earl of Surrey, replaces Kildare as Lord Lieutenant.

1522AD Butler, earl of Ormond, appointed Lord Deputy of Ireland.

1524AD A Royal Commission resolves the differences between Kildare and Ormond, restoring Kildare as Lord Deputy.

1529AD Sir William Skeffington is appointed Royal Commissioner.

1533AD Lord-Deputy Kildare summoned to court. Leaves his son, Lord Offaly as vice-deputy.

1534AD Kildare imprisoned in the Tower, where he dies. Consequent rebellion in Kildare, led by Lord Offaly.

1534–6AD Revolt in Ireland. Fall of Maynooth Castle. Arrest of Lord Offaly and five of his uncles, all brought over to England for trial and punishment.

1536–7AD Meeting of Irish Reformation Parliament. Execution of Kildare and his uncles at Tyburn.

1540AD Appointment of Sir Anthony St Leger as Governor of Ireland.

1541AD Meeting of Parliament that declares Henry VIII as King of Ireland. Launch of Surrender and Re-grant programme of land ownership.

1547AD Death of Henry VIII. Accession of Edward VI.

1548-53AD Garrison policy to surround the Pale with fortified positions carried forward by successive governors — Bellingham, St Leger and Croft.

1553 AD Death of Edward VI. Accession of Mary.

1556-64AD Thomas Radcliffe, earl of Sussex, Governor of Ireland.

1557-6AD Military colony established in Laois-Offaly. Murder of Mathew O'Neill, baron of Dungannon. Military campaign in Ulster to enforce the Surrender and Re-grant programme.

1558AD Death of Mary. Accession of Elizabeth I. But the reformation fails to take hold in Ireland, which remains firmly Catholic.

1560 AD Second Irish Reformation Parliament, which approves Elizabethan church settlement for Ireland.

1561-4AD Sussex carries out various campaigns against Shane O'Neill. Opposition to financial exactions within the Pale. Beginning of Elizabethan wars in Ireland.

1565-71 AD Sir Henry Sidney Governor of Ireland. Launches a military campaign in Ulster. Death of Shane O'Neill. Attempts to restore order in Munster.

1569-71 AD Meeting of Parliament in Dublin. Tyrone declared forfeit to the Crown. First provincial presidents appointed in Connacht and Munster. Local rebellions in Munster, Leinster, and Connacht.

1570AD Elizabeth I declared excommunicated by the pope.

1571–75AD Sir William FitzWilliam Governor of Ireland.

1572AD Rebels brought to heel in Munster and Connacht.

1573–4AD Private colonisation in Ulster.

1575AD Fitz Maurice FitzGerald voyages to the Continent to seek Catholic support and aid against the Elizabethan Government.

1575–8AD Sidney's second period as Governor of Ireland. Takes a more conciliatory line. Private colonisation ended.

1577AD Land Tax implemented, to try and increase revenues. Opposition from within the Pale community.

1578AD Sidney resigns and leaves Ireland, believing his position undermined by the Pale community.

1579AD Fitz Maurice FitzGerald returns with Catholic expeditionary force. Desmond murders a government official and joins the rebellion.

1580AD Rebellion in Munster and Leinster. Lord Grey de Wilton appointed Governor, ousts the Continental force from Smerwick, but is defeated at Glenmalure in Wicklow.

1582–3AD Suppression of rebels in Leinster and Munster. Desmond killed.

1584–8AD Sir John Perott Governor of Ireland.

1584AD Provincial councils restored in Connacht and Munster.

1585AD Parliament meets in Dublin. Confiscation of rebel property. Commission convened for the redistribution of rebel lands.

1585AD Hugh O'Neill,baron of Dungannon, created earl of Tyrone.

1588–94AD Sir William FitzWilliam Governor of Ireland for the second time. Spanish Armada defeated.

1589–90AD Bingham, president of Connacht, tries to extend Crown territory in North Connacht and South Ulster.

1591AD Elopement of Hugh O'Neill and the sister of Ulster's top Crown official.

1592AD Hugh O'Donell expels all government officials from Tyrconnell. He and Hugh Maguire oppose all crown interference and redistribution in their territories.

1593–4AD Opposition to government intervention intensifies. Tyrone still loyal though his brothers are rebelling.

1595AD Death of Turlough O'Neill . Rebellion of Hugh O'Neill, earl of Tyrone. Spanish support for the rebellion sought.

1596AD Spenser's *A View of the Present State of Ireland.*

1596–7AD Ulster rebellion intensifies. Rebellions in Leinster and Connacht.

1598AD O'Neill vanquishes the English at the battle of Yellow Ford, in Ulster. Rebellion spreads to Munster.

1599AD Robert Devreux, earl of Essex, in charge of suppression of rebels. Agrees truce with Tyrone.

1600AD Charles Blount, Baron Mountjoy appointed Governor of Ireland. The government forces rally.

1601AD Spanish military support arrives. But O'Neill and O'Donell, along with their Spanish allies are defeated by Mountjoy at the battle of Kinsale.

1602AD Carew restores order in Munster. Mountjoy penetrates into Ulster.

1603AD Death of Queen Elizabeth I. Accession of James I. Surrender of Hugh O'Neill to Mountjoy. English law enforced throughout Ireland.

1605AD Sir Arthur Chichester Governor of Ireland. Proclamations: that all persons in Ireland are free subjects of the King, and seminary priests and Jesuits expelled from the country. Pressure on all for religious conformity.

1606AD Foundation of St Anthony's Franciscan College. Government attempts to dismember Ulster lordships through judicial review. Settlement of Scots by private treaty on the Ards peninsula.

1607AD Flight of the Earls. O'Neill of Tyrone and O'Donell of Tyrconnell and others leave, and are declared traitors.

1608AD Beginning of the plantation of Derry by merchants of the City of London, and other Ulster colonies. Rebellion of Sir Cahir O'Doherty.

1610–30AD Geoffrey Keating writing *Foras Feasa* or *Éirinn.*

1611AD Publication of *An Teagasg Criosdaidhe.*

1612AD Publication of *A Discovery of the True Causes Why Ireland Was Never Entirely Subdued*, by Sir John Davies.

1613–15AD Irish Parliament endorses plantation scheme in Ulster and makes provision for the settlers to have full representation in future parliaments. State Church Meeting of Convocation, which adopts over one hundred articles of faith.

1616AD Death of Hugh O'Neill, earl of Tyrone, in Rome.

1621AD More plantation colony schemes for the Irish Midlands mooted.

1622AD Comprehensive survey of Irish Church and Government. Also of plantations.

1625AD Death of James I. Accession of Charles I.

1628AD Charles gives 'Graces' in exchange for subsidies, provides toleration of Catholicism — enraging his Protestant subjects.

1641AD Large-scale rebellion for the return of lands by the Catholic Gaelic natives, who are joined by the Old English Catholics in Ireland. 59 percent of the land is held by Catholics.

1633–41AD Viscount Wentworth Governor of Ireland.

1634–5AD Irish Parliament hears from Wentworth that he intends continuing the policy of plantations, and will ignore the 'Graces'. He then begins to establish Crown title to the province of Connacht.

1637AD Wentworth attempts to maintain control and discipline over the state church.

1640AD Opposition to Wentworth's rule.

1641AD Wentworth, (now earl of Strafford), is convicted of treason and executed in England. Rebellion in Ulster. Ireland slides into anarchy and chaos.

1642AD English Parliament passes the 'Adventures Act', seeking to suppress the Irish rebellion. Scots Covenanters' army lands in Ulster, commanded by Robert Munro. Owen O'Neill arrives to form an Ulster Catholic army. Civil war in England. The Catholic Confederacy assembles in Kilkenny.

1644–5AD Archbishop Rinuccini arrives in Ireland to give direction to the uprising.

1646AD Catholic victory at the battle of Benburb, County Tyrone, where Owen O'Neill defeats Munro. But the rebels fail to take the advantage. Rinuccini tries to prevent the Confederate Catholics from coming to terms with a Protestant monarch.

1647AD Parliamentary forces dominant in the English Civil War. Dublin conceded to Parliamentarians by Ormond.

1649AD Execution of Charles I. Cromwell arrives in Ireland, and captures Drogheda and Wexford after brief sieges. Death of Owen O'Neill.

1650–52AD Cromwell's conquest continues. Catholic landowners exiled to Connaught beyond the Shannon line.

1654–5AD Cromwellian plantation carried out.

1658AD Death of Cromwell.

1660AD Restoration and accession of Charles II, who declares he will both uphold the Cromwellian conquests and restore property to innocent Catholics.

1661AD Episcopal state church reconstituted. Investigation of Irish land-ownership .

1662AD Duke of Ormond becomes Governor of Ireland. A commission hears Irish claims for land-ownership.

1663AD Closure of the commission on land-ownership.

1665AD The 'Act of Explanation' obliges Cromwellian settlers to return one third of their land to provide for innocent dispossessed Catholics.

1670AD Synod of Catholic bishops in Dublin.

1678AD Moves against Catholic worship.

1681AD Execution of Oliver Plunkett, Catholic archbishop of Armagh.

1684AD Dublin Philosophical Society formed by William Molyneux.

1685AD Death of Charles II. Acession of James II.

1687AD Talbot, earl of Tyrconnell appointed Lord Deputy of Ireland. Begins replacing Protestant officials with Catholics.

1688AD James II deposed. Gates of Derry closed to James' troops. William of Orange invited to take English throne. 22 percent of Irish land is held by Catholics.

1689AD William and Mary enthroned. James II arrives at Kinsale from France. Siege and relief of Derry. Catholic parliament in Dublin.

1690 AD William III lands at Carrickfergus and defeats James II at Battle of the Boyne. James flees to France. Dublin taken by William. Sieges of Athlone and Limerick fail. Courts begin hearings against Irish who opposed William.

1691AD Catholic defeat at Aughrim and surrender at Limerick. Athlone taken by Protestant forces. Treaty of Limerick.

1695AD 14 percent of land held by Catholics. First penal laws carried out against Catholics.

1698AD William Molyneux writes a pamphlet against England legislating for Ireland.

1699AD Acts restricting Irish wool exports.

1704AD More legislation restricting Catholic landholding and public offices.

1713AD Swift becomes Dean of St Patrick's in Dublin.

1714AD 7 percent of land is held by Catholics.

1719AD Toleration Act for Protestant Dissenters.

1720AD Swift issues pamphlet rejecting English intrusion.

1728AD Act removing Catholics from franchise.

1750 AD Dublin Society formed.

1762–72AD Viceroyalty of Townsend.

1768AD Octennial Act, limiting the duration of Irish parliaments.

1772AD Relief Act for Catholics.

1775AD Henry Grattan is leader of the 'Patriot' Party.

1778AD More Relief Acts for Catholics.

1782AD Legislative Indepenence gained from Britain.

1791AD Wolfe Ton's *Argument on behalf of the Catholics of Ireland* published.

1792AD Catholics permitted to practise law.

1793AD Volunteers suppressed and arms restricted. Catholic parliamen tary franchise.

1795AD Earl Fitzwilliam becomes Lord-lieutenent of Ireland.

1796AD Insurrection Act. French fleet arrives in Bantry Bay. Wolf Tone on board.

1796–98AD United Irishmen plotting rebellion.

1798AD Martial Law imposed. Arrest of the Leinster Directory of United Irishmen. Lord Fitzgerald arrested and hung. Rebellions in Midlands and Wexford. Battle of Vinegar Hill. Death of Wolf Tone.

1800AD Act of Union passed, effective from January 1.

1803AD Emmet's rising. He is tried and executed.

1823AD O'Connell's Catholic Association founded.

1828AD O'Connell elected for Clare.

1829AD Catholic Emancipation passed.

1832AD Irish Tithe Composition Act.

1833AD Irish Church Temporalities Act.

1835AD Compact between O'Connell, Whigs and radicals.

1837AD Accession of Queen Victoria.

1840AD O'Connell's Repeal Association founded.

1842AD Davis founds *The Nation* newspaper.

1843AD O'Connell's 'Monster Meetings' for Repeal of the Union. Finally Clontarf meeting banned.

1845AD Blight in the potato harvest, leads to the beginning of the years of famine. Sir Robert Peel, then Prime Minister, imports Indian corn. Trevelyan permanent Head of Treasury.

1846AD Trevelyan begins selling Indian corn, but stops in summer because too many people want to buy. Repeal of Corn Laws. Attacks on food carts and food riots. Peel replaced by Lord John Russell as P.M. Public works begun, but halted in anticipation of the new harvest. But after the potato harvest has failed completely they are recommenced. First deaths from starvation reported.

1847AD Government soup kitchens deliver free rations. Fever spreading throughout the country. Small but blight-free potato harvest. Trevelyan ends soup kitchens, and retires to write a history of the famine. Responsibility for the poor thrown on local rates. Ireland is left to cope alone. Foundation of Irish Confederation.

1848-9 AD Worst years of famine. Battle at Ballingarry, an abortive rising. Young Ireland leader Smith O'Brien arrested. James Stephens flees to France.

1856 AD Stephens returns from France and walks through the country. Phoenix Society founded.

1858 AD Stephens founds organisation — The Irish Republican Brotherhood. Fenian Brotherhood founded in America.

1861 AD Funeral of Terence Bellew Macmanus. Stephens swears in more members to his Organisation.

1863 AD The *Irish People* newspaper is founded.

1865 AD Arrest of the editorial board of the *Irish People*. Stephens arrested, escapes from Richmond jail.

1866AD Stephens at first encourages but then calls off a rising. He is finally replaced by American Fenians. American civil-war veteran Kelly becomes 'Chief Organiser of the Irish Republic.' Sails from USA to Ireland.

1867AD Abortive raid on Chester Castle. Fenian Rising in Ireland. The rescue of Kelly from a police van in Manchester. Execution of Allen, Larkin and O'Brien. Clerkenwell explosion— the first Irish bomb on the mainland.

1869AD Disestablishment of Protestant Church in Ireland. Gladstone P.M.

1870AD Gladstone's first Land Act.

1875AD Parnell elected MP for Co Meath.

1879AD Threat of Famine again. Evictions. On the initiative of Michael Davitt the Irish National Land League is formed.

1879-82AD Land War.

1880AD Parnell begins his love affair with Mrs O'Shea.

1881AD Gladstone's second Land Act. Parnell imprisoned in Kilmainham.

1882AD Death of Parnell's and Mrs O'Shea's first child. Kilmainham 'Treaty'. Parnell released. Phoenix Park murder.

1886AD First Home Rule Bill.

1887AD Forged Parnell letters published by *The Times*.

1889AD Letters exposed as forgeries perpetrated by the journalist Pigott.

1890AD Parnell's divorce heard in court. Parnell deposed from the leadership of the party.

1891AD Second Home Rule Bill. Foundation of the Gaelic League.

1899AD Griffith founds *United Irishmen* newspaper.

1903AD Wyndham's Land Purchase Act.

1906AD Election win in England for the Liberals, with a huge majority, and no need to offer Home Rule to the Irish Party.

1909 AD Land Purchase Act.

1910 AD In two general elections the Conservatives and the Liberals are equal, with the Irish party holding the balance of power.

1911 AD The Parliament Act removes the power of ultimate veto from the House of Lords.

1912 AD Third Home Rule Bill. Solemn League and Covenant in Ulster.

1913AD The Ulster Volunteer Force founded. Also the Irish National Volunteers and the Irish Citizen Army.

1914AD The Curragh Mutiny breaks out. Gun-running in Larne and Howth. First World War begins. Home Rule Act goes onto the Statute Book. The IRB decides on rising.

1916AD Easter Rising in Dublin. Followed by executions. Finally at Christmas the first rebel prisoners are released, including Michael Collins.

1917AD All rebel prisoners released. De Valera wins East Clare. First World War ends. English General Election. Victory for Sinn Fein over the Parliamentary party in Ireland.

1919AD Dail Eireann meets in Dublin, and is not banned. Catholic Royal Irish constables killed by Dan Breen at Soloheadbeg. Killing of the police organised by Copllins.

1920 AD Arrival of the first Black and Tans, and other auxillaries. Kevin Barry hanged, the first of over two dozen executions carried out by the British. 'Bloody Sunday' and the Kilmichael Ambush. Burning of Cork by the auxilaries.

1921 AD IRA reverse with the burning of the Dublin Customs House. The king opens the Northern Ireland Parliament in Belfast. Sir James Craig is Prime Minister of Northern Ireland. Truce. Followed by the Anglo-Irish Treaty.

1922 AD The Four Courts in Dublin occupied by anti-treaty IRA. A general election in Ireland and a pro-treaty majority. The Four Courts attacked by Free-State troops as civil war breaks out. Deaths of Michael Collins and Arthur Griffith. William Cosgrave becomes President of the Executive Council. First executions of anti-Treaty IRA by the Free State in Dublin. Followed by the executions of Erskine Childers, O'Connor, Mellowes etc. Total by Free State to date = 77.

1923AD Civil War ends. The IRA dumps arms.

1924AD National Army reorganisation, cut-back, and mutiny.

1925AD Boundary commission collapses and partition is confirmed by tripartite agreement.

1926AD De Valera leaves Sinn Fein, founds Fianna Fail.

1927AD General Election in Ireland. Murder of Kevin O'Higgins. De Valera's Fianna Fail party take the oath and enter the Dail as opposition party.

1930AD Irish Labour Party separates from the Trades Union Congress.

1932AD General Election in Ireland. Fianna Fail victory. De Valera replaces Cosgrave as president of the Executive Council. The

Free State gets into an economic war with Britain. Land Annuities. IRA prisoners released.

1933AD Fine Gael Party founded under Blueshirt leader O'Duffy.

1934AD O'Duffy's resignation allows Cosgrave to become as Fine Gael leader.

1937AD Constitution of Eire.

1938AD Economic war with Britain ends with an agreement. Britain renounces naval rights in Treaty ports.

1939AD IRA bombing campaign begins in Britain. Outbreak of Second World War. Eire declares herself neutral. December raid by the IRA on Magazine Fort, Phoenix Park, Dublin. Death of Yeats.

1940AD Death of IRA hunger strikers in Eire. Anglo-Irish military consultations.

1941AD Worst German air-raids in Belfast and Dublin. Death of Joyce.

1945AD End of Second World War. Radio speeches given by Churchill and De Valera. General Election in Britain, victory for the Labour Party, who will hold power for the next six years.

1948AD General Election in Ireland, and defeat for Fianna Fail. De Valera out of office for the first time in 16 years.

1949AD Republic of Ireland declared. Accepted by Britain with guaran tee of support to Northern Ireland.

1954AD IRA attacks in Armagh.

1956–62AD IRA campaign in the North.

1965AD O'Neill-Lemass Talks.

1966AD Anglo-Irish Free-Trade agreement.

1967AD Foundation of Northern Ireland Civil Rights Association.

1968 AD Summer Civil Rights March. Derry Civil Rights march banned by Craig, Minister for Home Affairs, but is held in defiance and brutally broken up by police. O'Neill reforms announced.

1969AD More Civil Rights marches. People's Democracy Belfast to Derry Civil Rights March attacked. O'Neill resigns. Clark becomes Prime Minister. Police B Specials get out of hand in Derry and Belfast. August 14 British troops sent to Derry. Protestant riot in Belfast against the Hunt Commission's report on the RUC.

1970AD Dublin Arms Trial.

1971AD First British soldier killed by the IRA in Belfast. Clark resigns. Faulkener becomes Prime Minister, and gets Britain to agree to Internment. 342 arrested. By the end of the year 1576 have been interned.

1972AD 30 January Bloody Sunday in Derry, 11 killed. Stormont sus pended and Direct Rule imposed.

1973AD Sunningdale agreement. Assembly for NI established, with power sharing. Republic and UK both join the EEC.

1974AD Ulster's Workers Strike brings down Faulkener and Assembly. Direct Rule reimposed. Multiple killings in Dublin. Guilford and Birmingham pub bombings.

1975AD Northern Ireland Convention convened. Internment suspended.

1976AD Convention collapses. British ambassador in Dublin killed.

1978AD IRA fire-bomd kills twelve in a Down restaurant.

1979AD Earl Mountbatten and relatives killed in County Sligo. Eight soldiers killed at Warrenpoint.

1980AD Founding of Aosdana.

1981AD Death of Republican hunger-strikers.

1982AD Multiple murders of soldiers at Knightsbridge UK and Ballykelly in County Londonderry.

1983AD Futile All -Ireland Forum.

1985AD Anglo-Irish agreement at Hillsborough, generates vehement Protestant protest.

1986AD Referendum confirms Republic's constitutional ban on divorce.

1987AD 11 killed at Enniskillen on Remembrance Sunday.

1988AD SAS shoot dead two IRA men and a woman activist in Gibraltar.

1989AD IRA kills 11 bandsmen at RoyalMarines School of Music, Dover.

1990AD IRA bombs the London Stock Exchange. Little damage. Conservative MP Ian Gow killed by IRA car-bomb.

1991AD IRA mortar bomb 10 Downing Streetwhilst the cabinet is in session. Also bomb Paddington and Victoria stations in London. Mary Robinson becomes president.

1994AD IRA ceasefire brings hope of a solution to the problems of Northern Ireland.

1996AD These are subsequently dashed when Sinn Féin/IRA restart the violence.

INDEX